WATCH AND PRAY
A PORTRAIT OF FANTE VILLAGE LIFE
IN TRANSITION

WATCH AND PRAY
A PORTRAIT OF FANTE VILLAGE LIFE
IN TRANSITION

NANCY LUNDGREN
UNIVERSITY OF CAPE COAST

HARCOURT COLLEGE PUBLISHERS

Fort Worth   Philadelphia   San Diego   New York   Orlando   Austin   San Antonio
Toronto   Montreal   London   Sydney   Tokyo

Publisher	Earl McPeek
Acquisitions Editor	Bryan Leake
Project Manager	Angela Williams Urquhart

ISBN: 0-15-505933-5
Library of Congress Catalog Card Number: 2001092727

Copyright © 2002 by Harcourt, Inc.

Address for Domestic Orders
Harcourt College Publishers, 6277 Sea Harbor Drive, Orlando, FL 32887-6777
800-782-4479

Address for International Orders
International Customer Service
Harcourt Inc., 6277 Sea Harbor Drive, Orlando, FL 32887-6777
407-345-3800
(fax) 407-345-4060
(e-mail) hbintl@harcourt.com

Address for Editorial Correspondence
Harcourt College Publishers, 301 Commerce Street, Suite 3700, Fort Worth, TX 76102

Web Site Address
http://www.harcourtcollege.com

Printed in the United States of America

0 1 2 3 4 5 6 7 8 9   039   9 8 7 6 5 4 3 2 1

ABOUT THE SERIES

These case studies in cultural anthropology are designed for students in beginning and intermediate courses in the social sciences, to bring them insights into the richness and complexity of human life as it is lived in different ways, in different places. The authors are men and women who have lived in the societies they write about and who are professionally trained as observers and interpreters of human behavior. Also, the authors are teachers; in their writing, the needs of the student reader remain foremost. It is our belief that when an understanding of ways of life very different from one's own is gained, abstractions and generalizations about the human condition become meaningful.

The scope and character of the series has changed constantly since we published the first case studies in 1960, in keeping with our intention to represent anthropology as it is. We are concerned with the ways in which human groups and communities are coping with the massive changes wrought in their physical and sociopolitical environments in recent decades. We are also concerned with the ways in which established cultures have solved life's problems. And we want to include representation of the various modes of communication and emphasis that are being formed and reformed as anthropology itself changes.

We think of this series as an instructional series, intended for use in the classroom. We, the editors, have always used case studies in our teaching, whether for beginning students or advanced graduate students. We start with case studies, whether from our own series or from elsewhere, and weave our way into theory, and then turn again to cases. For us, they are the grounding of our discipline.

ABOUT THE AUTHOR

Born in Syracuse, New York, I spent my childhood moving west as my Baptist preacher father pursued his career. By my high school years we had arrived in Phoenix, Arizona, where my father worked for the Migrant Ministry and I finished high school. I undertook undergraduate work at the University of Redlands in California and completed at the University of Hawaii.

After college I married, had two sons, worked and pursued graduate work. The alternation of work, graduate study and child rearing propelled me into an array of places and professions. These included socialwork in Gary, Indiana; graduate school in psychology; therapist and general clinician in a variety of mental health agencies; social worker and director of a child abuse agency; director of a mental health agency, and a juvenile court investigator.

In 1984, I received a Fulbright grant to undertake my dissertation research in Belize, Central America, combining my specializations in political economy, child socialization, "race," gender and class, and the African Diaspora. This research allowed me to continue to develop my persistent interest in the reproduction of systems of social inequality. Subsequently, I returned to Belize and published material from that work.

After receiving my PhD in anthropology in 1987 from the University of Massachusetts in Amherst, Massachusetts, I taught at Antioch College until I left in 1996 for research and teaching in Ghana, West Africa, at the University of Cape Coast. At the moment, I am researching the political economy of cement in Ghana, tracing its origins as a building material, as well as its implications for identity, expression, and economic development. I currently live with my two dogs, three cats, and monkey in Cape Coast, as well as in the San Francisco Bay on my reconditioned World War II barge.

ABOUT MR. BAIDOO

Ato Baidoo was born in Akotokyir village in April, 1947, and had his education in Cape Coast. He is father of six and a staunch member of the Catholic Church. He worked briefly in Accra and Cape Coast before travelling to Nigeria in 1977. He taught physics and mathematics at Government Secondary Onne in the Rivers State, until he returned home in 1986.

He founded Tuwohofo-Holly International School, Akotokyir. He has been a regular exchange teacher to Kemet School, Florence, South Carolina. His hobbies are attending to people's needs and counseling. He is a great lover of peace.

ABOUT THIS CASE STUDY

"We want you to know the villages and their people in the way that Baidoo sees them and the way that I, with my Western, American-bred eyes, have seen them. We want you to know his village and those connected to it because they represent a spirit and a tradition and a collaborative lifestyle that we as a human species may not know again. Change is coming; it is inevitable. We want you to see the people of Akotokiyr and Abaasa and Nim before they change completely, before their way of life has been ultimately and irrevocably altered. We also want to explore the ways in which the new is incorporated into the old, and we pray that the combination will not completely destroy a way of life that has allowed a people to survive for thousands of years, despite continuous efforts since the beginnings of the industrial revolution in the 1400s to subvert such durability" (p. 13)

With these words, Nancy Lundgren states the purpose of this case study. What she leaves out is that which makes it possible for us, the readers, to understand what these words mean when applied to the time, the people, and the places she is describing. This case study makes an indelible imprint on the reader. He or she becomes a participant in the scene, whether in a home, a "palace" of a chief, a church, a public forum, in the market place, or in the author's own home. The blazing sun, the airless rooms with concrete block walls with roofs of sheet iron, the dust, flies, rough streets, the verdant forest, the streams, the open, running sewers, all become habitats of our minds as we read of the author's interactions with people in the small villages where she is living and working.

Nancy Lundgren is more than a participant-observer in the anthropological tradition. She teaches school, contributes money to community projects and helps arrange the necessary resources to complete the projects, and actually became

Queen Mother. A white woman, a foreigner, becoming a Queen Mother? This is un-precedented! It is both an indication of how much the community has changed and how much the people think of her.

The author brings us into each experience by telling us how she felt, how it seemed to her when it was happeningæand afterward. Not so many years ago, we were taught in graduate school to keep ourselves out of the dialogue, to never reveal our feelings, to keep all but the "objective" observations to ourselves. This began to change in the 1960s, gained momentum in the 1970s and 1980s, and is a full-blown stance today. We recognize how much the observer is part of the action, how every-thing the observer feels and thinks is relevant. Nancy Lundgren carries this strategy to its fitting limits. The result is a case study that is a study but also a story set in her biography . . . a life story.

This story goes beyond and behind analyses of culture change, urbanization, and modernization. The living reality of the situation is dramatically communicated. One begins to understand what is happening in Africa and other "third world" places to-day. This is a precious understanding that must be a part of any education worthy of the name.

We leave to the reader this case study. May you experience it as I, the editor, have.

George Spindler, Editor
Case Studies in Cultural Anthropology

CONTENTS

About Case Study   vi
About Author   v
Preface   ix

Chapter I   Our Story: If all the people were to carry the heavens, no one would become humpbacked: An Introduction   1

Chapter II   If you get your bundle ready, you will be helped to carry it: Community, Economy, Work   15

Chapter III   When a chief has plenty of milk it is the people who drink: Becoming Queen Mother   37

Chapter IV   The poor kinsman does not lack a resting place: Kinship, Marriage, Family, Clan   69

Chapter V   Nothing is as painful as when one dies without leaving a child behind: Children   101

Chapter VI   All human beings are children of God: Religion   127

Chapter VII   A person cutting a path does not know that the part that has been cleared behind him is crooked: Change   137

Bibliography   151
Glossary   155
Index   159

PREFACE

It has been a very long time since Boas and his students studied far away from home and since Evans-Pritchard and Radcliffe-Brown wrote in "the ethnographic present." Since their time, there have been years of discussion, inside and outside of anthropology, about the wisdom, value, possibility, or even ethics of trying to speak about a people, a culture, a place not of one's own. In this postmodern time when all concepts are being reexamined, when the very idea of representation is a charged and contentious project, there is newly fueled and energized discussion on the topic. Anthropologists are often in the forefront of these discussions, as the self-professed "experts" on "culture," perhaps the most contentious of the contentious issues around. Therefore, it is not without a great deal of soul searching and apprehension that I present this little ethnography.

I cannot here go into that long and sometimes painful discussion, but I feel that I must make at least two things clear about my position. First, I think that it is always good for us to look at ourselves, to scrutinize our activities, to revisit our long-held beliefs and assumptions, to be reflexive. For anthropology and for individual anthropologists, this is a good thing. Second, I am firmly committed to the practice of anthropology and to its potential value. We must not lose our history as a people, as the species, Homo sapiens. We cannot understand our collective selves by only knowing our individual selves. It might be better if we were all able to tell our own stories; but we know that that cannot be. Certain political and economic realities prohibit some of us from speaking for ourselves in a way that makes it available to our fellow species members. If we think of ourselves, as I do, as one people, one species, then it behooves us to know about each other as much as possible so that we can be mindful of our individual and collective needs.

I am aware of the danger, even arrogance, of such an undertaking as this. It is a powerful responsibility and I do not take it lightly. My methodology, thus, is one of engagement, constant reflection and comment on precisely the dynamic interplay of power and resistance inherent in all aspects of this kind of work. The imbalance of power is for me an ever-present presence, an embedded aspect of both the studied and the studier.

I first wanted to write an ethnography about my friend, Mr. Augustine Ato Baidoo's village, Akotokyir. It is a small village on the campus of the University of Cape Coast in the coastal town of Cape Coast. Cape Coast is in Ghana, a small West African country originally colonized by the British. I wanted to try to understand where we all came from so maybe we would better understand where we are and where we are going. However, it soon became apparent that I needed to extend this work to other villages nearby. The work then became one of the Fante of Ghana in interconnected villages as well as in the town of Cape Coast where I also have a faculty position at the University of Cape Coast.

The matrilineal Fante are members of one of the most populous ethnic groups in Ghana, the Akan. They are the dominant group in the Cape Coast area and have a long history in the region. They are Fante speakers, but also speak the national language, English. They live in towns and villages, are predominantly Christian, and earn their living primarily as traders, farmers and fishing people, but are found in all walks of life including government officials, teachers, university professors, lawyers, and doctors. Cape Coast, the third largest city in Ghana, has been a market town since its beginnings but has evolved as the principle seat of higher education. The town supports one of the four major universities in the country, the University of Cape Coast, as well as many old, well-established private secondary schools, drawing students from all over the country.

As I watched and talked and participated with the mostly Fante people of the Central Region of Ghana, I became more and more aware of the difficulties of representing any part of the life of a people. There are too many variables, too many perspectives, too much to observe. I, therefore, have tried to present the material, keeping myself always present, and as the "culture" and "cultures" unfolded for me. I wanted to convey, if not the actual reality, at least the essence of a people. I discuss these issues more specifically in the text. I believe that the way of life of these people is being rapidly undermined, if not completely destroyed, and I believe that it is important for the people of Akotokyir and Abaasa and Nim and Cape Coast, but also for all of us, to record as much of this life as we possibly can.

For making this work possible, I am especially indebted to Mr. Augustine Ato Baidoo, my partner, consultant, and friend; and Anthony Kwame Nkrumah, my translator in Abaasa, my inspired and inspiring "right hand man," and indefatigable worker for his people. I am also indebted to the people of Akotokyir, especially Mary Baidoo and the Baidoo children, Thomas Baidoo, Alice and Eric, and the people of Abaasa, especially Kobina Eight, Mr. Adams, Nana Mensah, Chairman, the chief's linguist, and my charming and wonderful friend, Adwoa. To Yaro, Sabonzee, Father Emil, Philip and especially my special child friends Eric, Samuel, Ezekiel, Adwoa, Afua, Kwesi and Kojo, I owe my gratitude for hours and hours of conversation, tutoring, support, friendship and advice. My little assistant, William Kwesi Yaro, with his honesty and decency and kindness, has given me strength and courage at times when I needed it most. I am grateful to the wonderful, warm, and helpful reception I have received and priceless information I have gathered from the women in the market, especially Jane, my students, people at the universities and in the churches and the miraculous people in Akotokyir, Nim, Abaasa and all of the other villagers and chiefs and elders and clergy I have met and learned from throughout the region. I am always gathering data, always taking notes and I could not have done this work if the people among whom I have worked and played and loved had not allowed me to do so. Everywhere I go, I am greeted with respect and acceptance and interest. This has made my work, not only possible, but terribly pleasurable. Ghanaians are proud of their hospitality, their kindness to strangers and, in this, I have found confirmation.

I have not been successful in describing the lives of these Fante people of Ghana. I have only been successful in writing down my observations. I have done this as honestly, as reflexively, as respectfully as it is possible for me to do. Mr. Baidoo helped me with children's drawings and stories, some of which are included in this document. He collected interviews and had them transcribed and wrote a brief history of his village. I did not use his interviews directly and we were unable to actually write the book together, but his spirit, his judgment, his balance, is here in all of it. On most occasions I have changed the names of people slightly to preserve their privacy. The names of many, however, including Mr. Baidoo and Kwame Nkrumah, are real.

On the other side of the Atlantic, I also have many debts. I could never have done this work if it had not been for the support, confidence, love, and intelligence of my good friend Marianne Whelchel. I learned, and continue to learn, from countless late-night and early morning conversations with my friend and colleague Nancy Fairley. Special thanks to my friends Kay and Azi for always being there and to my wise and sensitive Belizean son Daniel. I suppose my greatest debt is, ultimately, to my parents, who gave me freedom and thought I could do anything, even when it seemed crazy to everyone else. I learned early lessons in ethnography, in interviewing, in kindness, as I tagged along with my father to migrant camps, Navajo towns, Mexican villages, horse auctions, county fairs, always learning about people and how they live. My greatest intellectual debt is to my wise and demanding advisor at the University of Massachusetts, Sylvia Helen Forman, whose belief in women and in equity made it all possible. When my children were young, friends would sometimes marvel at how I could do so much while raising two sons, Trent and Kai, by myself. I always responded that I was lucky, I could not have done it if I had not had such good sons. With their grace, courage and humanity they give me the peace of mind to be able to think, the freedom to move, and the hope for the future so as to be able to act.

Having said all of this, I am ultimately responsible for what is in this work. I beg your indulgence for its inadequacies and hope that you will read it with charity.

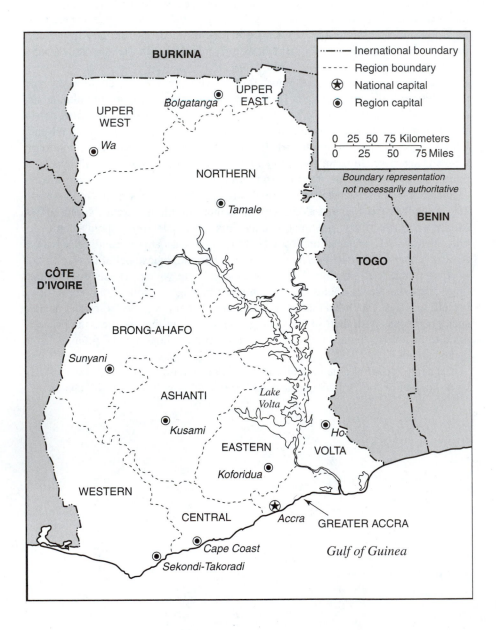

BURKINA

International boundary
Region boundary
National capital
Region capital

0 25 50 75 Kilometers
0   25   50   75 Miles

*Boundary representation
not necessarily authoritative*

UPPER
EAST

Bolgatanga

UPPER
WEST

Wa

NORTHERN

Tamale

BENIN

TOGO

CÔTE
D'IVOIRE

BRONG-AHAFO

Sunyani

ASHANTI

*Lake
Volta*

Kusami

Ho

VOLTA

EASTERN

Koforidua

WESTERN

CENTRAL

Accra

GREATER ACCRA

Cape Coast

Gulf of Guinea

Sekondi-Takoradi

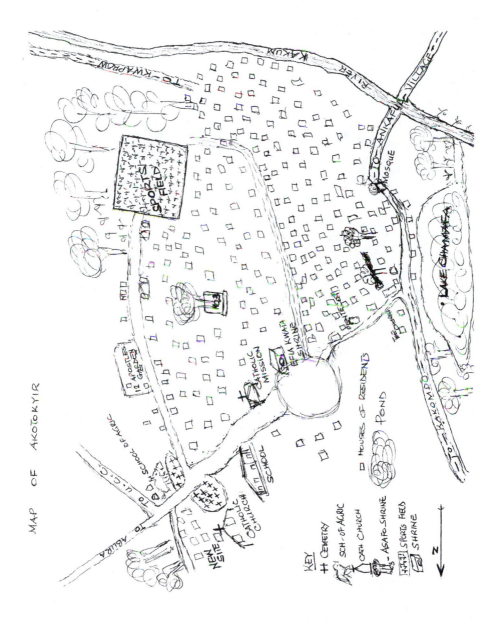

MAP OF AKOTOKYIR

1 / Our Story

If all the people were to carry the heavens
no one would become humpbacked

IT HAS BEEN a very long day—one of those days when the electrician comes at breakfast time as Samuel has his Northern Ghanaian wares laid out in the courtyard with his friend Francis, and Kwesi is madly washing, while Kojo is sweeping into my food and the puppy has torn up the newspaper I had planned to read in the quiet early morning hours. The electrician is polite and formal but does not have the actual fan he is to install. He needs a ride to the administration building where he will discuss it with his boss. I dress before I am ready, leave a bevy of children to clean and guard the house, and take the electrician. His boss is not in so we make a few stops and return without the fan but with the promise that he will return.

I try to collect myself to meet my eighty students who are crowded into a hot, airless, concrete room designed for 40 or 50. The class goes well as I scream the lecture, constantly wipe my dripping face, occasionally gag from the chalk dust that is too close because the students are sitting in rows within a foot of the blackboard where I have to fit. I borrow a student's tiny space for my notes and try to shout over the chorus of voices crowding in around the outside of the room to get seats for the next class. As class closes, one student grabs up my briefcase, another grabs my arm, and they yell, "Let's go!" as I hesitate in the midst of a virtual stampede of students.

Well, at least that is over; but I have to check my e-mail to see if my family has wired money, which I need because the check I received from Accra will not be cleared for at least fifteen days, I am told after waiting for an hour at the bank. I make it to town amidst honking taxis, broken down tro tros, and a cacophony of sounds and smells and sights that, when added to the dazzling sun, stifling heat, and billows of dust, give an almost surreal, mad carnival atmosphere to arrival in Cape Coast.

The Kotokuraba market is like most West African markets, a crowded, smelly labyrinth of tiny paths in between tiny crowded stalls and the sewage system, which is made of narrow, pungent canals. The market is a woman's place and it is filled with laughter and teasing and conversation and sharing food and sometimes even dancing. I am greeted with affectionate teasing about my short hair, poor Fante, and my whiteness, and I am embraced and kissed and touched by my special friends. They think my hair feels like the large rat-like animal they call a grass cutter, which is a compliment. I make them laugh and fuss and I try to listen to their little English as they patiently listen to my feeble attempts at Fante. I do some business here, pick up fish for my dogs and cats, get a few tomatoes, a tin of Nescafé, a few tins of Ideal for my coffee, and toilet paper, and I make my way out into the glaring heat where

Market

I stumble, dripping and grimy, to my "spot," where I can have some small refreshment and large conversation with my little friend and manager, Nicole. She greets
me with pleasure, grabs my heavy bags, chastises me for once again buying cloth,
and brings me my Club beer. Nicole thinks that I have enough of the wonderful, colorful Ghanaian Wax Print fabric I love. I say I could not find a few items I wanted,
so she demands my money and, treating me like a rather stupid child, runs off across
the street to the market where she will easily find what I need. For a few minutes I
relax in the protection of the small bar before I once again return to the sun and glare
and noises and dust and make my way to my tailor on the other side of town. He has
turned me into a grudging business partner and today we need to do some business.
He, of course, needs money. But I have none because my bank is now closed and the
money will not be there yet anyway. He greets this news cheerfully and assures me
that he knows I will be blessed with the money soon and that we will both be en-
riched. It will by all means be coming, he says.

I have only two more stops before I make my way home. It is dark when I return, but the lights are on in my house and I am gleefully met by the entire Nkame
family, including Father, who would like a cup of coffee and a chat in my breezy
courtyard. All of my dogs are leaping and barking and wanting to be fed. The cats
are also squawking noisily about food. I feel overwhelmed and want to cry. I need a
bath, a cup of coffee, some food, and a few moments of quiet. However, because no
one can imagine such a need as solitude, I am not allowed any. I finally get my bath
after an hour's chat with Father over shared coffee and bread with ground nut paste.
It is now about 9:00 p.m. I feel the need to attend to some paper marking and lecture
preparation so that I can write a bit tomorrow when I have no classes, but I am suddenly heavy with weariness and wonder if I can really manage any serious work.

It is a typical day, a typical homecoming, and it is after such a day that Kojo has
now remembered a note that had been delivered to me earlier that day. He had stuffed

it into his jeans pocket at about 2 p.m., he says, and apologizes for having only now remembered it. The note is from Mr. Baidoo. It says that they have had a death in the village. The wake keeping is tonight and they hope that I will join them in their mourning. There is no alternative. I have to go.

Sixteen-year-old Kwesi and I get into my newly acquired car and drive off in the deep dark of a moonless African night. The tropical foliage crowds in on us with its accompanying brilliant chorus of night creature sounds as we wind around the narrow, deeply pitted dirt road to the village. My fatigue leaves me as I near the ceremonial site and the scene energizes me. Before me is an improvised shelter of bamboo poles and thatch under which Mr. Baidoo sits proudly in his best funeral cloth. He holds his youngest boy, who is asleep, in his arms. Beside him sit the other Baidoo men, looking tall and solemn and sure. Other men, some in cloth, some in suits, some in African trousers and shirts, sit in rows behind Mr. Baidoo, who takes the role of head man, head patriarch, the presence that holds the event together in the absence of a chief. The women sit in different groups in rows under the thatch, leaving a large, sandy circle in the center. A group of women in black with red turbans are the special mourners and, as usual, the helpers, the nurturers. Surrounding the large circle of dignified, softly weeping mourners is the eerily beautiful sound of voices raised in song. The music seems to seep out of the dark forest from all directions, but I cannot see a choir.

As I approach the thatch and bamboo, I am cordially and formally greeted with a handshake by the Baidoos and other men and women especially known to me. They express their gratitude for my attendance and Ato explains that because the young woman who died was a chorister, choirs from many of the surrounding villages are joining in the remembrance of their sister. Her body, he says, is in the primary four classroom because no one has a house big enough. Her young friends stand around her and sing. Folks go in and out throughout the evening, paying their last respects. Ato says that his sleeping 5-year-old boy, Vincent, is not sure whether or not he will look at the body. His father will help him with either decision. We sit quietly. Every now and then Mr. Baidoo turns to me and explains something or we chat for a moment. Vincent is getting heavy, so Ato decides to take him into the house to bed but soon he returns, Vincent in his arms, saying that the child is not yet ready to go to bed. Vincent is wearing a cloth wrapped around his neck and covering his body in the style of young children ready for sleep. His father says that it is a bed, blanket, sheet, and pajamas all in one.

The choirs continue. Ato gets up, drops his now sleeping child into his brother's arms, and motions for me to follow. We go into the school room where the dead girl lies, dressed and made up to look as much as possible as she had just yesterday when she lived. Why did she die, I ask. She is so young. I remember her from just the Sunday before, singing in the choir. We don't know, Ato says. She had pains in her stomach. They found a taxi in the early hours of the morning, but she was dead by the time she reached the hospital, they said. He seems satisfied, so we walk around the room and out again to our seats. Later I learned that the death had something to do with an attempted abortion, but these things are not asked of or discussed. Too many people seem to die of unknown causes. Mostly people do not ask and doctors either do not know or do not tell.

Cape Coast

Ato picks his heavy young son out of his brother's arms and once again straightens the cloth around his thin, strong, bare shoulder, shuffles Vincent, and sits. The child awakens and says nothing. His father struggles with his long cloth, trying to reach his knicker pocket. "I want to get a toffee for Vincent," he quietly tells me. Finally he is successful and hands the sweet to the sleepy child who solemnly puts it into his mouth. The women come around with popcorn, peanuts, and sweets that we all share.

I ask Ato about his other four sons. Had he also been close to them when they were as small as Vincent? I wonder if because this is his baby, he is especially pampered and petted, but Ato assures me that each son has been close to him. They each followed him around and he bathed and fed and talked to them all. He says that he had been very close to his eldest son, Elvis, now a second-year student at the University. In fact, he says, he had just talked to the young man before he went off to Kumasi to study, and reminded him of a story. He said that when Elvis had been small and in the University Primary School, his father walked to pick him up from school every day at 1:30. One day, the young Elvis looked a bit glum and thoughtful and his father inquired as to his disposition. The boy told his father that for some time now he had been a bit ashamed because his father walked and many of the children rode in cars. But now, he said, he is fine because one day "we shall have a car, and theirs will be old and used and they will have to walk. But," he went on, "we shall stop and pick them up in our car, even as they have not picked us up." So, Ato told me in the late tropical night, he had reminded Elvis of this story as he was going off to the University. "You will want to remember to pick up the others when you finish with your University education." With this advice he sent his firstborn away from the village, for the first time in his life, on his way to getting his own car. It is Ghanaian. It is the Sankofa, the symbol of the bird bent backwards over its tail, which means: *"Do not forget where the worm was found."*

Cape Coast

Our conversation is interrupted by the appearance of a small delegation of elderly men who look dignified in their cloths and sandals and their strong, bare shoulders. They seem agitated and speak in loud and animated tones to the Baidoo men. Thomas, the elder brother, speaks back. The old men become more agitated. Thomas gets up from his seat and speaks assertively to them. Others join in and there is a verbal and gesticulating dialogue for 3 or 4 minutes. Finally Ato shifts his son in his lap, straightens his cloth, sits his 6-foot body up tall in his chair and calmly and quietly says something to the men. A few words are exchanged and the delegation moves on. Ato is unruffled; the child continues to sleep and the wake-keeping activities are undisturbed.

What has happened, Ato now thoughtfully tells me, is that a few of the more rowdy young men have been having their own wake keeping that has been loud and raucous, with noisy drumming and singing, all of which has been disturbing their own wake keeping. We told them, he says, that if they want to continue, they can come, and the Baidoo-led group will leave the place to them. "But," I protest, "Where would you go?" Ato looks straight at me, grins ever so slightly and says, "We aren't going anywhere." But, he says, the elders who had come mostly agreed with them and said that the young boys were misbehaving and would be stopped. However, in true Ghanaian style, there had to be prolonged and ardent, if agreeable, argument and conversation about the entire issue. The boys could beat their drums and sing their songs in another part of the village so as not to be a disturbance. So that solved that.

However, there is an epilogue. A short while later a young boy, reeling a bit and looking somewhat worse for the weather, swerves over to Ato, leans into him, and speaks into the man's face. Baidoo does not seem at all disturbed. He utters a few words and gestures for the boy to leave; after a mild protest, the young man stumbles off. Baidoo turns to me with a chuckle and says, "Has the world gone mad? What are we coming to? People have madness. This boy," he says to me, "has had the nerve, after all of the conversation and uproar, to ask to borrow my boys' drum." He is incredulous. What a crazy thing. This boy, who has been chastised by the elders of both his own and Baidoo's group, now wants the injured party to contribute to the perpetuation of the offense. It all seems too crazy and funny to Baidoo, and he chuckles a little more as he turns his attention elsewhere.

Now the choirs begin to soften and stop, people continue to sob softly, and the lights go off. It is dark and still. Soon our eyes become accustomed to the dark, and we see in the middle of the circle a small table, a large ledger book, and a man standing. Ato turns to me and whispers that now they will call the role of the choristers. The man begins. As each name is called, the chorister calls out, "Here." When they come to Afua, she does not answer the call. Her girlfriends run out after her calling, "Afua! Afua!" But she does not answer, and they cannot find her. They go on with the role call until all have answered but Afua.

The man in the center now begins to speak. It is a eulogy, I gather. It revolves around the scripture taken from Mark 13:31-37, which says, "Take heed, watch and pray: for ye know not when the time is" (Mark 13:33). Watch and pray, because you never know when the master of the house will come home. This was a young girl, a vibrant girl, but she was taken by God, and God will know when it is your time, so you had better be ready. You had better always have your life in order. Only God decides when it is our time, and it is the right time. So remember to be careful in your life. Live your life. Enjoy your life. Have peace in your life, knowing that when you go, it is time, it is the moment. So be ready, have lived your life well, have taken care, have been watchful, and have kept in touch with your God. Tomorrow, like our own beloved Afua, you may be taken, so you had better watch and pray today.

And so I leave. It isn't over, but it is now about 2:30 a.m., and I am physically and emotionally tired. The wake keeping will probably go on all night, Baidoo tells me. The Baidoo men and women, the choir master, and my self proclaimed "husband" (of which I have many) all shake my hand and formally thank me for coming.

It was a moving and beautiful farewell to a beloved member of the entire village family. Baidoo knew what he was asking when he wrote his note, and I am grateful to him. He knew that I would learn from this occasion and that I would know more about his people from it. And he, of course, was right. I learned, as I had learned many times before, of the great capacity for the human spirit not only to survive, but also to thrive against assaults to the body, assaults to the mind, assaults to the spirit of a people. I want to know how they do it. How do they have so much dignity? So much compassion, such patience, such great capacity for forgiveness, for cooperation, for individual pride, for individual analysis?

These are the "backward" people of whom the world speaks. These are the "people without history," without culture, without God. These are the "underdeveloped," the "primitive," those who refuse to become "modern," the people who deny "progress." These are the people who refuse to practice "family planning" and don't know how to plan and don't know how to take care of their young. These are the people the world wants to "help." These are the people the world thinks cannot govern themselves, so they must be governed, cannot regulate themselves, so they must be regulated, cannot control themselves, so they must be controlled. These are the people who must learn how to work, how to take responsibility, how to defer gratification.

These are the people the world wants to teach. These are the people we come to "help." We are so sincere, so eager, we helpers. But what does it mean to "help"? What does it mean to be *able* to help? We know that we feel a little debased when we are forced to ask for help and when someone offers. We may need to accept, but we vow that one day we will not have to take "hand-outs." We will buy our own children their shoes; our children will turn to *us* for advice. Are not children the ones who are dependent, who need to be taken care of? Is it not the parent, the strong, the powerful, who gives, who helps, who tells? Is it not the child, the weak, the powerless, who has to take, who cannot offer help but must accept it, who has to be told, not to tell? Do not the children yearn for independence? Do not they cry for input? Do not they fight to have their say? Do not they struggle to get power, to be free from asking? Do not they want their own income, their own room, their own space, their own dignity? What does it do to the soul of a woman to be a perpetual child? What does it do to the soul of a people?

We "helpers" are invited to a celebration. It is the 75th Anniversary of the Akotokyr Catholic Church begun by Mr. Baidoo's great-great-grandfather. The splendor of the event is almost indescribable. It is a hot, humid, overcast day. The Bronyis are invited, as are my friends and I. There are four of us. Four white women. We are dressed appropriately in our newly acquired and tailored semi-Ghanaian clothes.

As we come around the corner of the farm, the fat jersey cattle are lazily eating in the verdant pasture. The leaves of the bush and trees are colored from the bright red clay of the road. The gate is open. We turn into a jubilant crowd of children, mothers with babies on their backs, teenagers, grandmas, grandpas, and fathers with scrubbed and shined, beribboned and suited young ones. Some have on t-shirts announcing the event, clean and ironed and carefully tucked into pressed trousers or new cloths. They are shouting and clapping and making music with rattles and sticks. Although the red earth is billowing up from the slight wind, the few taxis, and our car, it never seems to destroy their shine, their cleanliness.

My new little white car has been carefully washed as usual by Kwesi. We slowly move through the crowd lining the road to avoid the potholes and gouges dug out from the pounding of many rains. The crowd is ecstatic. It is as if the four white women in the beautiful white car have appeared just in time to provide the role of dignitaries to bless and empower their celebration. We are welcomed as a king, mayor, or president. They wave, many shake my hand as a welcoming greeting, and they are all smiling and laughing; even the children are jumping and shouting.

As we approach the Baidoo immediate family, Ato smiles sedately and greets me proudly and proprietorially. I know that I have come through for him in a manner exceeding his expectations. He is, as usual, straight, tall, and dignified in his white t-shirt, clean and creased gray slacks, and polished black-tied shoes. His brothers, almost as tall, just as thin, in similar attire but for the celebratory shirt, flank him with their children in their arms or at their sides, or looking also tall, thin, dignified. Never ones for gaudily effusive behavior, they shake my hand, bowing ever so slightly. Baidoo looks on, the patriarch approving of his people.

We are embarrassed, awkward. We know that we have not earned this proffered reverence and power. We can see the shabbiness of their dress beneath its clean and Sunday-new presentation. We feel the scorching heat and the dust of the road and the presence of the small, bare, sandy, chaotic-looking village of shacks ahead. Some of the children look thin and tired, with flies circling around their exposed sores. We see the incongruity of the situation. We are not dignitaries. My friends have no connection to the village. But we are professors from abroad, and we are white. Unaware of the true history of colonization, slavery, and continued imperialist activities, or naive about its continued presence and actual proximity in time, my friends think it odd, out of place. They share the American blindness to the modernity of the colonial. Kofi says he is "a colonial man"; he is a colonial man because he grew up in the "real" colonial times—and he is not an old man. *He* knows it is still the colonial times; he is still a servant, and he serves mostly white people who come from the colonial core. That is why he is such a good man, why everyone loves him so much— he "knows his place" and he knows himself, he would say.

But we want to deny our place, my friends and I. We want to act as if it were different, that we are different, and we are like Kofi and the villagers. We feel uncomfortable when they play out the colonial scene in our presence. Why must they treat us differently? Why is the occasion so important to them? We know that it isn't so important. It is a tiny village without a real church. The dust of the ground and a few bamboo poles and thatch is their church. They have a public address system that crackles and hisses and spits out words and music that is too loud for the setting. The choir has robes of heavy dark red cloth and satin. The priest wears a long, polyester vestment. We are nearly breathless in the scalding heat, the glare of the sun off the sand making our faces drip and our cotton clothing stick to us. How can they stand those garments in this heat? It does not fully register that this was the dress of the "mother" country. It belongs to an earlier era, to the dark, dank, cold, and drafty halls of the European houses of worship. When it came to Africa, the adjustment was never made for the tropics. The vestments had, by this time, acquired their symbolic value and therefore could not be replaced.

The altar boys also wear long, red, polyester gowns with collars of satin and lace. They look like the gowns worn in the Catholic churches of the foreign missionaries, or in photographs of the Vatican or the "mother" church in Europe or America, but they are worn and tattered. The lace has holes; the satin is torn. The choir robes are shiny and worn from too many hand washings and from the sun. Is this a masquerade? What is this ritual? Why is it not "traditional?" This is grotesque. Everything is out of place.

We arrive amid cheers and cries of joy and are placed on velvet seats. One chair has arms. It looks like a throne. My friends refuse to sit in it; they make me do it. They do not want to participate in the ridiculous charade the people are forcing on us. They do not know that this *is* colonialism. We *are* participating in it. We *have* participated in it. Perhaps they know at some deep visceral level. Perhaps that is why they are so uncomfortable, but I don't think so. It is simply that we think as Americans. Why shouldn't we? We are American. We were trained in American schools and American houses and American churches. We are good people. We are decent. We care about the poor. We want to help. We have been taught what it means to "help." But when we are here, things are different. What are we to teach amidst this chaos, these paradoxes (a word they use a lot)? What is the paradox, I want to ask. There is no paradox. There is colonialism.

What can we teach this tall, proud, dignified, 50-year-old man? He is the chief. He listens to his people and he solves their problems. He has fathered six children and every day of their lives he has struggled for them. He walks miles into the town to buy their food and clothes; he walks miles to the school to talk to the headmistress, to plead for his daughter so that she may be allowed to go to the school. He rides hot, crowded, unsafe tro tros to Salt Pond, Accra, and Takoradi—anyplace that he can get help. He talks to priests and bishops and he brings his cousin, who is the Diocesan accountant, to hold mass. He walks in the blistering sun to my house, sometimes more than once a day. He walks to the Chalets where good-hearted for-eigners are waiting to help. He pleads with the contractor to let him have the roofing sheets with a small down payment before the rains come and ruin the house he has built over time, block by block. He looks for help wherever he can find it. He is the headmaster of the only school in the village; he started it because the village chil-dren had to walk too far to go to kindergarten and primary school in their hot little uniforms, perhaps carrying a piece of bread and some water. He searches to find teachers who will teach for almost nothing. He entreats the education board for books. He goes to workshops on curriculum and rides the tro tro to Accra to pick up books that were sent by some charitable group for village children. He has to pay 50,000,000 Cedis for the gift. He has to scramble for the money. He goes to his bank for a loan from a mate who now works in the bank, but he has no collateral; he has only his good name and the responsibilities of a childhood mate. He sits at the coun-cil with his child in his arms, gently removing him each time he must stand and care-fully returning him when he sits again. He loses sleep because his first born son, a man, we would say, is in pain from an infection, and he sits with this child all night.

What will we teach this man? He is a village man, an African. He needs our help. He grows plantain and cassava on his small plot of land. Each morning at 6 a.m. his wife walks to a far village to teach, and she comes home to sew, to pound fu fu for the family to eat, to wash clothes for the next day, and to tend to the farm. Shall we teach them the virtues of hard work? Shall we teach them how to manage their money? Shall we teach their sons, who have managed to attend the best senior secondary schools in the country and who are studying biochemistry at the univer-sity in Kumasi? Shall we teach them English, these people who speak English and Fante and one or two other neighbor languages? Shall we teach dignity to this man who stands straight and proud and tall in his gold and black cloth at the wake keep-ing, the wedding, or the funeral, representing the strength of the leadership in the vil-lage? Shall we teach this man whose wife and children manage always to have the appropriate shirt, the special Kaaba and slit, the proper senior brother slacks, the pol-ished shoes and the oxford cloth shirt?

I am thinking all of this as I sit in the dust on my lopsided, torn velvet throne, and the choir is heard faintly over the hill. We look in the direction of the small, pink, windowless cement block school; the outdoor toilets of the Baidoo family; the rolling, rocky, undulating land that holds the small, crooked, sometimes crumbling, thatch- or asbestos-roofed structures that are the village. We see the procession. Everyone is still. We hear only the bleating of a goat, the cackling of a chicken, as the priest, in his flowing white vestment, leads the solemn altar boys, who carry a wooden cross, and the choir. It is chilling: the beauty and power of their voices, the light beating of the drums, and the elegance and dignity of their ascension into our midst. They take their places across from us and bring forth an anthem. When they finish, the priest chants his response behind a long table lovingly covered in a white tattered cloth and adorned with candles flickering in the wind, someone's old, proud, and beloved Kente cloth providing a backdrop. The choir, the priest, and the con-gregation move gracefully through the ceremony, each participating confidently so as not to interrupt the rhythm of the meditation.

Baidoo in cloth—Akotokyir

The sequence finishes with the choir—loud, clear, confident, bringing forth a composition of the young boy choir leader, which is a Christian hymn, a Gregorian chant, and an African anthem all in one. In the silence that follows, we are stunned. The priest gently rises, floats to the podium that has been acquired for the occasion, and begins as his gowns flow gently around him in the soft, hot breeze. He turns sweetly to we three women and tells us quietly in perfect, soft, accented English something to the effect of how pleased they are to have American guests with them today. "Having spoken with them before the service, it seems that they are eager to

Mr. Baidoo and Mary at store—Akotokyir

know about Ghana. We are pleased about their interest. As a part of this admirable interest, they are learning the language. So, as you know, we say that the best way to learn to swim is to jump into the water. So you will have the opportunity today as we hold our service in Fante." He smiles at us and the crowd as he says this, nods his head to us in acknowledgment, and proceeds with the service. Nothing more is ever said about it.

In typical British Ghanaian fashion, he elegantly uses the language to formally recognize us and properly enter us into the service, although letting us politely know that he does not intend to defer to us by using English. He chants, the choir answers, and we sit and stand and some kneel as the service rolls along. The tempo changes from meditative to worshipful to instructional to noisy to joyful. We dance along with the others to share their tradition of dancing to the altar to give the offering. It becomes quite exciting as men, women, and children show their dancing skills and as a competition ensues among the members of birth day. During this exercise, which is usually one of about two offerings, a speaker calls out the days of the week, by the Kofis and the Adwoas, the Essies and Kwesis all have their turn to see if they can give the most to the offering that day. Every child at birth has a name announcing the day of his or her birth. Girls born on Sunday are always Essie and boys born on that day are Kwesi. So they give their offerings by their day and name, making it a competition to see who can give the most.

When we arrive and meet the crowd lining the road, they are, in actuality, not waiting for us, but are preparing to greet the brass band that they have hired to help celebrate. We are a bonus. The band finally arrives, accompanies the crowd to the celebration area, and finishes the mass as the crowd dances their last offering. The priest, in good spirits, smiling and clapping, calms the congregation for the conclusion, prays and chants, and we are finished. The choir sings the benediction and, again singing in loud, clear voice, processes back out the way they entered. The priest follows the altar boys, who file out in the same serious and devout way they arrived. By this time the crowd is ready to shift gears and the other, secular part of the celebration is to begin. It is about 2 p.m. We have sat for over two hours through the hot noon hour with the sun directly above us to this mid-afternoon hour when the sand of the village has heated up like an ocean beach.

We are soggy and sticky; our hair is wet and limp and messy. We are impressed, but slightly cranky. It is hot and humid as only a tropical afternoon can be, and the shabbiness and poverty and odors and sounds are beginning to overshadow the beauty and pageantry of the event, reminding us once again of the "paradoxical moment." Our host is disappointed. He had expected us to stay all day. He is puzzled. Why are we leaving so soon, missing the brass band and the dancing? Can't we sit in his little airless cement office and converse awhile, and perhaps be treated to a mineral? Another time, we say. We will be back. He is mollified. In his trusting Ghanaian way, he believes we will soon be back. But I know that in all likelihood, my friends will not. I know that it has taken too much effort. It is not the Africa they have come to see.

This book is about Eric Wolf's "People Without History," and about Wallerstein's periphery. It is about the people who have been called "backward," "underdeveloped," "Third World," and sometimes even more pejorative names such as "savage," "primitive," or "tribal." This book is, in many ways, a joint effort between a member of a village and a trained anthropologist. We have worked and played and shared with each other for many hours over a period of two and a half years. We want to present the preceding scenes so that they make sense and so that the felt experience of the colonial becomes evident in every part of every day.

We want you to know the villages and their people in the way that Baidoo sees them and the way that I, with my Western, American-bred eyes, have seen them. We want you to know his village and those connected to it because they represent a spirit and a tradition and a collaborative lifestyle that we as a human species may not know again. Change is coming; it is inevitable. We want you to see the people of Akotokiyr and Abaasa and Nim before they change completely, before their way of life has been ultimately and irrevocably altered. We also want to explore the ways in which the new is incorporated into the old, and we pray that the combination will not completely destroy a way of life that has allowed a people to survive for thousands of years, despite continuous efforts since the beginnings of the industrial revolution in the 1400s to subvert such durability.

We have been as honest and clear as we can be, although we recognize that our own lenses allow us to distort our vision in an effort to convey a message about a people and a way of life that are unique and precious and in many ways in great peril. The spirit of the people, nevertheless, is powerful. They are colonized in ways both economic and ideological, but they are not without agency. They do not succumb easily. They struggle. And one of the most important things about them is the way each one struggles differently. Americans believe that we are all individuals, that we think for ourselves, that we are independent-minded; but we often seem to merge together into an American consciousness that pales compared with the vivid colors of these individual philosophers and theoreticians I meet every day, manifesting as unique and individual forms of struggle that have been crafted out of pride, necessity, tradition, and remarkable patience and endurance.

Every photograph, every painting, every story, every ethnography, frames one small piece of the artist's vision. The artist hopes that with this one work, finished, framed, bound, we are representing a part of the whole of the scene. Ethnography is not art, but it, too, can only provide a small glimpse into the whole; it is limited by the vision, the lenses, the perspectives of the viewer. This limitation does not lessen the relevance, however. There are two main perspectives and countless secondary views presented in this work, making it both more complicated and, hopefully, more complete as each of us brings our unique perspectives to bear on the reading of the text (to borrow slightly from Geertz). We also place the present within the context of the past, connect the present periphery to the present core and use a variety of forms of information to present our story.

2 / Community, Economy, Work

If you get your bundle ready, you will be helped to carry it.

I AM TALKING to my tailor, Mr. Esoteric. His real name is Philip, but we call him Mr. Esoteric because it is the name of his shop. He is wearing corduroy trousers and an old shirt of vaguely African style. He is a very good tailor. He works all the time to support his young wife and two small children. He is a prudent man, a religious man. His two girls are the only children he plans to have; it is too difficult, he says, to support more these days. He is not a philanderer; he does not drink. His aspirations are modest. He wants to take care of his family, educate his girls, and provide for them a better future than his own. Recently, the family moved to a nearby village where they can live more cheaply and grow a few vegetables. He has contemplated raising chickens. His wife sometimes buys items in nearby villages and takes them to market to sell.

Today we are discussing his most recent plan. He wants to purchase a car and use it as a taxi. The tailoring business is no good anymore. It does not allow him to earn even a minimal living. He finds it difficult to provide school fees, clothes, and books for his girls; to provide food; and to pay the rent for his small shop. Like many Ghanaians, there were not resources for Philip's family to send him to high school. His father had eight or nine children from two different wives and was a farmer with little income. So Philip managed to obtain a situation as an apprentice to a tailor.

However, now there are too many tailors and seamstresses because the cost of high school and university are prohibitive for most and jobs are few; trades are therefore a much sought after alternative. There is another problem, one of even more consequence and with more long-term implications. That is, the steady flow of *foos,* used clothing from outside the country, mostly the United States. This attire is cheap and much in demand. It is gradually replacing the traditional wax print cloth, which has meaning attached to the colorful designs, and the Batiks and the tailors and seamstresses. Now instead of tailored trousers and African-style shirts, men's and boy's sport jeans and flannel shirts and the ubiquitous denim. Women, especially the young, are out in short Western skirts, blouses, and even jeans and denim; these clothes increasingly are replacing colorful, individually tailored, more modest long skirts (slit); big sleeved blouses (Kaaba); and head ties. Even Philip is wearing his corduroy trousers. It doesn't make sense. The corduroy and denim are too hot for the tropical heat, and they have no meaning within the African traditional cultural context.

I am wondering aloud to Philip why they have not resisted this clothing importation, or why a government would import a commodity that so clearly undercuts their local economy and affects such a large portion of their workforce? The entire clothing industry, from designing, producing, and selling cloth, to sewing the fabrics

into attire, includes a large part of the laborforce, particularly women. Soon, I esti-
mate, the entire clothing industry will join the food industry in relying almost exclusively on imported, rather than local, products. Philip says that the tailors and
seamstresses have an organization but that this issue has not explicitly surfaced. It is
insidious, how this works, I reflect. At first an enterprising entrepreneur imports used
clothing (the term *foos,* I am told, means literally, "dead white man's clothes"). It is
cheap, and it matches the models people see on television or in the few magazines
they acquire. The young people, especially, love America, things American, and
things "modern." People gradually begin purchasing this clothing and substituting it
for the more old-fashioned African wear. Then more is imported, more worn. Mrs.
Baidoo wants to buy a large bale of it to sell. People can afford it, they buy it, and
she can make a little extra money. Before we know it, there is less and less of the old
and more and more of the new. The young people will forget how to wrap a man's
cloth and how to sew a woman's kaaba and slit.

Philip just shrugs his shoulders and smiles. "This is progress. What can we do?"
It is as if a large wave swells, flows over a culture, and washes parts of it away. People seem to have no control. It just happens. Later, perhaps, Philip and the other tailors and seamstresses might protest, they might even join together in a union and
demand that the government regulate these imports. However, by this time, people's
tastes will have changed, their activities will have changed, their desires and needs
will have changed, and they will welcome the new items, will see them as a natural
part of their new participation in the global culture. The new clothes will have taken
on new meaning; the old will have lost some of its meaning. For the present, however, I notice that the new is merging into the old in innovative and creative ways. It
seems odd to my American eye to see a man in tight spandex jeans or tiny village
children in a pair of green and yellow Birkenstock sandals. Men happily sport
women's blouses, women use old nighties as dresses or blouses. Men arrive at a village council meeting with a man's dressing gown, a work shirt advertising Bill's
Auto Shop with the name John on a front pocket, or a dressy, flimsy blouse unbut-
toned halfway down the front. Tiny girls appear in church with boy's jeans and dress
shoes or at village events equally content with dresses meant for a picnic or for a
party. American men might wince at wearing a pink shirt, pink and purple flowered
shorts, or even a flowered shirt. But here, if it is pretty, if it is Western, if it appeals
to the wearer, it is worn. On my return to Ghana from the United States, I brought a
pretty little pair of violet, hot pink, and green shorts for my eleven-year-old neighbor, Adwoa. I bought them in the little girls section of an American store along with
a lavender t-shirt. Before I was even unpacked, her sixteen-year-old brother arrived
at my house in the shorts. I had to check myself to keep from gasping. It would never
have occurred to me that a teen-aged boy would ever wear those shorts. He and his
eighteen-year-old brother fought over who would wear them. Even their father admired the shorts.

There are rules in a culture about attire, just as there are rules about everything.
The rules have to do with who can wear what for what occasion, and they are remarkably rigid. It shocks us when the rules are broken. When I wear an "up and down" (a
matching long shorts or trousers and shirt usually worn by men) that is designed for
men, people are polite but surprised. My Ghanaian children are embarrassed, telling

me that the people in the village are asking whether I am a man or woman. My seam-stress objects when I ask her to sew a kaaba and short slit (one that is below the knees but not to the ankles). When, some years back, I first confronted her with such a propo-sition, she refused, did not know how to do it, and did not know what I wanted or why I would want it. We foreigners to Ghana often love the fabrics, the colors, and the de-signs, but we are uncomfortable with many of the styles. So we style our own, usually in a comfortable Western fashion but with Ghanaian cloth. But, like the jeans in church, the mechanic's shirt at the council meeting, or the "female" style jeans on a man, our attire does not make sense in the Ghanaian context. People are forgiving and kind, but they think we are odd. We all know what will happen if a beach costume is worn to a university lecture, a church outfit is worn to a high school class, or funeral attire is worn to a wedding. It usually will not do, even in this age of unisex, for men and women to wear dress obviously meant for the other gender.

Most of us learn early in life the crucial lessons regarding dress and social be-havior. If we do not master it by the time we are adults, we have failed to grasp one of the central, critical symbolic expressions of our culture. We probably even will be considered crazy. Dress designates class, gender, age, and ethnic background, among other things. It is always specific to place, activity, and social group and conveys im-portant information about us. Each culture has its own codes of dress that every child must learn if he or she is to function successfully in the culture. By the time we are adults, we take it for granted, and we think what we wear is a natural and ratio-nal response to the necessities of life. The codes shift slightly, styles change, but any cultural member has internalized the basic rules to the extent that they can easily ac-commodate fluctuations.

When we are thrown into a new culture, then, it is difficult to make this very im-portant symbolic shift. Most of us continue to do what we have always done. We con-tinue to place ourselves with our attire according to our gender, our culture, our class, and other aspects of ourselves we wish to convey. If we are forced, for some reason, to adhere to the dress codes of another culture, we almost surely will make mistakes. We sometimes make offensive mistakes, sometimes only foolish ones.

Ghana, in company with many other countries, has been forced to change its clothes. It has been forced by the pressures of a global market economy, new telecommunications systems, secular and religious ideology, education, and a con-cept called "modernization." If it does not change its clothes, it will be called "back-ward," "underdeveloped," and "traditional," with hints of "primitive" and "savage." If it does change its clothes, however, it does so at a very high cost, the cost of its own independent economy and the cost of its own cultural identity. Its identity, called "culture," is thought about as a museum piece for tourists or for entertainment on the stage. Philip wears his corduroy trousers and worries about how to feed his family while his very livelihood is being taken from him by his own desires and interest in getting ahead, sending his girls to Western-style schools, and his need for capital. Philip's modest and reasonable desire to manage, to send his girls to Western-style schools, to get ahead a little, to accumulate a little capital, and to wear his corduroy trousers militates against his own achievement. He must change his clothes to sur-vive and not be labeled "backward," and in so doing, he undermines his own ability to survive.

Africans must compete in an increasingly globalized market that requires them to change their clothes and "modernize." In the process they must lose their traditional ways. They cannot continue to wear their traditional cloth to work in the bank; they must wear an oxford cloth shirt and tie. To do business with the West, they must look Western. So, as Ayittey (1998) says, Africa lives in two worlds, the "traditional" and the "modern." Many people have said this, but they say it believing that one is simply a different form of the other, that they function by the same "principles" and "logic." The traditional is an earlier form of the modern, on its way to being modern. However, in reality they are two different systems with two different rationales. They are not easily blended. It is easy to put on the dress of another, but sometimes when we do this, we make mistakes. The rules are not the same. Although cultures are constantly changing, the rapid changes of the past three hundred years have been unprecedented in human history, and the need for a culture to change so quickly in the service of another also is unprecedented.

The theme of the modern versus the traditional is one that plays itself out in many forms in Ghana. It plays itself out in every arena of sociocultural life, it seeps into personal relationships, economic relationships, religion, love and romance, family life, child rearing, education—everywhere. It takes the form sometimes of the old versus the new, Africa versus the U.S., traditional versus modern, or "primitive" versus "civilized." Sometimes it takes the form of "Black" versus "White" or sometimes "underdeveloped" versus "developed." These categories go together, and how they play themselves out forms the stage on which all aspects of the culture are acted out. They are the central themes of today, the resolution of which will be the realities of the future.

The Electricity Poles (Abaasa)

We all sit, once again, in the temporary chief's palace. I have become queen mother of the village and, as such, sit many times in this fashion. The chief has "run away" to Kumasi and is yet to return, so we use one of the best houses (really just a room) for our business. Africans are often thought to look alike, just as white people are thought to look alike in this age of "race," defined by something called "color." But as I look around the room, I am struck by the differences. Kwame Nkrumah, who is my translator, reminds me of my brother. I feel that it is somehow providential that my interpreter shares the name of Ghana's first president in this village where chance has brought together such an unlikely mix. It is chance or providence. They have told me that it is God who has brought me here, here to this translator of language and culture who has the name of the great African leader and who looks like my brother. It makes me wonder. My brother has tan skin although that of Mr. Nkrumah's is a deep, dark brown, but the similarities in the soft expression of the eyes, the full black beard, gentle manner, and almost sweet face are more obvious to me. He is about 5'10", tall and thin, a size I would call medium. Although there is a kind of sweetness about him, there is also an underlay of deep intensity, maybe brooding. He is my unofficial linguist because his English is better than most and because he is so involved. He is a preaches on Sundays at the Twelve Apostles Church, is a farmer, is sometimes a teacher during the week, is always at the chief's council meetings, always takes the lead on community matters, and is an outspoken leader in the broader community. He walks with a limp caused by a diseased hip joint that causes moderate to severe pain throughout the year, yet he has always been an active man and is proud of his background as an exceptional football goalie.

Next to Mr. Nkrumah is Mr. Adams. He is always called Mr. Adams. He is a much taller man with skin the color of caramel, somewhere in between my brother's and Mr. Nkrumah's color. He has large, round bright eyes and an intense, interested face. He smiles easily, displaying a set of perfect white teeth. He reminds me of a professor friend of mine. He is a sober man, a preacher, and sometimes a teacher, whose presence lends an air of stability and sanity to the group. He is dignified, humble, and sensible.

Across from him sits Nkrumah's junior brother, Kobina Eight. Children are given many names in Ghana. One of them reflects their gender and the day on which they were born. Kwame is the name for a Saturday-born boy. Kobina is a boy born on Tuesday. If there is more than one in a family, something else is added, thus, Kobina Eight. Nothing about them suggests to me that they are brothers. Kobina does not speak English very well, but he speaks Fante fluently and does not mind expressing his opinions. He is a friendly, joking kind of man who smiles most of the time, a wide, cheerful grin, punctuated by slightly protruding teeth and wide gaps where teeth used to be. His face is more angular than his brother's and not as handsome as that of Mr. Adams, but it is alive with energy, enthusiasm, and intelligence. His eyes are always moving, and his very slim, tall body seems also alive with energy. He is an excellent dancer, an exuberant man, and an able, cooperative participant in village life. Although he has grown children, Kobina gives the appearance of a young, agile, sometimes goofy boy.

Next to Kobina sits the chief's linguist. He has been the linguist for the past twenty or more years and is an elderly man of indeterminable age. He is perhaps seventy, perhaps older, but he does not know, and it does not matter. He is one of the elders. He is a very small man; he and I can see eye to eye, which means he is probably not much more than 5'2" or 5'3". He is thin with a craggy, dark, truly ebony face. His eyes are small and piercing. He is almost an ugly man, except when he speaks, when the light in his eyes and the wisdom in his face give him a charm and beauty of his own. He rarely speaks, allowing everyone else to carry on the conversation while he sits in quiet contemplation.

Next to the chief's linguist is yet another unique and interesting man. He is young, perhaps in his thirties, though he, too, could be taken for a young boy. He is somewhat taller than Mr. Nkrumah and thicker than Kobina. He wears a clean Izod shirt and dressy long trousers most of the time. This is in contrast to the often tattered, open shirts and torn, dirty shorts of many of the other men. His name is Kwaku, and he has a smooth, clear face that is a color somewhere between that of Mr. Adams and that of Kobina. His face is open and looks like that of a man without any worries. It is a calm, pleasant, unlined, oval face. He reminds me, in his polo shirt, of a newly graduated college man or a young businessman. He is slightly athletic appearing but without the usual American macho athletic look. He is polite, gentle, in the typically Ghanaian masculine style that American men might refer to as somewhat effete.

Then there is the "chairman." He has his own style, his own look. His skin is a shade or two darker than Mr. Adams's and his face is furrowed, angular, and large. He is a large man, tall, and big boned with huge feet. I noticed his feet accidentally one day as he sat near me while we waited for the meeting to start. I was so struck by their size that I caught myself commenting to him. He was not offended, maybe pleased, and agreed that, yes, they are large. He has matching large hands and large personality. He is the chairman of the council, but perhaps partly because he likes apeteche too much, he does not seem to play as critical a role in community affairs as do Nkrumah, Adams, or some of the others. His face is not smooth, and his eyes do not have the large openness of those of Adams, nor does he have the sweetness of Nkrumah or the cheerful smile of Kobina. He has the face of a man who is not at peace with himself. There is a certain handsomeness in his face that is overshadowed by a look of sadness, anguish perhaps.

There are others, of course. Most of them are thin, but they vary in height, body build, eye and nose shape, and skin shade. One of the elders is Muslim. He has a very long, straight nose curving downward, small round eyes, high cheek bones, and skin like milk chocolate. He has beautiful, long fingers on hands that have been used and worn. The men have come from many different parts of Africa and have mixed and blended with many different people, so even when they are brothers, their faces are a personal blending of shade, tone, and shape.

I notice these interesting and unique faces, hands, and feet while we wait patiently for all to assemble. Finally, there seem to be enough. There are maybe twenty or thirty men who attend council meetings, but the configuration changes from time to time, usually averaging around ten. There is the stable core: Mr. Nkrumah, Mr. Adams, the chairman, Kobina, the linguist, and usually Mr. Mohammed. Frequently there is the chief's senior brother, my husband, Mr. Akrah. But the rest of the group is fluid, including over time almost all of the adult men of the village. The women join us now and then for specific purposes, but they are not regular members of the council. Traditional gender roles keep them away.

We begin the meeting as usual, clearing the air with greetings, formally welcoming me, the stating of our purpose in meeting, and discussing how things are in each of our villages. Usually I am given a beer, two Cokes, or a Coke and a malta. After these amenities are observed, we sit down to business. Today we are discussing the electricity poles. The village has no electricity, as is the case of many villages in Ghana. The government has an electrification plan in place, but the people of Abaasa are anxious and would like to expedite the process if possible. They have been told that if they obtain a plan from the electricity company and purchase the poles, the government, with the help of some nongovernmental organization (NGO), will come to finish the job. The issue of the poles has been on our agenda for some time now. The village has obtained the plan and are now looking for the poles. They have been told that each pole will cost approximately 300,000 Cedis. They will need twenty-five poles at a total cost of approximately eight million Cedis. This is equivalent to approximately 400 U.S. dollars. The minimum wage in Ghana at this time is 2000 Cedis, or less than one U.S. dollar, per day. Some of the members of the community work as laborers for wages, but most of are farmers. The villagers sometimes sell charcoal, which they make; palm nuts, coconuts, or oranges, which they grow. However, most do not have anything to sell and therefore rely primarily on their own farm produce for survival. This consists mainly of cassava and maize. They sometimes farm for cash to earn money for clothes, shoes, school uniforms, school fees, and whatever else they must purchase. It was beyond my comprehension how such a village was to acquire these twenty-five poles. It was also beyond my understanding how such a village could be expected to provide them.

Nevertheless, the village had agreed, I was assured, that the poles would be obtained. At one point, they had wanted a grinding machine so that they could grind their own cassava and maize, pay a small amount, and use the proceeds for the village. As it is now, they use a grinding machine that belongs to someone from another village and must pay each time they use it. I said that perhaps I could buy such an item as a gift to the village. It was to cost approximately 2.5 million Cedis. But now, they said, I should instead use the money for the purchase of the electricity poles. I had agreed reluctantly because I thought that the grinding machine would be more helpful. It also seemed to me a dubious activity to obtain poles, put them in the ground, and then wait for some unknown period for some unknown benefactor to produce lights for the village. However, after weeks of discussions, I was convinced that they were convinced of the wisdom of this endeavor and therefore would proceed as quickly as possible. After all, everyone wants electricity. The children can learn better, they said, they can use the television and radios without car batteries, and they would have lights for nighttime use. Eventually, they would even have refrigerators and cold beer.

Today, we are discussing the poles available at Jewkwa. Jewkwa is a larger village about 3 miles down the main road from Abaasa. They have poles to sell, and Abaasa would like to buy them. They will sell them for 100,000 Cedis per pole instead of the usual 300,000. The community is divided into two groups, Nkrumah explains to me, the men and the women. Each group is to earn money. They will add this money to my money, and we will buy the poles. The people in Jwekwa already have electricity, but they made their own poles in anticipation of help from the government. In the meantime, an NGO or the World Bank (no one seemed exactly clear) had come along and put in electricity, providing poles and all. Now Jwekwa has about seventy-five useless poles of which Abaasa wants twenty-five. I wonder what would happen if we obtain the poles and the same thing happens to us. How do we know that the government will bring the electricity, and how do we know that someone will not come along with help, poles and all, and we in Abassa will be left, as was Jwekwa, with extra poles? "Oh, this will not happen," they assure me. "We need the poles right away." I am skeptical. "What is the hurry?" I ask. "Who has 2.5 million Cedis at this moment with which to purchase these unwanted poles? Will they be taken if we do not hurry and buy them? Are they sure they want to spend the money in this way?" I am confused. They seem sure. I try to make it clear that this is one gift, and that another one will, in all likelihood, not be available. I am, after all, not an agency, not an NGO. I do not have 2.5 million to give every day. Maybe we should check on other poles. Maybe we should ask the electricity company if they have old ones. Maybe we should wait until we know for sure that the government is coming with the wiring, and so on. Where is the villages' contribution? Do they have it? How could they possibly get it? I have heard that in situations like this, the village figures the cost of the item and then levees each member of the village, in residence and outside, so that they acquire the necessary funds. Shouldn't we do such a thing?

The chief is not here. My Fante is still miserably poor. Only Nkrumah seems to understand English well. I feel overwhelmed. I need guidance. But who is there to ask? I have asked everyone I can think of, but no one seems to know what to do. My questions seem mostly irrelevant to the village. There is an assembly man for the district, Mr. Clarke. He speaks good English, is somewhat sophisticated, and is responsible for representing the seven villages in our district to the regional and eventually the national government. He thinks the villagers should be levied. He offers to go with me to the local electric company to ask them about the qualifications for the poles. Mr. Clarke believes that the electricity company has extra poles that they will sell for less money. We go there. Nkrumah and Adams go there. We each speak to different people, and no one knows anything about how to obtain inexpensive poles. The poles should be made of wood or of cement with an iron rod through the middle. They are to be a certain height and will rest a certain number of feet into the ground. These poles cost about 300,000 per pole. We are back where we started. Jwekwa has cheaper poles, and Abaasa needs them to demonstrate that they are serious about electricity. They are anxious and are in a hurry. Many villages will want the poles, they say.

So, there is an uproar of sound in the small room. The men are animated in conversation. They stand up, gesture, argue, and then suddenly burst into a peel of loud laughter. "I'm coming," says Nkrumah to me, every now and then, to assure me that he will soon translate. They are discussing the poles, the money, Jewkwa, my contribution, and the villagers' contribution. Mr. Mohammed takes the floor. Suddenly, all are quiet, and all eyes are on him. He takes his time. He deliberates and takes long pauses while he fingers his beads. I do not know what he is saying, but it sounds profound. It seems as if he is summing up. For about an hour they have been discussing, exhorting, shouting, talking over each other, laughing, and gesturing. Now, in the silence, the old man stands, wearing his skull cap and Muslim dress, and his craggy face and bright eyes make him seem wise like the ancestors. His words are important. He speaks for some time, sitting in his chair, and then leans back, still fingering his beads. He is finished. Nkrumah turns to me now. "Queen Mother," he says, "What the old man has said is that you are right to worry, that you should not spend your money without knowing what it is for, that we should go with you to Jewkwa so that you, yourself, can see the poles and talk to the people." So, in two days we will go to Jewkwa. Someone will inform Jewkwa that we are coming. I will return to Abaasa, and we will go to Jewkwa. It is settled.

Two days later I arrive in Abaasa when the sun is high and hot in the sky. We sit in the makeshift chief's palace, once again waiting for the group to gather. They give me a warm beer to welcome me. I sip on it as we wait. It is so quiet that I can hear the flies buzzing around the opening of the door. Clothes sway on the clothesline outside. There is an occasional bleat of a sheep or crow of a rooster. Women move about noiselessly, carrying wood or hanging clothes with babies on their backs, wrapped in their mother's cloth. Some of the women, usually the older ones, have abandoned a top, and some wear only a bra. All have a cloth around the bottom. It is hot and still. The activity of the village goes on without drama, without noise, without disturbance. As I sit in the small room and look out on the women and the front of the mud house,

Kwame Nkrumah (far right) with committee members—author's truck—Abaasa

I can look out the door and see the chickens, goats, and flies. It feels like time has stood still and time stands still. There is no rush. There are no honking horns, jangling radios, clanging televisions, or even crying children. I know that the children cry, that some people have radios and tellies, and that people quarrel, but you cannot tell it when you are here. When you are here, there is a stillness, a slowness, a sense of endless time. It is clean in the village. There is no refuge. There are no politine rubbers (polyurethane bags) flying about. You can hear the flies. Why do these people want electricity? Why do they want to disturb this peace? Will it bring them happiness? What will it be like if they have more tellies, more radios, and refrigerators? Will they be happier with cold beer and cold soft drinks? Will the children spend more time studying than they do now with the light of a lantern?

I have asked these questions. I asked the school children as they piled into my truck coming home from Junior Secondary School (J.S.S). They, like their adult counterparts, answer my questions quizzically. Of course it will be better, they say. We can learn better, they say. They know that this is a part of progress. They know that this is development. Everyone needs to develop, they say. But how will everyone afford a tellie, I ask. They are surprised. They will get it. It will just happen. Will it be good?, I ask. Of course it will be good. Tellie is good. But when I watch it myself, it seems bad, filled with the worst of the West and bad imitations of the worst of the West, mostly the United States. It is filled with the usual violence, illicit sex, and images of women and men in situations and clad in dress that is completely foreign to the situations and dress in the villages and even most of the towns in Ghana. How can this be good, I ask myself? Why do children need electricity to learn? Can't they do it after school? Can't they do it during the day? Will they use the evening hours?

My thoughts are interrupted. It is time to go. We go to Jewkwa: Mr. Adams, Mr. Nkrumah, Kobina, and I. When we arrive, it is late. It is almost 4 p.m. Someone wrote that there is no dawn in West Africa, and there is no dusk. There is no dusk in Ghana. The sun stays high and hot and piercing until 6 p.m. when it suddenly disappears. By 6:30 p.m. darkness has descended. So, although 4 p.m. looks like the middle of the day, it is really the end. The people in Jewkwa have finished their work for the day and have begun to relax, as have the people from Abaasa. Soon after we arrive, it is clear that no real discussion or observation of poles will take place today. Our people start to demand a lower price for the poles, and their people begin to argue. Our people begin to lose their tempers, and their people do likewise. I am barely out of my truck, but it is decided that we will come back to speak more officially to their own district assembly man and members of the community. "Where is the chief?" I want to know. "Where are the elders?" We cannot just turn over 2.5 million Cedis to these people in the street. No, we will return. "But, what about the libation?" one of the Jewkwa men ask. I quickly understand, begin to hand them two 5,000 Cedi notes. Nkrumah angrily grabs back one. This begins another round of argument, tempers are beginning to heat up again. I begin to move my truck, the rest of our men jump in, and we dash off down the dirt road.

I am praying as we leave that the next encounter will be more orderly. And it is. The next week we return to Jewkwa to complete the deal. This time we are met by the assembly man for the district within which Jewkwa sits. We walk across the sandy road, around a half-completed cement house, and through a yard with chickens squawking and children running, staring, and calling out to the brunyi (white woman, or foreigner) as we pass. We enter a building resembling the rectangular cement rooms of Abaasa but somewhat larger. The assembly man, who is referred to as "Assembly Man," is tall, young-looking, and serious. There is another man, an elder, who directs us. Other men sit around. None of them wears a cloth. There are no stools or goat skin rugs. The assembly man is dressed neatly in khaki trousers, a plain Western-style shirt, and good leather sandals. Everyone else is in Western attire. There are no formalities. There is no ceremony, no libation, and no questioning of purpose. I am surprised because I have never been to such a meeting in a village in Ghana. Clearly this is a business meeting. This does not have to do with the chief, the elders, or ritual or ceremony. This has to do with straight business. The assembly man does not seem like a patient man. He wants to sell his poles, and he wants his money. This seems clear. He says that he has the poles. We can see them if we like. The price is 100,000 Cedis per pole, and there will be no further bargaining. I ask a few questions about the price and quality of the poles, trying to be sure that we are doing the right thing. He answers my questions but seems annoyed. His English is perfect. My people look at me anxiously. They are afraid I will change my mind. We decide to confer outside.

Outside I try to explain once again my reservations about quickly grabbing these poles at this price. "We have not looked at other poles," I argue. They say they are selling the poles for the cost of the materials, but are not including the labor. This is a good deal, we are told, and my people agree. "But," I persist, "Why should we pay them for the cost of the materials? If this is the case, Abaasa could buy their own materials and make them themselves." In other words, I reasoned, we are not getting any particular bargain, and Jewkwa is stuck with seventy-five poles they do not need. They surely will sell them for less. My people are disturbed. I seem to be missing the point. They want to buy them. The people of Jewkwa are being good to the people of Abaasa. They are offering us a deal. They are not charging for the labor. The labor was contributed by these very men from whom we are buying. I realize that my arguments are in vain, so I stop. I say that I have my money and that if they want to use it in this way, I am ready to complete the deal. They are happy. We go in, inform our hosts, hand over the money, and are ready to leave. Afterwards my people comment on the fact that the people of Jewkwa did not even given us a drink or greet us properly. But they do not dwell on this bit of sloppy hospitality. We have our own libation by lamplight in Mr. Adams's tiny square room, shake hands, and celebrate our victory.

It is dark by this time. While I drive home, I reflect on the negotiations. In America, we are practiced in stratigizing for the best price. We think about how to get the most for our money. We feel that it is wasteful, careless, and almost sinful not to do so. I am not very skilled at this activity. I am not a businesswoman. But even I wanted to push harder. The logic of their purchase evades me, as the logic of my skepticism evades them. Why did I not see that this is a very good deal and that the people of Jewkwa are trying to help us? I realize that we have this difference partly as a result of our different relationships to labor. In my country, the labor is hidden; we never see it. It is in Taiwan, Mexico, or maybe even New York or Los Angeles; but wherever it is, it is neither seen nor mentioned. The laborer is unknown to us. We do not think about the time or working conditions that went into the product. We think of our advantage. We think of supply and demand. How many products does the seller have, how many buyers? If we know there are plenty of products, the price should be lower. If there are few buyers, the price should be lower. If it is rare or if everyone needs or desires it, it will cost us more. But here the laborer is sitting right before us. The labor cannot be ignored. It is perhaps a cousin, a brother-in-law, or a senior father. The man doing the bargaining put his own hard labor into the product, and his own village mate, his own relative, or his own friend is there before him, assessing that labor. We have been given a gift. The labor has been given for free. How could we possibly ask for more? Can we exploit these people who sit before us and who have known us and our fathers and will continue to know us and to marry our sons and our daughters? It has never been clearer to me that the item we bought is the combined labor of these men and women and that of this fact they are aware. I am not used to this kind of thinking. They are not used to mine. How can they bargain with me? How will they compete? How will Ghana compete in a world that thinks the way I do? They have not fully caught on to the principles of capitalism. This is what the newspapers say. They need workshops and seminars to learn about it.

More Poles

God Did Not Create an Evil Person.

[Gyekye 1996, 189]

I had not been to the village for a while. When I arrive, it is late, almost 4 p.m. I had gone to the Catholic church in the morning and then stopped by to see Baidoo. He has just arrived from the U.S. and is settling back into everyday Ghana life. It is always

difficult coming back, I think. It is anticlimactic. The preparation for travel, the limi-
tations of travel, and the preparation for return are all exhilarating. There is a sense of
purpose, of adventure, and of meaning. Preparation is essential for the trip and therefore makes preparation activity essential. The questions of meaning and purpose are
temporarily in abeyance. The urgency of the moment makes life meaningful. But the
return is a return to what you have left. The same problems, the same debts, the same
quarrels, and the same demands on time, money, and patience. The realities of your
existence are, if anything, even clearer, put into relief by your recent absence. The
poverty of Ghana, the inconveniences, the frustrations, and the ever-present and constant need are more obvious in contrast to the smoothly running, clean opulence of
the North. You miss it, but now the heat, the dust, and the filth are oppressive. Your
responsibilities are still there. Your doubts, fears, and mortality are still there.

So Baidoo is settling in. He seems tired and scattered as he sits in his beautiful
new blue cloth. He says he has been somewhat ill since his return. It is probably
malaria, the ever-present, insidious disease that, once in you, never seems to leave
fully. He cannot go to Abaasa with me today. He has too many obligations. So I go
on alone, later than I had planned.

There is more activity than usual when I arrive. The huge electric company truck
is just leaving, people are scattered about, and I see most of the council members out
on the dusty, rock-strewn road, here and there, as I drive my ailing Pajero into the
village. Nkrumah meets me eagerly, agitated. There has been a terrible accident, he
says. The electric company came to place the poles in the holes dug by the village.
All have been put into the ground with the exception of two. He takes my hand, and
we go to the spot where one of the yet to be placed poles lies on the ground. It was
here, he says. They were carrying the pole on the small, hand-driven cart when it
tipped, and the pole fell. Everyone scattered, but an old man could not run and was
struck across his leg by the pole. It is about 8 feet high and 10 inches in diameter. It
is made of solid cement with a steel rod running down its middle. The pole crushed
the man's leg, splintering it. They have taken him to the hospital in town. It just happened. Everyone is disturbed. We stop by and greet my "husband" on our way to the
temporary chief's palace. He is recovering well from his recent illness and looks
sprightly and somewhat devilish as he greets us. He expresses appreciation for my
help and prays for its continuation. "Do not turn your heart elsewhere," he says.

When we sit to discuss the event, many men are present. The ones who have taken
the patient to the hospital have just returned and we are interested in news of his condition. I am greeted and welcomed. A warm Club beer is set before me as a welcome. There
has been an accident, Nkrumah tells me and the others, but the poles have been put into
the ground, and otherwise things are fine in the village. The messengers share their news.
We are told that the man has been placed in the hospital. They will repair his leg and put
it in a plaster cast. It costs 2000 Cedis for the visit, 3000 for a consultation fee, and 80,000
as a down payment on the setting of the leg and hospitalization. In addition, they must
purchase a toothbrush, toothpaste, a washcloth, a comb, and other small items for the
man's personal hygiene. He also requires help for his food and bedding. There are few
relatives around, but a nephew somehow materializes, and he will buy the items and send
for a sister in nearby Saltpond. The village is responsible for the cost of the man's accident. They express gratitude that it was not a more severe accident; for example, it was

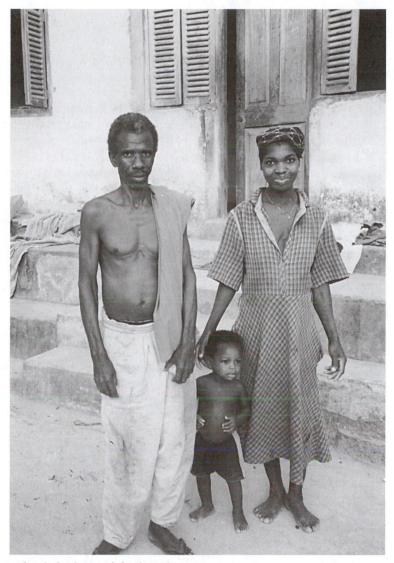

Recovering from broken leg—with family—Abaasa

not his head instead of leg, or that it was not a small child. Nevertheless, it is difficult news. Part of the difficulty, as usual, is the money. The village was struggling to find the money for the poles and to bring electricity to the village, and now they are encumbered with this added expense. I express my condolences, and we all express sadness, frustration, gratitude, and anxiety for a short period. Mohammed suggests that perhaps they should try to retrieve him as soon as possible from the hospital and bring him to the village for local cure. Nkrumah explains to me that they have very good local doctors who can set broken limbs and have good medicinal herbs for curing. The local cures are very good, he assures me. I am familiar with the curing capabilities of local healers and nod agreement with their plans.

Nevertheless, this creates yet another obstacle to the electricity procurement program. The village must pay all expenses incurred while the injured man is unable to work, including hospital bills, medicines, food for the man and his family, and extra items, such as milk and a jacket for cold evenings. After several weeks we collect the man from the hospital. The fee is 700,000 Cedis. The average laborer receives 2,000 Cedis per day and most of the Abaasa farmers do not make that, so this is a huge cost for them. It amounts to approximately 250 U.S. dollars at the time, which seems like a very inexpensive hospital stay to most Americans. But to the village it was an unimaginable amount. I try to negotiate with the hospital, who respond that they cannot run a hospital on nothing. Because it is obvious that most of the people using the hospital, either in the hospital or as out patients, are villagers just like those from Abaasa, the hospital clearly cannot afford to give away its services. Together we acquire the requisite amount and take our man home. It is not clear to me what would have happened to him if I had not been there to help.

When we bring him home, everyone rejoices. However, he is in a cast to his hip and requires medication for pain and for a sore that has still not healed. He is to have the sore dressed every few days, but it seems impossible to figure out just how that will happen. Transportation in and out of the village is expensive and difficult to procure. Taxis are reluctant to travel into the village, and when they do, they charge exorbitantly because they are afraid their vehicles will be ruined. The man cannot walk and has to be accompanied. At one point the leg begins to swell, so we return him to the hospital where they remove the cast and discover infection. He receives a new, lighter cast, a new fee, and is sent home to return in another 4 weeks. During this period, it is decided that his care will be turned over to the local healer, who removes the cast and applies his own medicines. The last time I see him, he is feeling fine and standing although he still cannot walk. Later, Nkrumah tells me that he dreamed that the man could stand, and that day he went to the house, and the man stood.

We are now free to discuss another problem on the table. This has to do with me, the assembly man, money, and the electricity project. All are assembled as usual, we greet each other, they welcome me, and I state my mission as usual. We are in the middle of a problem. I explain the problem to the village, but we do not agree on the solution. I am annoyed. I feel betrayed. One of their (our) own has cheated me. He has taken my money, used my time, and inconvenienced me. He said he would help me with my car. He spent too much on the repairs and often kept it too long, clearly using it for his own purposes. I was busy, and it did not seem like too much, so I let it go. Then he went too far. He said that he took it to his mechanic, who told him what repairs were required. The items totaled 700,000 Cedis. This is a huge amount of money. Looking back, I realize how foolish I had been. No one around me in Cape Coast had ever or would ever see such a large sum. But I was frustrated with the car, wanted to get it repaired and on the road, and wanted to forget about it. So I gave him the money and sent him off to Accra where he said he would purchase the items. In the end, he never went to Accra, never paid his mechanic to repair it, and acquired a few of the items in Cape Coast without paying for them. He kept the car for several days and returned it clearly in the same condition as when he took it. When I suggested this to him, he flew into a rage and ran off. Nearly every time I drove the car after that, someone came up to me saying that I owed them for a piece of equipment or repairs.

Because the same man owed me about 300,000 Cedis already, the sum is now an alarming amount. Not knowing what to do about it but thinking that, at this point, something has to be done, I ask for advice. Mr. Baidoo says that I should tell the village so that they can bring my man before them and that they, by all means, will ensure justice is achieved. But justice is not what is accomplished, at least from my point of view. I explain my story. Mr. Clarke explains his. He does not explain exactly his actions, but he says that because I am his mother, queen mother of the village, how it would be possible for him to do such a thing to me? How could he lie to his own mother? This does not convince me, but it seems to convince them. After long deliberation and discussion, most of which is not translated, Mr. Mohammed speaks. The village, he says, understands my problem. They understand that Mr. Clarke has done a very bad thing. They agree that he should be chastised, and they have done so. However, he says, I should now try to forgive him. We must all live together, we must all work together, and it is not good to have bad feelings. I am crushed. I say that it is a great deal of money, that I do not have large sums of money, but that, more than that, I have been deceived, cheated, and betrayed. They agree, but I must forgive him, they say, and we will go on. I am not satisfied, but it is late, they say, and Mr. Clarke has far to travel on foot, so we must continue another time.

Today I am returning to finish the conversation. This time, however, Mr. Clarke is not there. The atmosphere is tense, but I am ready. After the protocol has been observed, I say that I have something to say. I begin with a story. You have parables, I say, and we also have them. I tell them one of ours, as they tell me theirs. This one is about the goose that laid golden eggs. I tell them the story. When I finish, I say, "I am that goose. Mr. Clarke is the one who stole it. I give small gifts now and then. Some day, who knows, there may be another golden goose born, or I may lay more eggs. But Mr. Clarke became greedy and took too much and has now killed the golden goose." I continue, "Now if you need money for the remaining electricity poles or for help with the school or help with a doctor visit, you will need to go to Mr. Clarke because he has my money. Until the million Cedis he owes me is used up," I say, "you can go to him for help."

There is deadly silence while this news registers, then a burst of conversation. They talk for a long time. Nkrumah does not interrupt to translate. Then, Mohammed, beads in hand, sits on the edge of the chair and, in a calm voice, punctuated by long silences, speaks. Nkrumah does not interrupt him. When he stops, Nkrumah turns to me. He says that the old man has spoken. The old man wants me to think and reconsider. I am much esteemed by the village and all of the people around. All of the villages around know that I am the queen mother, and whenever I do something for them, it is known. When electricity comes, it will be known by everyone that I have given lights to the people of Abaasa. I have done great things for the people, and God will bless me and reward me. So I must not worry about this issue. They are on my side. They know that Clarke has done wrong. They know that I have been good and done well. They understand my story, and they like it. However, I should also know that they, too, have their proverbs, and one of them says that you do not let go of the hand of your friend in the middle of the stream.

Nkrumah says this softly with his rolling, accented English, and I look at the face of Mohammed. His eyes are smiling in his deeply cragged tan face. I feel ashamed, and I think he knows that I would. He looks calm, confident, and sure. After Nkrumah finishes, the old man speaks again. Nkrumah again translates. They have another parable: "When a ball is bounced against a wall, it bounces back at you." This time the old man is smiling outright. What can I say? Afterward, I think, "What a clever old man."

The Government and the Perils of Acquiring Electricity

I give them the rest of the money for the poles, but our problems are not over. They have to make large, deep holes by hand with shovels and picks. They are finally all finished, except for one. That one is delayed because they run into solid rock. With a pick and hammer, the men spend many more days chipping away at the hard rock.

There are other problems, but none of them deter Abaasa from its quest for electricity. We speak to regional and state electricity people, to the district manager, and to the minister of parliament. When we visit the minister of parliament at a funeral, in his cloth in the pouring rain, he says that the village should receive services, but they are waiting because the village is to be moved. I protest because the village was told it would be moved seven years ago, and now they are still waiting. Well, he says, we need to get a letter from the water and sewage people stating whether or not the village will be moved. So we go to the water and sewage people. Yes, they say, it is true. The village is being considered for removal because a the dam is to be raised will cause the village to flood. But in all likelihood that will not happen because the dam was built in 1928, making it old and unable to support any more water. It is also perhaps too old to be lifted, as the plan demands.

In the meantime, Abaasa is waiting. So the water and sewage man assures me that he will send a letter to the district chief executive who will inform the minister of parliament so that Abaasa can be eligible for government services. As it is, the school is in disrepair, there are not enough seats for the children, and not enough teachers. The road is barely passable, which isolates village, and transportation of their small amounts of oranges, charcoal, and cassava to market is almost prohibitive. There is no indoor plumbing, and the two bore holes dug about 10 years ago are falling into disrepair. A part of the metal pipe that lies underground has corroded, so the pump no longer works. They show me the broken pipe, saying that there is someone who might be able to fix it, but it costs 200,000 Cedis that the village does not have. They tell the children not to use it. They continue to use the river and the one remaining bore hole for the water needs of the village. They prefer to spend their money on electricity. Electricity is the most important need.

Finally the electric company puts the poles in position. We pay them, and the village provides fu fu, goat meat, and drinks. They also add a sheep, bananas, and locally-produced gin for the men to take home. We pour libation, and everyone rejoices. Seventeen electrical poles now reach proudly to the sky throughout the village, representing movement and progress. Again, I go to the electric company, and our man looks at me and says, "Oh, yes. You are Asebu Abaasa. I remember you." I offer that I suspect he will tire of seeing me there, but that I need to come. He replies, "I'm already tired of you, Asebu Abaasa, but I will do what you want anyway." We will see.

PROGRESS

I personally feel the whistle for the human race was blown by God for both blacks and whites from an equal standpoint of view, but whether it is lack of stamina, speed or tiredness, whichever one cannot tell why the white race is far ahead of us. Our traumatic traditions have crippled our legs making us staggering behind the race. I sometimes pity those who call themselves traditional activists, of which many are prominent educationists of this great nation. Inasmuch as one should respect the re-ligion of one another—that is, freedom of worship—there are aspects that need to be discarded. How can we progress with people still advocating for the revival or sustenance of Trokosi? Why do people still practice female genital mutilation, wid-owhood rites, and other outrageous traditions? Notwithstanding the fact that some of our traditions are worthy of preserving, most of them must go, because they are simply outmoded. If one takes a look at how fast these whites are developing day in and day out, these retrogressive traditions are not mentioned in their world. How can the land be observed for a period of weeks without making noise, with no serious farming business activities going on? It is high time we got primitive ideas scrapped off our progressive spectrum. As we are preparing to enter the new millennium with the reduction of economic hardships, political stability, and tranquillity, there is much left to be desired. We must be armed to achieve targets of Vision 2020 with optimism. Indulgence in too much tradition cannot do.

[Stephen Aidoo
Quarshie, Asamankese
The Mirror, Ghana, July 10, 1999]

The starting whistle blows, the race begins, and Africa is far behind. This news is heralded throughout the land, from both sides of the ocean. The International Monetary Fund and the World Bank lament the fact and impose structural adjust-ment policies to try to bridge the gap. Africans, in public and in private, argue the mystery. Why should Africa be underdeveloped while America is developed? Why should black people be so far behind white people?

By all accounts, the African economy is in shambles. (Ayittay 1998; Watkins 1995; Saul and Leys 1999; Davidson 1992)

Half a century ago, the Bretton Woods conference created the World Bank and the International Monetary Fund (IMF) as the twin pillars of what was to be a new world order built on the foundations of full employment, prosperity[,] and coopera-tion. Nowhere is their failure more starkly apparent than in Sub-Saharan Africa, where the economic policy horizon has been dominated by IMF-World Bank Struc-tural Adjustment Programs for more than a decade." (Watkins 1995, p. 93) The re-sult is that "Africa is fast becoming the Third World within the Third World: its cit-izens poorer, less healthy and less educated than their counterparts in Latin America and Asia." (Watkins 1995, p. 96)

"In most places in Africa, telephones do not work; they 'bite back.' Electricity and water supplies are sporadic. What are called roads are often passageways truncated by crevasses large enough to swallow a truck. Hospitals lack food and medical supplies. Doctors even have difficulty finding paper on which to write pre-scriptions. Often patients are requested to bring their own blankets and bandages. Communicable diseases such as yellow fever, malaria, and cholera (once believed vanquished) have reappeared with a vengeance. In the cities, many banged-up and unrepaired vehicles move sideways in a crab-like manner. Even government buildings have reached advanced stages of dilapidation. Broken windowpanes abound while offices reek of mold, rust and dust. (Ayittey 1998, p. 9)

Foreign aid is a way out. However, this is not without its own problems.

Aid-giving has now become such an integral part of this co-existence that some of us developing countries have been made to believe that our very survival and progress depend on such apparently benevolent hand-outs. In fact some countries may not even be assured. Such aid-dependency syndrome does surely kill self-confidence and initiative. A plethora of agencies, especially the so-called NGOs have lately surfaced, all proffering aid, said to be free of any encumbrances in every aspect of human activity. These agencies operate oftentimes in blatant disregard or contravention of local custom, law, and religion. It is these particulars which have to be subjected to strict scrutiny and surveillance.

[S.E. Quarm, Daily Graphic, Ghana, July 22, 1999]

"Development," however, has begun for better or worse. And what is a country to do? We live in a global world in a global economy with global rules. Structural adjustment is a fact of life and aid programs are a necessary, albeit complicated, part of local economies. Daily the newspapers announce workshops on how to understand time as an asset and the virtues of the new technology. Never mind that the electricity does not always work, that the humidity rusts and corrodes at a phenomenal rate, and that time is yet to be completely tamed. There are speeches, articles, and radio programs extolling the virtues of free enterprise and private ownership and warning against the dangers of "tribalism" and backwardness. Nevermind that local survival still depends on sharing and family ties, and the fragile infrastructure is held together primarily through the lingering remains of a highly effective, local "traditional" governance system, replete with chiefs, queen mothers, tribal councils, and the inalienable rights of the elders. Progress is washing over them to cleanse them of the old and sweep them into the new.

When Great Britain colonized Ghana, the local populations were horticulturalists. They were organized around lineages, clans, tribes, chiefdoms, villages, and kingdoms. Their slash-and-burn method of growing protected the soil while supplying the needs of the group. They gave birth, fed their people, maintained order, danced, sang, married, and buried their dead. As they have been increasingly drawn into the world market, they gradually have neglected the internal market to produce for an external one. They need money now, money to send children to schools, to buy them shoes and uniforms and school books, and to purchase items they no longer produce. Different products have served the needs of the export business over the years. At the moment, the chief export crop is cocoa. Timber is gaining ascendance. When the market no longer requires a product or the soil becomes overused and the product is of inferior quality, the market rejects it. It is the way of the market.

So, as is the case of much of the world's populations, Ghana imports most of what it consumes and exports most of what it produces. It is also the way of the market to sell dear and buy cheap. So Ghanaians must sell cheap and buy dear. The same is true of labor. Labor is bought cheap. The average laborer makes approximately 5,500 Cedis per day, or under 1 U.S. dollar. They cannot any longer produce what they

Mr. Baidoo's school

need, so they must purchase it at a high price. However, wages are low. Most people do many things to keep themselves going. They have a job or two, plant a few crops, sell something, and engage in complicated exchanges with relatives.

The Baidoos are perfect examples of what we might call a mixed economic strategy. Mr. Baidoo manages to run his school despite the fact that the fees are very low and many of the families never pay. With this money, he sends his children to school: one to fancy boarding school, one to University, and one to training college. He had chickens in the past, but said it did not pay enough. They have three farms, one in a neighboring village (Abaasa), one behind the house, and one on land that belongs to Mary. Mary does much of the planting and harvesting, although they all help. Sometimes people or the government give small gifts to the school, and sometimes Mr. Baidoo goes to the bank for a loan. Sometimes he borrows from a brother, but more often a brother or sister or nephew borrows from him. He is trying to add to his school and complete his modest house. For this he sometimes gets a bit of cement or roofing sheets and then performs the labor himself. He also pushes to find cement, steel rods, and wood to finish the Catholic church, of which he is a very active member. The church sometimes gives the community materials, and they work together to build. All of these projects are coterminous. Recently a friend built a small wooden kiosk in front of the Baidoos' house. Mary runs the little store with the very few items they can manage to obtain. Sometimes there is a little bread, ice cream, and crackers. Other times there are matches, cups, and tins of meat. The shop is building up slowly.

The Baidoos are savvy and forward-thinking. They want more for their children than they have had. Like Mr. Esoteric, they want a new world. It is not that they do not love Ghana, their ancestors, or their traditions. It is just that they do not like poverty. They do not like to see their children hungry or their wives without cloth.

CLOTHES AND MONEY, THE MODERN
AND THE TRADITIONAL, AND THE COLOR OF CHANGE

I always try to argue with my development class at the university that mud- and thatch-roofed houses are more adaptive in Ghana than the preferred cement-and-tin roofed ones. I always lose the argument. I also lose the argument that there is nothing inherently more beautiful about skin with little melanin than skin with more melanin or about straight hair than curly black hair. Things European and Western are modern, things African are traditional. The traditional is better left for museums and the stage. For real life, the modern will do. While driving down the road one day, Kwesi looks around him in dismay, pointing to the dirty gutters, the potholed road, the crumbling buildings, the poor begging men and women, and the half clad children darting to and fro. "If this were America," he says, "It would not look like this. Americans would fix it up in a minute. They would not allow this to happen." I am speechless. How can I explain the colonial history of Ghana, the import and export inequities, the IMF and World Bank, the world market, and the politics and economics of the situation? How can I explain that it is not magic, that America and white people do not own some special power that enables them to transcend history and economics and politics to create enormous capital. It takes enormous capital to clean the streets, to build tall buildings, and to keep beggars from view, not particular cleverness or special sensitivity. Capital is created. It does not care about the amount of melanin, the curves of the face, or the texture of the hair of the individual to whom it is affixed. It can be created by anyone under the proper conditions. But to a small boy in Africa, there is a clear correlation between progress and development and Western, American, or whiteness, in some abstract sense. He knows about colonialism, and he celebrates Ghana's independence. He knows about the slave trade because he sees the slave "castle" almost every day. He even knows something about economics; he has learned it in school. Then why can't he put it together? Why does he think that it all happens magically? Do I dare tell him that what the white man, the American, has built has been on the labor, the resources, and the poverty of his own Africa? I do not dare, and he will not believe me anyway.

And he is not the only one. In some ways, Mr. Baidoo, Mr. Esoteric, my students, Mary, and Yaro all believe in the god of little melanin. Somehow there is a magic essence in the white man that allows him to dominate and prevail. When I ask people about the term *brunyi,* I always get the same reply. It means someone white, but it is a good thing, they hasten to inject. I tell them that white people are usually offended by this title. Oh, but it is not meant as a bad thing, I am assured. It is good. They think that if a brunyi is among them it is good luck, it is a blessing.

There are almost eighteen million people in Ghana. Forty-four percent of these people are Akan, the group of which the Fante are a part. Not all of these people think alike. However none of them, in today's Ghana, can avoid confrontation with what it means to be a Ghanaian, an African, and a person in the context of a world filled with the contradictions of modern and traditional, black and white, developed and developing, first world and third world, and rich and poor. What continually amazes me is the individuality, the care, the dignity, and the intelligence with which the men, women, and children I know confront these contradictions. As I am leaving

Mary Baidoo in shop—Akotokyir

Accra to fly to America on a recent trip, I am in a taxi cab with 17-year-old Charles and 18-year-old Kwesi. The cab driver is a young man of about 30. He immediately engages us in conversation, saying that he has a wife and children and that he wants better things for them but that it is not easy. It is difficult in Ghana today, he says. There seems to be no way out. The only way is for Africa to unify (as Nkrumah clearly prescribes) but no leader today in Africa can do it, he confidently assures us. Samuel, never one to be shy about his views, speaks up from the back seat. "Excuse me," he says politely. "I know that you are my elder, are older than I am, have lived longer, and know more. I hope that I do not offend you if I speak. But perhaps you forget, because you are older, that there are some of us who are still young. We have hope. Among us, there might just be one of those leaders. We are still young. We need time to grow. But one of us may be the one, like Nkrumah, to lead us. One of us might be the one to bring Africa together." We careen around a corner with traffic loud and threatening around us and arrive at our destination. When he cheerfully waves us out of the car, the cab driver smiles broadly and says something to Charles that I interpret as "touché."

3 / Becoming Queen Mother

When a chief has plenty of milk, it is the people who drink it.

A Chief is a Chief by the People

SCHOLARS OF AFRICA have differed in their interpretation, theoretical orientation, and general approach to Africa. However, not since some of our anthropological forefathers—structural-functionalists R. Radcliffe-Brown (1950), Myer Fortes (1949), Daryll Forde (1950), and E.E. Evans-Pritchard (1951)—have they disputed Africa's inexorable ties to what Frank (1967) and Wallerstein (1980) refer to as the Core/Metropolis, or to the dilemma, terror, or inevitability of her change (Ayittey 1998, Davidson 1992, Appiah 1996, Gyeke 1996). Change is inevitable, but how are we to evaluate the kind of change that has come out of the imperialist colonization of a people and their cultures? Shall we applaud it as progress? Shall we deride it as cultural genocide? Shall we accept it as inevitable?

This topic of change, its effects and its responses, is the underlying theme of the research that I am undertaking in consultation with Mr. Augustine Ato Baidoo of Akotokyir village. He is the headmaster of the only school in the village, the chairman of the Catholic church, the father of six, and the unofficial head of the village in the absence of a reigning chief. His village is one of several that occupy the large sprawling campus visualized by the late Kwame Nkrumah as the intellectual Mecca of, if not all of Africa, at least all of Ghana. Mr. Baidoo's ancestors came to this exact spot, and this is where the family has remained through the years of British rule, their liberation, and the exhilarating and hopeful times of one of their great heroes, Kwame Nkrumah.

As times change, so do leaders and today's president. Flight Lieutenant J. Jerry Rawlings has a necessarily different agenda. He is looking more toward the West, both as a model and as a source of aid to Ghana's inevitable incorporation into the global economy. The village system of chiefs, elders, and matrilineal or patrilineal organization survives precariously with the national legal, political, social, and economic processes. The economies of farming, fishing, trading, and sharing increasingly give way to the competitive, profit-dominated global and local market economies. The changes are not new, but they seem to increase in speed as technology increases in precision and scope.

It was with these changes in mind and with my interest in history, inequality, and the reality of our human connections that I looked for a place where I could record, in ethnographic style, this moment and past moments in the hope of capturing a part of our collective history that may in time elude us. Salvage anthropology is most often attributed to Franz Boas and his students (i.e., Mead 1928, Sapir 1921, Benedict 1934, and Kroeber 1939), and we do not think of it so much in these post-modern times. However, I suppose that many of us anthropologists and citizens of the world, when confronted with the dichotomies and change-related stresses apparent in places like Africa, are stricken, as was Boas, with the sheer horror of the potential loss of yet more cultural systems.

Exploring the Cape Coast area, I found Mr. Baidoo. From the moment of our meeting, he took hold of my ideas, my concerns, and my inquiries, and he more or less took over my research. Thus my methodology, which is essentially one of participant observation, developed a new dimension. Now I am engaged in what I would call a reflexive anthropology with a local expert as my guide. He is interested in telling the story of his village, and together we gathered much of the data for this work. We have interviewed elders of the village, both men and women. We have collected stories and drawings from the children. Together we have participated in rituals, both public and private, have conversed for hours, experienced family exchanges, and encounters with almost every aspect of village life we call culture. He is the insider; he is the one who has the culture in his land, his compound, his family, and his bones. He corrects me and guides me, and together we sort out the meaning of what is now our collective culture.

Although much has been done in our work together, I am continuously reminded of how much more there is to know. It feels a bit like an onion, as one layer is peeled away and yet another one appears. I gain a deeper and broader sense of understanding as each layer reveals a new dimension, and even Mr. Baidoo, in response to my searching and probing, is forced sometimes into a new or newly-remembered knowledge of his own people and his own cultural sense of things. So together we explore the culture, and we plan how to present the picture. The people of Akotokyir and Abaasa are eager to tell their story and let themselves be known and understood by those who do not know them.

Therefore, even though the layers of cultural understanding will never be wholly peeled away, we want to begin to document the history and contemporary lives of these Fante people, as well as their ties to global politics and economy and their understandings of, and responses to, the rapid and contradictory changes they experience. Can we answer these questions: Is this progress? Is this ethnocide? Is it inevitable? Are the choices being made really choices? Can it be said that the Fante people are informed? Do they decide their responses to the changes, or are technology, multinational corporations, global trade, and global media new forms of power replacing the earlier imperial tactics of conquest and military aggression? Is this development and modernization really progress? Will all the people of the world come together into a world culture free from the devastating effects of poverty, illness, hunger, discrimination, and war?

W.W. Rostow (1962), a noted development scholar, suggests that the final stage of development for a nation is high mass consumption. Is this the end we seek? Shall we all participate more fully in the production and consumption of more and more consumer items? Will all people in the world, the people of all the Akotokyirs, and the Abaasas enjoy the use of the Internet, washing machines, home fax machines, lawnmowers, VCRs, 45-inch television sets, clothes from Paris, and cars from Germany?

And what of multiculturalism? Where does this fit? Will all cultures maintain their own culturally-identified means to accumulate such items? Will they use them in culturally sensitive ways? How will Akotokyir fit these new items into their systems of matrilineality and the chief's council? When will they learn enough of the language to understand the new consumer items? Will they stop speaking Fante? How can they keep their culture and lose it at the same time? How will the people of Akotokyir respond to such inconsistencies, such inequities, and such threats to their being, which are couched in the language of progress?

In our work together, Mr. Baidoo and I have not answered all of these questions. However, we have some insight, much data, and many more questions to ask. Although this will in some ways be a lifetime project for us both, we would like to gain some closure by putting into coherent written form the results of our work thus far. Our work together has taken us to other villages where we have connections in interesting and complimentary ways, and I have traveled to Northern Villages where I have observed that the Tallensi people, studied originally by Myer Fortes, are still remarkably similar to the people he knew.

There are several scholars of Ghana who grapple with all of our interests. Ayittey (1998) recently published a work that directly addresses the issues of change and the political and economic turmoil to which Ghana is being subjected. Appiah (1996) likewise writes of Ghana but from a slightly more personal point of view, having lived his life between Ghana (his father's home) and England (the home of his mother). Gyekye (1996) is a philosopher whose thorough coverage of Ghanaian life is wonderful. All of these works, coming from Ghanaians, are invaluable resources and give insight and perspective on Ghanaian life.

I cannot hope to present any aspect of the Ghanaian reality in the same way as can a Ghanaian. What I can do is add a perspective from outside, the particular vision that comes from confronting a culture as a newcomer. My method of participant observation and intensive, long-term engagement at the village level with the constant guidance of a non-specialist Ghanaian also offers me a different perspective. Although women scholars, such as Aidoo (1967), Prah (1997), and Clark (1994), contribute to the information from Ghana, their voices perhaps are not heard as loudly as those of the men. I believe my female colleagues will agree that a female perspective from an on-the-ground focus is one that, compliments the often male-dominated scholarship, not only in Ghanaian and African work but in scholarship in general.

We all owe a great debt to the early pioneers of work in Africa: Radcliffe-Brown (1950), Evans-Pritchard (1951);, Myer Fortes (1949);, Dyrll Forde (1950), Paul Bohannan (1964), and Melville Herskovits (1964), to name a few. I also take as my mentors the Pan-Africanists, such as Amilcar Cabral, Maurice Bishop, Walter Rodney, and W.E.B. Dubois. I perhaps owe a more theoretical debt to the following scholars: Basil Davidson (1992), Clare Robertson (1990), Bernard Magubane (1981), Claude Ake (1981), Manning Marable (1983), Emmanuel Wallerstein (1980), Marvin Harris (1994), Ashley Montague (1974), Maria Mies (1986), and Maria Patricia Fernandez-Kelly (1983). I sincerely hope that this work adds to the above research. I also hope that this document will be available for not only the people of the villages, but others who may never have the pleasure of sitting with the chief's counsel, participating in a village funeral rite, or being carried on a peroquine in a queen mother festival.

BECOMING QUEEN MOTHER: AN INSIDE VIEW
INTO TRADITIONAL POLITICS AND GOVERNMENT

There is no extensive literature on the actual lived experience of a chief and still less on the queen mother. On March 15, 1998, I become the official queen mother of Asebu Abaasa and immediately plunge into the world of chiefs, subchiefs, paramount chiefs, and linguists. This is also the beginning of a new relationship between Akotokyir and Abaassa, a relationship leading us to other villages and other chiefs, highlighting the futility of thinking about a village, a town, or even a country as a self-contained, isolated entity. The experience highlights for us the ways in which we—Baidoo, Abaasa, and I— are in truth related.

Of course my experience as a queen mother cannot ever be equated to that of a local Ghanaian queen mother of the royal line of her village. Nevertheless, immediately the village and village leaders take me as their real queen mother and expect me to behave like and fill the role of the queen mother. In fact, it is a great shock to me to gradually come to realize how much they take me to themselves and how thoroughly they expect that I am their own real queen mother. When Nana (the chief) turns to me during an early meeting and says that we speak as one, that whatever I do will be in his name, and that we are essentially the same, it suddenly dawns on me that this is a serious obligation and honor and that I am to be treated no differently than any other queen mother or, in fact, Nana himself. They assume that I know and share their cultural values and norms and therefore plunge immediately into the business at hand. When I leave for a brief trip to the U.S., they pour libation for me and pray to my God and to theirs that I will be safe and return to them soon. Nana says to me that "to be honored in one's time makes one's life complete."

I am also called Nana, and they do this with the ease of those who take the role and the title for granted. Having grown up in a culture completely devoid of such levels of nobility, I have yet to feel truly the deep reverence, awe, and respect with which they treat us. As an American, of course, it is uncomfortable to be adored, to have people follow you around fanning you and dowsing you with powder and perfume. I am not supposed to move without an entourage, and people are to bow to me holding their hands in a supplicating manner, casting their eyes down, and almost whispering, "Nana, Nana." I am slowly, I believe, realizing that I must behave in the manner of a superior, almost supernatural being, or I will be roundly chastised by my elders, by other chiefs, and by my council, and I will be an embarrassment and humiliation to them. They already hear murmurings from other villages that they "threw their stool away" by giving it to a brunyi, and are anxious to prove these rumors false. I am a true Nana and I must behave like one. I really thought that this would be mostly a ceremonial title and had no idea the responsibilities it actually implies. I am willing to honor my commitment, but it is a treacherous business. It is a bit like being a two-year-old, struggling to catch up, to hear the words, to understand the implications, and to learn the rules. The problem is that I am not two, and they do not realize the extent of my ignorance. It is a delicate dance to gain information without undermining their confidence and trust while also being seen as their leader.

This is all greatly exacerbated by the fact that almost immediately after my formal enstooling ceremony, my chief "runs away." Well, he doesn't run away exactly, but he goes to Kumasi, a town in the center of the country, ostensibly to earn some money, and does not return for nearly 2 years. Therefore, I am told at least once every time I visit that I am now the chief. In the absence of a chief or subchief (which we do not have), queen mother is it. I am now the leader. I am supposed to know everything and everybody. I am supposed to help them with their decisions. I am to know why and when the gong gong is rung, why there is a chairman, a chief, elders, a linguist, and a secretary. I must know how to dress, how to sit, when to take my shoes off and when not, and to whom to give allegiance and to whom not. I spent my entire adolescence, as did my other female peers, being told by my mother and my own elders that "nice girls" keep their legs demurely together. Now, I must sit with them spread wide, my back straight, and my hands firmly on my thighs in a position of power and confidence.

I have many assistants, but most of them speak very little English, have no idea what I do at the university and cannot put themselves into my shoes any more than I can put myself into theirs. So I am not a typical queen mother. I am a struggling one, but in the struggle and as an outsider, I can see it all with fresh eyes and perceptions. My faithful guide, Baidoo, is an invaluable resource and always at my side although, as we shall see, it has its rocky moments.

Finding a Bird Cage—The First Step

Abaasa is a Fante village, on the edge of one of the few remaining tropical rain forests. It is inhabited by approximately 150 adult males, and females and children too numerous to count. My journey to becoming a queen mother begins with a bird. Charles says that he has a nice bird for me. He has been talking about it for a long time. I finally say that he should get one for me. He says they are found in the forest, and they are beautiful colors. I have in mind a parrot, lovebird, or maybe even a toucan—something with rainbow colors. When he brings the bird to the car, its feet tied in ropes, I can hardly look. At nightfall, the air is dripping hot and sultry, and the streets are a mass of people, horns, taxis, carts, women with loads on their heads, and children darting around among the cars. The road, dusty and rutted as usual, takes my full attention. No lights, no stop signs, and no rules makes traveling the downtown Cape Coast roads treacherous at the best of times. But at dusk, after a long day, with my hair and clothes plastered to my skin and my eyes full of grit, it takes all of my attention and endurance. So it is not until we reach home that I see that what Charles has lovingly gotten me is a pigeon. It is a beautiful pigeon with brown and beige wings, but it is, nevertheless, a common, everyday pigeon. Oddly enough, we decide that we should get another one, and we call them Rebekah and Jacob, Charles's idea.

For some days after the acquisition of the pigeons, we are in search of a cage for the birds. Somehow I continue to think of the birds as rare African specimens in need of a cage. Several options are absent-mindedly explored. One late afternoon Charles declares that he knows just the right kind of cage. I allow myself to be led, as so often I do, by the uncanny reason and persuasion only a 15-year-old boy can muster. He says that the place is just a little way away on the other side of town. So, off we go. We have Kojo, Kwesi, other small boys, and their sister Adwoa, happy to go anywhere with the anticipation of a possibility of diversion and food.

Main street—Abaasa

We travel to the other side of town and then through Pedu and Abura until we are on a stretch of open highway. I am a confident and trusting person and respect the minds of small boys, but I begin to get ahold of myself and wonder out loud why this cage place seems to be outside town on a highway. "Oh," says Charles, confidently, "it is not far." "Just 'a stone's throw,'" Kwesi says, referring to one of our standard jokes arising out of an incident in which I was taken off for many miles by an old man who kept exclaiming, "It is just a stone's throw away." So I continue for several "stone's throws," and Charles eventually says I should turn. "Now we are almost there," he says, "and this road is very good, so we should be there in a minute." Well, a road traveled by foot is a very different thing from a road traveled by automobile, as I can attest to as a result of this trip. The road is an enlarged footpath with holes that could swallow my little car and gullies that appear like glaciers, as well as ruts, mud, hills, rocks, and weeds. We slip, slide, and jerk down the road, occasionally scraping the undersides of my little city Renault and eventually gouging a hole in the muffler, before we swing around a curve, up a huge hill, and gaze down on the village of Abaasa.

Despite the dubious quality of the road, the trip is one of unmitigated beauty. The land rolls up and down through lush tropical forest, occasionally revealing a long vista of bright blue sky, blazing sun, and lush green mountains. There are hills of orange trees, coconut palms, banana trees, royal palms, and an assortment of huge, old, twisted, elegant trees. Abassa appears hot, quiet, and beige as we drive up one of these splendid hills, reach the small Church of the Twelve Apostles, and emerge over the edge of another long, rising hill. Beneath us, Abaasa looks like a cluster of neat, carefully tended, but randomly strewn toy houses of clay, mud, and tin. Some are carefully built of the more pricey and desirable cement. The village is quiet. The sun reflects off the tin roofs and the treeless, zigzagging sand pathways. There is no hustle and bustle. No horns honk nor do hawkers cry out. Flies lazily swarm around the little village that seems almost like a mirage in the distance as we lower ourselves slowly down the jagged precipice.

Truck making factory

A bird cage? Here? In my mind, I quickly give up the idea of a bird cage but I know that I have found something much more important. We stop the car. Charles confidently gets out, orders me to stay put and runs off into the heart of the hard-packed dirt hills and valleys of the village. He soon returns, declaring jubilantly that the cage maker is there and agrees to start on our cage immediately. I follow Charles up a steep incline, over a hard-packed dirt gully, and up another hill and arrive at the cage factory. It consists of a small clay and thatch house, in front of which is a scrambled pile of wood and two very small boys with machetes. One boy appears to be around 9 years old, and his assistant appears to be a spirited, busy 7-year-old. "They will make the cage," Charles beams. "They will make it with this wood and the machetes only."

By this time I have really lost interest in the cage, but sit down to watch the procedure. As I sit, engrossed by the quiet of the village and the agility and expertise of the two tiny boys, a swarm of people gradually begin to assemble around me. Children begin to appear, mothers poke their heads out of small concrete or mud dwellings, and curious folks, young and old, pour out of the buildings and down the slopes to my side. There seem to be hundreds of children, and they keep multiplying as we sit. There are tiny, medium, and large boys, nearly naked and carrying sticks and rusted wheels. There are girls, equally naked except for a little tattered panty or piece of shorts. There are little girls who carry their small siblings on their backs with colorful Ghanaian cloth, sporting pink or gold earrings in their pierced ears. They are, like children everywhere, beautiful. Each has her own eyes, hair, and smile. Most are tiny and thin, but some are stout and chubby. Some look at me solemnly, appraising me; some jump with abandon; some stand by shyly; and others rush toward me, calling and laughing, as if to embrace me. I can never resist the charm of sweet little child faces, so I respond immediately with smiles, waves, and jokes, speaking my little Fante. They reward these gestures with shouts of glee, more clapping, poking, staring, pointing, and the inevitable, "Brunyi, brunyi," respecting my whiteness and foreignness.

One of the young women comes forward and begins gesturing and speaking some English. She is sad, she says, because she has not gone to school and cannot speak English. But I do not speak Fante, I communicate to her, and we are in Fante-speaking country. Nevertheless, she mimes her sadness at her wretched fate. I mime it back, and everyone laughs. Periodically the children have to be pushed back to keep from smothering me, but my new friend and a few of her cohorts is undeterred in her determination to communicate with me. As I look around, I realize that almost everyone here is either a woman or a child. The women, like the children, come in all sizes, shapes, shades, and personalities. Most are thin, with long graceful limbs and an equally thin baby on their backs. Some have on only a bra on top, some have a t-shirt, but all have a worn and tattered Ghanaian cloth wrap covering the bottom of their bodies to the ankles. Their faces are friendly, intense, and focused as if they do not want to miss a moment, a gesture, or a breath of this new creature. They are not shy, though, and full of jokes. The Fante love to joke, I am told, and I have experienced it. Even without the language, joking is possible. I find that especially the women love to joke with me and in this way establish a kind of non-verbal bond, a kind of sisterhood, an understanding of the womanness of us all. My hair is cropped close to my head, and I wear no earrings, both unthinkable in a woman my age. But they point at my hair with approval, and when I gesture that there is none of it, they concede my point with exuberance. I also have on a skirt that by their standards is far too short. They comment on this also, but I am used to it by then. As I walk through the market or on the streets in Cape Coast, the women constantly tease me about my hair, my fat stomach, my clothes, my undressed ears, and my bare legs. So I join them in the fun, and they clearly enjoy it.

After about 2 hours of this, sitting on a stone in the hot sun, I begin to wonder about my cage. It clearly will not be finished today. So I plan to return tomorrow when it "by all means" will be finished. I extricate myself from the pressing crowd and make my way with my three small boys down the hill to my car. The crowd follows, of course, cheering and laughing and singing. As I pull out in my little car, I reflect on the scene. What an unexpected treat. Purchasing has never been so much fun and so rewarding. I am a celebrity. I have done nothing to earn it. How can people be so pleased about your mere presence? And then I ask the perennial European and American question: Do they call me brunyi because of the racism that is unrecognized, or do they call me this, as Mr. Baidoo and others say, simply to denote that I am a foreigner? Does it mean simply "white man," or does it mean "someone different from me?" Or does it mean someone from Europe or America? Most brunyis are insulted, and the Ghanaians cannot understand why. The children are taught and encouraged by their elders to stand on the street as you pass and in a sing song rhythm, in chorus, to call out, "Brunyi, how are you, I am fine, thank you." They love to sing it, and the recipients hate to hear it.

But today as I leave the cage factory, I feel good, appreciated, recognized, like I have created a little fun and change in the village life and I received pleasure. How can anyone honestly say that they do not revel in the attention of others? I feel myself blossoming, becoming my better self as these generous, sincere, and appreciative people urge me on. It is one of the enigmas of colonialism and race. Racism is imbedded so deeply in the fabric of life that it does not even have a name. It looks like love. It looks like respect. My children say that they are teasing me and making

Children playing—Abaasa

fun of me, and they don't like it. Sometimes, they say, the people wonder in Fanti if I am a man or a woman. The children are embarrassed. I say I don't care, but they are disturbed. They say I must care.

The next day, we head back to the village. On the way, I pick up a large rubber ball, some pencils, biscuits, a bag of sweets, and some balloons for the many children I saw yesterday. My boys think that I am foolish to do it. Charles is becoming more and more grumpy. It seems our trip has backfired. He didn't expect it to turn into such an affair, and he is not sure he likes it. But he will not miss it.

As I enter the village for the second time, I give the gifts to my friend who was among the first to surround my car. The cage is still incomplete, but this time there are cars, tro tros, trucks, and buses made of the same soft wood, hewn with the same cutlass, and nailed together with nails fashioned from the same wood. From all over the village, little boys come with their cars. They push the cars with a bamboo stick, emerging slowly at first and then more rapidly like a swarm of locusts. Everywhere you look, from behind every rock, down every hill, and around every corner, comes a small boy with a car. And they are wonderful works of art. Each one is different, and each one has its own special cargo, a bit of paint or piece of old newspaper to decorate it, or scraps of orange for lights. I am amazed. They all want to sell them, of course, since they discovered my interest in such things. But it is mayhem. There is no way to buy one or two, but who can buy all of them, and who would you pay and how?

As I contemplate my new dilemma, Kojo comes up to me and quietly says that a man wants to talk to me. I look over and see a row of rather old, wrinkled, raggedy men sitting together on a bench. I say, "Later," because I am busy and have enough on my hands. We continue with the bargaining. My friend is in full swing, enjoying being the clown for her local and foreign audience. The women keep up a lively banter with me as the cars continue to flood in.

Kojo, who is a quiet, good boy, tries again. "The man is the chief's linguist," he says almost inaudibly. "He wants to see you." "Why," I ask. "I don't know," Kojo replies sincerely. Finally, I finish the negotiations, yet the bird cage is still far from finished. I have forgotten about the old man, and they tell me to come back tomorrow and bring paanu (bread).

Abaasa

THE CHIEF'S PALACE: RACE, DIFFERENCE;
UNDERSTANDING DEMOCRACY; COMING HOME

Chieftainship is people.
The King is the people. To respect the king is to respect oneself. He who despises our
King despises us. He who praises our King praises us.

The next day I bring paanu, and this time I speak with the linguist. "The chief wants
you to be queen mother," he says. I think he is joking and take it that way. "But we
are very serious," he says and leads me to the chief's palace. The palace is quite wonderful. It is an old mud and wattle room, approximately 15 feet by 15 feet. The roof

is tin, but the ceiling is mud and wattle. Nana Mensah sits on his stool with a black and white cloth around his thin frame, his eyes large and deep. He looks somber on his stool, his feet clad in the traditional large flat sandal and resting on his sheepskins. According to the custom, we remove our sandals at the door and greet the Omanhene with a slight bow. Around him is his council, a group of men. They are farmers, and their weathered faces, rough hands, and various infirmities attest to the ruggedness of this life. Most of them have on old shorts (or knickers, as they are called) and shirts from America. The shirts have things printed on them like: "John's Lube Shop," "Mike" (inscribed on the pocket), "How Many Kinds of Buns Are There?" (with pictures to offer suggestions), "Tony's Pizza Men's Ball Club," or "My Kid is the Best in Olympia High." One young man has a t-shirt with "Joey's Little Sister" inscribed on the back. The shirts seem ludicrous in the setting and in the context of the solemnity of the occasion, but they do not detract from the dignity and decorum of the meeting.

The men sit quietly after formally greeting the chief and wait for all to arrive. The room is furnished with benches and stools in a circle around the edges of the room. In front of the chief is a table on which he has an old cloth, a razor, a comb, a torch, and an assortment of other odds and ends. In the corner behind him is another table containing a similar assortment but with an old and dusty container of plastic flowers. Several photos of elders hang on the wall, along with a calendar with Christ in the middle and a few other religious hangings.

We wait for some time. There are some young men, some of middle years, and some who are very old and draped in their traditional cloth. When all seem assembled, my own linguist, Kwame Nkrumah (the only one who can speak much English), turns to me and explains that they will now begin. They exchange greetings in Fante of a stylized nature. Mr. Nkrumah turns to me and says that it is their custom to begin by stating your mission and by letting each party know how things are in their villages. Everything is fine in his village, he says. I reply likewise and say that I have been summoned and am there for that reason. The chief then smiles for the first time, looking at me with calm, gentle, friendly eyes. We are now ready to begin. We are clear about our mission and none of us have left behind serious problems that might distract us from the present business.

I sit at that first of many meetings to come, watching and listening in pleasure and admiration. I am not a romantic by nature, not enamored with the "good old traditional ways." I am not one who wants to go back and find the "real" people or look into my roots. I am basically a good, solid, skeptical intellectual, and I coldly overanalyze the most sacred of human affairs (as I sometimes have been told by my students). But I am struck, and continue to be impressed, by the ways that these people live together and treat each other with a respect for their person and a dignity that is difficult to explain because most of us do not see it. They argue and often become quite heated, but they are essentially kind and gentle with each other. They are sensitive and do not want anyone to lose face or to be offended. I observe this, and I am told it. Usually I am considered to be a rather non-assertive, non-aggressive "nice girl," which I have been groomed carefully to be. But I often feel like a boorish, clumsy elephant as I go through my life in Ghana. I am too loud, too fast, and too impatient. I am in a hurry. I want to push, to be confrontational, and to say what is on my mind whether the person is ready to hear it or not. Sometimes I get angry,

Woman and child—Abaasa

and I want to tell the person. But I am admonished not to do it. Ghanians tell me not to embarrass him or her, to be patient, to be cool, and to wait. They say I should not tell a person that you think he took advantage of you because he will be embarrassed. We do not want to offend her, I am warned. It is a new way for me even though I am not pushy by Western standards. I thought I was considerate, I thought I was easy, and I let people be. But this is a new kind of sensibility. It is a wonderful kind of caring and forgiveness. Americans are critical, and we are judgmental. But these people I meet in Ghana do not judge. They think you have a right to your own views. You can believe the way you want to; you do not have to look like me, talk like me, worship like me, or believe like me.

So I sit, watch, listen, and learn. I watch the ways that they solve problems without having to leave anyone feeling unheard or on the "wrong side." It is a different way of being, one I continue to try to understand and one that I continue to find hope in and admiration for. There is always an agenda, but it is never on paper. There are always hours of animated discussion, and the chief hardly ever says a thing. Gyekye (1996) say that "the principle of popular government was firmly established in the African political practice," and here it is before me.

This first day the agenda is to explain to me their reasons for wanting me for queen mother, what this will entail, and how we will proceed if I agree. They say that they have seen me in the village with the people and the children and that I look like a generous, good person, the kind that should be queen mother. Of course, as my cynical little boys remind me, the fact that I am a brunyi who is rich probably improves my character a great deal. It a dilemma I have yet to solve and one that we brunyis must confront every day. It is a new experience for us, but an old one for those on the other side of the fence. Am I a real person or just a white woman? Am I the same as all other white women? Do you really like me, or do you want to exploit me? Do you want to know me as a whole person? Are you being nice to me because I am white and probably rich? We want to scream out: "I am not a brunyi, I am Professor Lundgren or Dr. Smith, Marjorie, Mary, or Bob!" Don't you care? Can't you tell us apart? Am I invisible like Ellison's invisible man? Do I just become "that white lady"? Don't I have a name, a face, or a personality? Will I lose *me* in your perception of me as being like all white people? Will you assume automatically that I am good, bad, rich, or beautiful? I know that I am not a beautiful woman, yet over and over again beautiful African women say: "I will trade you my head for yours," or, "You are beautiful. I want a child who looks just like you." What do they see? They see only my whiteness—my fine, straight hair and my blue eyes—yet they think I am beautiful? Do they look at their own course, dark hair; dark eyes; and brown skin and miss the beauty?

Yes, this is a new experience for those of us who are used to being in the majority, being the ones who have an identity, a name, a face. We are the ones who daily, casually say: "You know, the black woman," "The black one over there," and worse. Is she automatically ugly? Is her hair too curly? Are her lips too full? Does she look like all black people, and can you really not tell *them* apart? But most of us do not learn from this experience. We say, "Not me. I am not the one who calls you ugly. I am a good guy. Why pick on me? I am one of you. I am with you. We are brothers and sisters." But when the Africans fail to see the goodness in us or fail to differentiate us from all other white people, we feel cheated and run away. We ask: How could you do this to *me*, your friend? I am just like you. But centuries of colonialism, inequities, war, and slavery have taught the African differently. Thanks to Oliver Cox, W.E.B. DuBois, Walter Rodney, Julius Nyere, Amalcar Cabral, Fidel Castro, Basil Davidson, Wallerstein, Ayittey, and even Martin Luther King in his last years, we are introduced to the vivid realities of the colonial experience and the torturous lessons of white superiority and beauty.

This form of racism should not be a surprise to us. We are all taught it, and only fools or martyrs do not learn the lessons well. We learn them at the end of a whip, a rope, and a man's penis. Whether we are the ones welding the whip or the ones being whipped, we all learn the same lesson. Some of us are beautiful and powerful, and some of us are ugly and powerless. White women are pure, virginal, and precious; black women are worthless, debased, and ugly. As Toni Morrison eloquently tells us, they lived in an old store front, and no one could have convinced them that they were not ugly. In Ghana, no one would say this. They are proud, strong, independent, and confident. Yet it creeps in even here when a white woman shows up like a miracle in the midst of a dirty, poor African village. Many people tell me that I am sent to them by God and that I am a special gift God has bestowed on them.

Perhaps the most important questions is how can I, someone from another culture, another continent, and another village, be their queen mother? Or, more to the point, how can a person identified as white, as European, be the queen mother of a people who are separated from me by the words *black* and *African*? Am I not contributing to the colonialism we all abhor? Am I not "steeling their stool?" I did not think it was serious, but when I realized how serious it is, I had to think deeply about these questions. But they want it so much. They want to add some notoriety to their little village. I believe that they (or at least some) sincerely feel that God sent me, that I am meant to be there, and that I am inevitably their real, predestined queen mother.

My "husband" says that we are, after all, all the same. And my friend Yaro frequently admonishes, "People are people." He sees them come and go from all over the world, and when it gets down to it, he says, people are people. And of course we are all one, and we are all people, all *Homo sapiens*. We *Homo sapiens* have a long and tortured history of racism and racialism (Appiah, 1992). We know that we are not biologically different in the ways we continue to be classified. Should redheads with freckles, light skin, and blue eyes be a race? The discussion of the realities and myths of racism cannot be developed fully here. However, long lists of scholars (Appiah, 1992; Montague, 1962; Fanon, 1974; Ellison, 1975; Harris, 1985; Marable, 1994; Gates, 1986; Prah, 1999; Dubois, 1983; Mazrui, 1986; and Wallerstein, 1983, to name a few) have agreed with my husband, that we no longer can support, biologically or philosophically, a notion of individual, immutable races with catalogues of accompanying characteristics, nor can we argue that the brains of women are somehow different than those of men.

We are forced into categories, shaped into caricatures of ourselves, separated by distance and culture, and separated most severely by a false immutability, by a falsehood that is more true than the truth. My linguist looks like my brother. His brother, who looks nothing like him, reminds me of a friend of mine. Mr. Nkum, one of my favorite people, is kind, generous, funny, helpful, always concerned with my comfort. Is there too much sun in my eyes? Shouldn't I have something cold to drink? Did I remember my bag? Are they walking too fast?

And then there is Mr. Quashie. He is cosmopolitan and almost suave. He has worked on ships all his life and has traveled the world. He is not awed by me. He is not impressed, but he is pleased to know me. He wants me to be comfortable because, even though he has been in places far from Abaasa, this is his real home. He extends his home to me with an ease and generosity that moves me. Everything here belongs to me, they say. I am invited into their midst, to be one of them, just like Mr. Nkrumah who comes from another village and the Muslims who dress differently and worship differently. We can all be a part of the village, and we all have a part to play. The parts are different, but they are all necessary. A popular Akan proverb says, "One head does not go into council." This means that "wisdom is not in the head of one person." If wisdom is not in only one head, then one head only cannot go into council (Gyekeye 1996, 116).

In every part of their lives, Ghanaians are communal, collective, and make decisions by consensus. One of my students tells me, "We are never alone. We are always with a group." However, although many believe that this communalism some-how militates against individuality, I am constantly intrigued by the individuality of the people I meet, by their confidence, their willingness to advance their own theo-ries, their singular analyses of the world, and their unique ways of coping with circumstances that would make most of us sit down and wait to die. This kind of in-dividuality in the midst of community is expressed in another Akan proverb that says, "The clan is like a cluster of trees that, when seen from afar, appear huddled together, but which can be seen to stand individually when closely approached." It means that "if one is far away from a cluster of trees, he sees all the trees as huddled or massed together. It is when he goes near that he recognizes that the trees in fact stand individually." (Gyekye 1996, 32).

So, with all of these reservations, I decide to take them at face value as they ap-proach me to be queen mother. I take them at their word that they think I am the kind of person to be a queen mother. I think that eventually I will have an identity, and we will all learn something. So, although at this first meeting I am still skeptical and still not sure it is serious, I am curious and interested. As the weeks go by with many long discussions, I come to understand the importance of our meeting. The councilmen create reasons, I begin to notice, for me to return again and again. We need time to get to know each other. Through the process of this decision making, they interview me, and I interview them.

However, my small boys, especially Samuel, do not take it all so easily. They are not so sure. "It is not Christian," they say. "They will do JuJu on you and take all your money," Samuel says. They insist that it is not a good thing to do, and it will get me into trouble. They say: "Something terrible might happen to you. They only want your money. You don't know. You are not Ghanaian. We are Ghanaian, and we know." But in my bones, I think it is a good thing and have no fear.

Meetings

Each meeting takes between 2 and 4 hours. Every person's voice has to be heard. They are all so different, I note as I look around the room. Some are light and joking and smile a lot. Some are somber and quiet. Some are animated and excited, and some are formal. Some (usually the elders) speak slowly and at great length; they pause, dramatically re-peat endings of words, and speak almost in parables. On his stool, the chief sits and watches in his cloth, with legs spread and hands on his knees. When everyone finishes, the chief sums up, declares the decision consensual, and again sits silent. At the end of the meeting, permission is asked of the chief to leave, he makes a gesture of approval, formal dismissal words are said, and we file out of the palace door.

At one such meeting, I bring photos of the village for them to see. They take them eagerly, laughing, pointing, gesturing, and arguing. Others come in from outside to see until the gathering reaches a crescendo of noise, excitement, and activity. Gradually, everyone sees the photos, the conversations become more subdued, and there seems to be a natural decrescendo. At this point, I notice out of the corner of my eye a barely perceptible gesture. Nana moves his hand slowly back and forth. His body does not move. He does not say a word. But the photos begin to move until they are in a pile, the voices are still, and all eyes are on the chief.

A good chief, I am told, must first come from the royal family. Then he must have qualities of a calm nature, good judgment, and the ability to listen. He is not arrogant, boastful, or full of pride. He is humble. He has good personal habits. He does not drink to excess, fight, lose his temper, smoke, or chase women, yet he must have

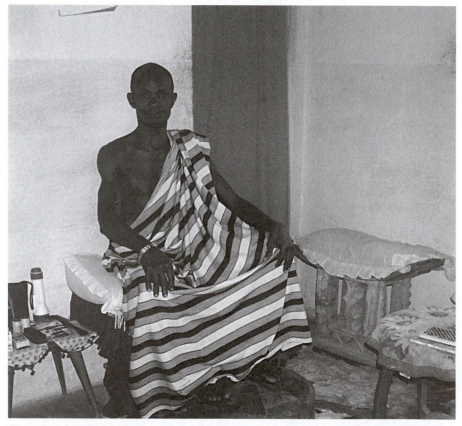

Nana Mensah—Chief—Abaasa

at least two wives. When a new chief takes office, he is told what he must do through his spokesman, the okyeame, and he must agree:

> We do not wish that he should curse us.
> We do not wish that he should be greedy.
> We do not wish that he should be disobedient (or, refuse to take advice).
> We do not wish that he should treat us unfairly.
> We do not wish that he should act on his own initiative.
> We do not wish that it should ever be that he should say to us,
> "I have no time," "I have no time."

[Gyekye, 1996, p. 112]

He must serve the will of the people. As I watch, meeting after meeting, I witness the degree to which the chief serves the people.

> In African societies, the will of the people is usually expressed formally in the councils of the chiefs and in other assemblies where people are free to express their opinions. Matters are never settled until everyone has had a chance to speak; and to carry out any program requiring the sanction of the whole clan or group. They talk and talk until they arrive at a consensus.

[Gyekye, 1996, p. 111]

I do not have to read Gyekye to know this. I can see it before my eyes. They talk and talk and talk. They talk and argue, gesturing elaborately. They stand up, point, and rush across the room; someone says something funny, and the room explodes with laughter. It goes on for 1 hour, 2, 3, until it seems that all are finished. But Nana continues to wait. And, yes, someone has something else to say. Only then does Nana calmly make his statement and they are finished. To them, "democracy means continuous and active participation of all the citizens in the affairs of government." (Gyekye, 1996, p. 116) It happens at all levels, and it begins right here: in the village, in the chief's palace.

On my first visit, they describe what they expect, say that I should contact my relatives and friends and bring them along next time if possible, and we agree to meet at a later date. They want to be sure that my relatives, as their own, are aware of the appointment, understand it, and agree with it. They do not want my people to feel that they are doing something secretive, harmful, frightening, or threatening. They want everything out in the open and known by all of their people and all of my people. I do not want to tell them right off that basically "my people" consist of two sons, who know me well enough not to be very surprised at anything I might want to do, and two brothers, whose whereabouts are not always known.

By the second visit, I ask more specifically about the job description and term of office. "Oh", they say, "Once you are queen mother, you are queen mother for life. You, your children, and your grandchildren will all have this as your home and will always belong to the village." One of the elders, the chief's senior brother, says that I resemble his niece and that my ancestors surely come from this village. God has brought us together, he says. He says that he would not mind being my husband, and as he leaves, he turns and with a twinkle in his soft, light eyes says, "You have carried your bundles alone too long; now I am here to help carry them for you." How does he know? How can he know that I have, indeed, carried my bundles alone for such a long time, and it never occurs to me that anyone can really help me carry them. It strikes such a deep chord in me that I, not a weepy sort, feel a bit of a lump in my throat.

Connections: Abaasa and Akotokyir

And so, after much conversation, they give me the bare outlines of a job description. I am required to be available always, serve as one with the chief, try to help the community, and, as mother of all, choose the next chief. But there is a problem. I am afraid to tell my partner and friend, Mr. Baidoo. It all seems to happen so quickly, I make so many decisions, and I am so busy with lectures and students that, somehow, it always slips my mind when I am with him. Finally, it can wait no longer and it comes out. He is stunned. He seems hurt and incredulous. It must feel like a betrayal. But he quickly rallies himself and says that it is impossible, it will not happen, and he will stop it. Of course I will not, cannot, do it. Mary, his wife, who rarely says a thing, is quite articulate the next day, saying that it is quite impossible, it will never do, and it will not happen.

The next time we meet, Baidoo says that he has decided to send the people of Abaasa a "broom." This is serious. A broom is a call to action, a request and not a demand, to meet. It is very serious and in the past has been the precipitator of serious altercations between groups. I don't know what to say, what to do, how to respond. Later, as I visit Akototyir, Mr. Baidoo meets me solemnly, almost tearfully. He says that the night before the elders of the village came to him and chastised him roundly for letting this happen. They blamed him for losing me, for not offering me a similar honor, and for disgracing them by having me go to another village. He tells me that only his brothers supported him and that he nearly lost his temper before the whole thing was over.

This is a serious error. How could I have done this to my partner and friend? I am in a mess because, in the meantime, the people of Abaasa administer the first set of installation ceremonies. They sell me a sheep and, during one of our meetings, unexpectedly lift me up and carry me to the marketplace while I am fanned, perfumed, and powdered. There, with the chief and his council, dressed in their usual tattered work clothes and bare feet, and some of the community members, they pour libation and pray to God that we will all be well, that this union will be fruitful and that God will always be with us all. They thank God for bringing me to them and thank him for his wisdom and mercy. They say this as they pour Schnapps from a small cup onto the bare earth.

After they pray, they turn to me, hand me the cup of liquid, and entreat me to now pray to my God. It does not matter to them to which God I pray, and it does not occur to them to question whether or not, in fact, I have a God. I delve more deeply into the issue of God later in the text, but basically everyone in Ghana has a God. Virtually all Ghanaians recognize the existence of and need for a protective entity to guide, protect, and watch over them. On this day my prayer is much like their own;

I ask to be blessed, to be protected, to be granted wisdom, and thank God for this fine moment, these fine people, and the gift of coming together.

Then it is time for the sacrifice. It is not a frightening thing, not a mystical thing, and not an evil thing; it is simply a way to thank God and to share a gift. And, probably not incidentally, it is a way to share the precious, scarce, and much needed protein. I pay a hefty sum for the beast, and at the end of the ceremony, every single part of the animal is carefully cut. Then handfuls are put into palm leaves and divided among the people.

One of a few Muslims who lives in the village slaughters the sheep. Although the ceremony calls for the sheep to be slaughtered at my feet, they defer to the possibility of squeamishness on my part and, without embarrassing discussion or fanfare, delicately take the animal outside. When the sheep is slaughtered, it is brought in and taken around the room by its feet so that spots of blood appear around me. The butcher grins from ear to ear, bows lavishly, and in general shows great delight and approval. He continues to be one of my most demonstrative supporters. After this part of the ceremony, there are a few speeches. I am asked to indicate my sincerity, my loyalty, and my promise not to abandon them, and they, in turn, speak of my natural connection to the village, my rights and duties to the people of Abaasa (who are now my people), their desire to have me become a part of them, and the great wisdom of God for having sent me to them. Just as suddenly as they swept me up from my stool in the chief's palace, they now lift me again and return me to the stool. From this moment on, my chair is a traditional stool.

The ceremony is over. They are pleased with my performance. My husband says that when they picked me up the first time, he watched my face and it did not show fear. This is a good sign. It demonstrates trust and confirms their initial belief in the inevitable and ancient connection between us.

So, what can I tell my dear friend? It all happened so fast. I just think that I am enjoying a rare moment in the process of a village holding on to the dignity and maturity of their role in the world as they simultaneously struggle with the demands of a foreign world.

Akotokyir has no chief at the moment or a real queen mother. Their chief died some time ago, and there is some dispute as to the proper successor, a common problem. The man who had been chosen, says Baidoo, came to visit one day for a ceremonial event, and the men of the village tried to stop him from leaving by first placing stones under his tires and then by pulling him bodily from his automobile. Unfortunately, the man is quite stout, and when he wrapped his arms around the steering wheel of the vehicle, all of the six men pulling could not extricate him from the wheel. He drove off leaving only a cloud of dust behind.

This may account in part for the lapse in what they consider to be their stool duties. At any rate, the lack of proper royalty at the moment does not make this any easier for Mr. Baidoo to endure. Mr. Baidoo, being a reasonable and patient man, however, readily forgives me my transgression. We discuss it at great length, and there now seems to be no need for a broom. Mrs. Baidoo continues to complain, but we carry on as usual. As the time nears for the ceremony, however, Mr. Baidoo makes it very clear that he is to be in attendance, that he will ride with his wife in my car, and that I will therefore go as a part of their family and the village of Akotokyir.

The enstooling actually was accomplished in that earlier, somewhat private affair, but the festival, the carrying of the new queen mother on the paloquine under
the umbrella for the whole village and surrounding villages, will be a public, jubilant, and extravagant affair. They tell me that chiefs and queen mothers from all
around attend, they hire a real brass band from a neighboring village, and there are
food, drinks, dancing, and drumming.

The first order of business, however, is the t-shirt. I am instructed that I
must make a shirt with my photo emblazoned on the front and queen mother of
Asebu Abaasa written on the back (Asebu is the name of the district of which
Abaasa is a part). Nana Mansah III, my stool name, and my title of professor go
somewhere on the shirt. There is great deliberation about the design of this
shirt, the number, the order of the words, and every other detail of the dress. It
soon becomes obvious to me that this whole event is quite costly and that I am
expected to shoulder the largest share of expenses. I am eager to be cooperative
and demonstrate my sincere support for all aspects of village life, but the
thought of my face displayed on the front of a large number of t-shirts worn
around the area and the serious cost makes me panic. My heart sinks in direct
proportion to their heightening enthusiasm for the shirt as we take part in many
sessions discussing the details. Finally, I meekly suggest to the happy crowd
that even though the shirt would be nice, we can perhaps spend the money in a
more interesting fashion. For example, I offer, we can get something for the
school or the children or put it toward a larger project for later. My linguist
puts this before the group to the usual passionate round of responses. The chief
finally speaks, and my linguist interprets. "The elders and Nana," he articulates,
"are very happy about your suggestion and think that it is an excellent idea."
Silence. Then, he continues, "Now, about the t-shirt. . . ." Involved discussion
once again ensues.

On each occasion, whether we discuss whom to invite, what to eat, or who
will get the brass band, I am struck by the rapt attention with which each person
beholds the current speaker. No one looks at a watch, out the window, or about
aimlessly. If Nana speaks, they sit perfectly still, gazing at him with absolute attention. When one of the very old elders speaks, there is the same steady stare,
the same encouraging nod of the head, and the same alert attention. Many times
they argue, point fingers, and get up from their seats, but they always listen to
everyone. No one is denied a voice, and no one is ignored. I never see Nana try
to curb the conversation, to direct it, or to influence it. They are not shy. They
speak their minds, but they never fail to show respect the minute Nana so much
as raises a finger. He never argues, he never raises his voice, and he never inter-
rupts. Until a particular topic has run its course, he sits patiently, watching, waiting, and concentrating. I try discouraging the t-shirt one or two more times, but
Nana never imposes his authority to support my own against the will of the majority, yet I think he certainly can. They are determined to have the shirt, they all
agree, and it is going to happen. Since that day, much to my horror, I see my badly
photographed and blurred face beaming like a chubby elf on t-shirts in all parts
of Cape Coast and the surrounding villages. One day I am in church and there,
standing before me, facing the crowd in prayer, is a young man, dressed neatly in

Sunday trousers and shoes with my face peering out of his clean, pressed Nana Mansah III t-shirt.

More about Government and Politics

The day finally arrives. Our meetings are worth all of the hours sitting inside the hot little palace, sometimes drinking a warm Coke, beer, or Malta along with a little apeteche. I learn a great deal about the political, economic, and social structure of the village and all the others surrounding. There is not a final authority, there are layers of authority. You are hard pressed to find anyone making a definitive, declarative statement on any issue. Americans are almost without exception furious about this seemingly vague unwillingness to make a concrete final statement—this apparent inability of Ghanaians to take action based on a decision. There is always room for another opinion, another level of authority, and another contending view.

In the case of the village, there are several avenues for resolving an issue, solving a problem, or planning. If there is a dispute, one's first recourse is to go to one's relatives. This can be the head of the larger clan, a senior member of the lineage, or a member of one's immediate family. In the case of marriage, according to Baidoo, each partner has his or her own confidante or dispute manager. They go to this person first if there is a marital problem. Usually such family matters can be resolved within the extended family. This family is so extended that only the family members really know who they are, and they stretch in all geographical directions. Furthermore, the boundaries of family change depending on who is describing them and why they are being counted. It is not something one can describe easily, nor is it customarily necessary to do so. So, to ask "How many children do you have?" or "How big is your family?" is to miss the point.

If a dispute cannot be resolved in this way, usually the next step is to take it to the chief. This is done customarily with each party escorted by its own supporters. It is held in the chief's palace in the presence of village elders, the linguist, the council members, and, if possible, all of the contending parties. The session is held in a formal way similar to our planning meetings. Formal greetings are made back and forth, and the parties each state their mission and inform the body about the well being of their home village. The linguist speaks for the chief unless the chief finds it necessary to speak himself. I have been to several of these meetings in different villages, and the format is always the same, with changes only in numbers of participants, amount of libation poured, and the presence or absence of certain members who may not be in residence or be appointed at the moment. The parties face each other, each on opposite sides of the room. The chief and his retinue, which is sometimes referred to collectively as Nana, sit on one end of the hall and sometimes around the periphery, or the chief sits on a platform with his linguist on another lower platform at his feet. The elders then sit on either side and the rest of the party on the sides. Nana is attired in a cloth that is usually regally beautiful and ceremonial, and it is wrapped traditionally across one shoulder (leaving the other bare), flowing to the floor with ample space for the spreading of the chief's legs. He often wears gold around his neck and on his fingers and wrists. His feet rest on his skins in large, often elaborately carved sandals, which sometimes are decorated with various pieces of gold and gems of different kinds. Depending on the occasion, all of this is more or less extravagant. The linguist and elders are attired similarly but less lavishly. They may hold staffs, and the linguist holds one with the sign of the clan on the top. For example, in Akotokyir and in Abaasa, the staff is topped by a parrot. Sometimes there are drums.

The parties then state their issue, and the usual discussion ensues. The chief's role, as usual, is to listen. When a decision is made about the nature of the event, a punishment is meted out to the offending party. This conventionally takes the form of a bottle or two of Schnapps, a goat or two, or a chicken. One chief tells me that he does not allow any fighting in his village, either verbal or physical. If an offender does not respond to his disciplinary requirement, he tells them that he will hand them over to the local authorities, and they can do with him what they may. Usually this threat of state intrusion is enough to keep control within the domain of the chief.

THE CELEBRATION

We have spent the usual long hours in deliberation and now the day has come. Money plays a large role in the discussions, as it does in all discussions, because there is none; today in the new world of modernity, everything costs money. These are farmers. They never needed money before. But we work all this out and plan for the food, the use of the paroquine in which I ride, the brass band, the drinks, the invitations, and, yes, the t-shirts. The chief's palace is replastered on the front and painted. There is a bamboo and thatch shelter in front and several other shelters to protect us from the piercing sun that shines relentlessly on the treeless village.

They tell me to be there by 8 a.m. I have rented a tro tro to carry my overflow guests who arrive at about 9:30 a.m. Mr. Baidoo and Mary are with me as is my neighbor, who sees himself as family. Mr. Baidoo is in a fine blue cloth, looking dignified and regal. Mary has a new printed Kente Kaaba and slit. She is as short and round as her husband is tall and angular, and her face is soft, smooth, and pretty. She looks like the sister of her 20-year-old daughter. She is included rarely in any of our conversations, about which I wonder. Since then I have discovered that the reason she does not talk with her husband and I much is that she simply does not like to talk, she says. It makes her tired, she says. But I also discover that when she wants to, she can talk quite well, and she has sensible and thoughtful contributions to make. Today she surprises me by her charm and dignity and quite competently is taking on the role of social facilitator.

We are escorted to the lodgings where I will later spend the night. As my guests arrive, they are added to our assemblage in the small square cement block room. It recently has been painted a cobalt blue and seems to have new linoleum on the floor. The curtains, which are made of a pretty, flowered, light fabric, also look new. The room has newly made wooden furniture, a short sofa, three or four chairs, and a coffee table in the middle, covered with a clean, lacy white cloth. The covers on the furniture are cloaked in clear plastic, which seems to be the custom. The room is cheerful and unusually clean and neat. There is a double bed to one side that is adorned in a pretty, pale green cover with matching pillows. An exquisitely beautiful young woman with a wide charming smile revealing a very straight row of perfect white teeth, enters and welcomes us. Then we sit and wait. And wait and wait and wait.

When we arrive, they are still working on the plastering, the front verandah is yet to be created, and the poles for the other shelters are being erected. My charming group of councilmen are in their usual attire. It is difficult to ascertain that an event will occur here today. So as the morning wears on, we sit in the little room, boiling. I soon am escorted out of the room and taken to another house where there is a small courtyard with a much appreciated breeze. Here, I meet many men in their cloth, all of whom are anxious to see this new brunyi queen mother of theirs. Many of them come from different parts of Ghana to their home village for the event. At around 12:00, I receive a plate of food, and my neighbor joins me. I do not know what happened to the Baidoos or my other guests. We all chat as best we can. I introduce myself to a man named Mr. Saigo who has been there before and is sophisticated and a very competent English speaker. I apologize all the time for my poor Fante, but everyone dismisses it as nothing to worry about, which is generous but does not make me feel much better. At any rate, Mr. Saigo is a kind interpreter, and when I begin to explain who I am, he says politely, "Oh, yes, I know your credentials."

Finally the time comes for me to dress. I go to the Pentecostal church and there, in the company of only women, I am dressed for the occasion. Adwoa, the young woman who played and joked for me when I first visited the village, is to carry my stool on her head, leading the procession. I also have two little girls who accompany me on the paroquine. Their hair is cut in the style of the queen mother (mine was already as short as it could get), and they are wrapped in beautiful, colorful cloth that matches the bands in their hair. They have gold (not real) earrings in their pierced ears, gold chains, leg bands, and bracelets. They are shy, about 9 and 7 years old. Adwoa's hair is up in a fancy do with gold sprayed around it. She is being wrapped in her cloth and jewels for the celebration. It reminds me of girls getting ready for their wedding. Everyone is talking, laughing, and joking. They are taking off clothes and putting new ones on in a casual, friendly, "girls only" sort of way. Several work on me, under the scrupulous eye of Mary Baidoo. They wrap me in layers of Kente (this is real) and adorn me with gold and jewels. It is then that I receive the special queen mother bracelet that, according to them, belonged to the first Nana Mansah.

As we dress, the small children try their best to peer into the room to see what is going on. The women have to constantly shoo them away, cover the windows with cloth, and threaten them with their lives if they do not leave. As my friend and neighbor, Mr. Yaro, says, "Children are children." And, it seems, women are women. I am quite sure that I look ridiculous, and photos of Margaret Mead are forcing their way into my consciousness, as I tried to remain calm and act as if everything is normal. It does not help much when one of the older women asks Mrs. Baidoo if the friend of mine who is there is my daughter. Now this woman is very tall, slim, African-American, and almost my age; I am short, extra white this day, and have gained significant weight in the last few years in a very non-muscular, American kind of way—too reminiscent of the figure of, yes, Margaret Mead. My friend howls with pleasure, and we both look at each other in astonishment. My hair is gray, hers black, and I gesture to her, over the heads of the women, that the dye is coming out immediately. To this she responds with unrepressed pleasure, and we both enjoy a wonderful laugh. It seems appropriate to the mood of the occasion, which is festive, fun, and exciting, with a real feeling of sisterhood. No one seems to mind that my friend and I are not Ghanaian, no one seems to be bashful as they scrutinize my bra straps atop the Kente and decide to take the whole thing off. We are all women together, with curlers in our hair, bras on and off, dresses up and down, laughter and scolding, and general merrymaking.

Finally the dressing is complete, and we emerge into the glare of the midday sun. There is a truck waiting. Mary, my friend Janice, the little girls, Adwoa, and I all cram in, and we drive up the dusty road to the little primary school. There we disembark and enter one of the small classrooms. My stool is brought to me and unwrapped to exclamations from the crowd that has gathered in the room. It is a beautiful black stool with copper studs adorning it and the symbol of the Gye Nyame, meaning "only God," in a lighter wood. They are proud of it. They got it far away in Accra. It takes my breath away.

We sit for some time, waiting for the brass band to gather, the people to assemble, and the paroquine to arrive. Finally, I was escorted out of the building and into my sled like paroquine adorned with a huge fringed umbrella. In my Kente I sit with my legs out straight in my new huge queen mother sandals, and they hand me the traditional sword. They have told me that I have to "dance" in the paroquine, and the chief once briefly, stiffly demonstrated the dance. I am to gesture to my right, then to my left, then up to God, and back down again (in a graceful manner), telling everyone that "on my right and on my left, all belongs to me" and that God is watching over us all. So, I begin to dance, the brass band begins to play, eight men (who have been drinking apeteche since at least dawn, I am sure) hoist me up, and we were on our way. The two little girls are positioned in front of me, also having been instructed to "dance.". At one point, much to the delight of the crowd, the eldest child stands up and dances on the unsteady conveyance. She is a charmer, and the village is proud of her.

I am carried down the road while the brass band plays and various followers dance, shout, blow the horn, and chant. Some of the women are dancing for me to give me clues, which is a blessing because my dancing lessons are limited. Furthermore, I am sitting with outstretched legs, carrying a sword, wrapped in Kente in the sweltering heat and piercing sun, and I need all the help I can get. Unfortunately, in the dressing process someone failed to tie my cloth, so as they jostle me and as I "dance," my Kente keeps slipping, threatening to drop at any moment. Of course they would not mind, or probably even notice, but I, in my Western, modest head, am nervous and keep hitching up the Kente in between movements of my arms.

I am tired by the time we ascend the hill and enter the village. Then, suddenly I realize that I am being taken through the bamboo and thatch shelters, and if I continue dancing and swaying, I will be decapitated or seriously damaged. So I quickly slide down in the sled, barely avoiding the top of the thatch. I pop up again on the other end, only to be confronted quickly by another. I try to appear graceful as I slide my body down under the thatch, but I can't imagine that that is accomplished. By the time the men deposit me in front of the "market" where the ceremony is to transpire, my legs are wobbling, I am slightly dizzy, and I can hardly walk. The combination of the heat, the heavy Kente, the jostling of the paroquine, and the pressure on my thighs during my constant "dancing" has taken its toll. However, I manage to stumble up into the enclo-

Queen Mother celebration—Abaasa

sure and be led to my stool to the accompaniment of women fanning me with towels and throwing perfume and powder over me. I sit down with relief, appreciating the respite from the heat and glare of the sun and a solid place to sit.

Mr. Baidoo is in a position of honor, along with his wife. He leans over to me and says, "Remember, when you speak, tell them that you do not come alone. You come with your family, who is also of royal heritage. You come with your people. Do not forget to tell them." I am very grateful to him for that. I am happy to do as he says. I feel pleased that there is unity between the villages and an acceptance of us all as a part of one large family. Mr. Baidoo discovers that, not only are the Abaasa people Fante, some even related to Mary, but they are also Parrots, the clan of the Baidoos. So we come together. We extend our networks and the Baidoos feel a part of it. The Abaasa people treat them as special people, as royalty, and as my family. From that moment on, there are links between Abaasa and Akotokyir, and I think that we are all pleased about the outcome.

The ceremony continues. They pour libation and entreat God to watch over us and to help us in our work. They thank God for bringing us together and blessing us all in this way. There are speeches, palm wine and apateche, and finally the word from Nana Mensah—that we should all adjourn and continue with the celebration. The women fan me and escort me back to the church where we change our clothes once again, this time quickly, and I am escorted back to the house where I will spend the night.

I am served food, my friends leave, and I am brought a lantern and asked if I want a bath. I do. They take me to the "shower." It is a cemented structure with walls but no roof, where you can stand and have a bucket bath. One of the women brings me a cloth in which to wrap myself and a wonderfully cold bucket of water. By the time I bathe and return to my "home," I cannot move. People are on the streets dancing, singing, drumming, and drinking, but I am finished. I danced for a short period after the ceremony when the women joined me, waved over my head with cloths, clapped, and were pleased overall. But that is all I can do for the night. One of the men tells me that the women are impressed with my dancing and that several men and women say that I dance in the paroquine better than a real Ghanaian. Well, I am happy to hear these kind words, but it is hard for me to believe that my awkward movements have anything of the grace and style that I have seen in the dancing of both men and women on many occasions in Ghana. But it means, at least, that I have passed the test and have successfully fulfilled my role in spite of the fact that the role is quite unclear to me at the time.

I am tired, but the room is airless and the night extremely hot. I hardly sleep until about 5 a.m., at which time they ring the gong gong to tell the village that the queen mother attends all of the churches that day. They wake me up to let me know. The night before, I had said to Nkrumah, who is also a pastor of the Twelve Apostles Church, that I wish to join him in the morning because I am staying anyway. The plan has been that I stay for a football game planned for the afternoon. I have not realized that, in true Ghanaian style, I cannot visit one church without visiting them all. In this little village there are five churches. This means that I visit all five on Sunday morning. No one should feel left out.

THE NEXT DAY

I have not planned for church but for a football (soccer) game, so the only clean garment I have to wear is an "up and down," which is a long knicker with a matching Ghanaian style top. This will not do for church. Therefore I am forced to return to the attire from the day before, which is white, dirty, and soaking wet because it has been left in the rain. So I don this "dress" and wait for church, which I am told begins around 9 a.m. They have already brought me breakfast and helped me to the bamboo pole toilet and the bath house by the time the chief arrives in my house at about 11 a.m. He wonders if I have any more of the beer I brought. He is dressed in his cloth and accompanied by many of the council men who now are dressed in their Sunday long trousers and clean, ironed shirts. Mr. Nkrumah arrives in black trousers and a white long-sleeved shirt, with Bible in hand, looking very much the preacher. We converse for a while, and then there are some murmurings to the chief, people look at their watches, and then they look at me. "The chief's watch has stopped," they say, "which is why we are so late beginning church." The chief looks again at his watch and then at me helplessly, and everyone decides that we should start off. The chief is Pentecostal, they say, but we will begin in Nkrumah's church, the Twelve Apostles. The 14-year-old small boy who stays with me, leans over and whispers, "There are twelve people in the church. Do you suppose that that is why they call it the twelve apostles?"

I am placed on the stage as the special guest, and Pastor Nkrumah reads from the Bible and gives a very short sermon. This is all in Fante. They sing a typical European hymn in a rather stilted way without accompaniment, and then the pastor asks me to say a few words. I am really out of speeches by this time and not sure about the kind of thing that is expected. So I repeat a bit of what I said at yesterday's ceremony about working together and all helping to improve Abaasa. This was translated into a speech about unity that seemed to strike the right chord, and they refer to it again and again, "Remember what queen mother said: We must have unity." Because it was well received the day before, I refer to it again at church with nods of approval from the group. I accidentally hit on a problem area for them, which seems helpful to me. I also say something about being in the presence of God and looking to him for guidance. It is then time for the collection, and we all file out to the next church.

This service is a more "traditional," with drumming and rattles and dancing. The music is beautiful in the open thatch and bamboo church, as it begins to drizzle outside, making the hills look greener than usual and the clay a deep, dark red. The women sing a cappella in the chanting style, which seems typical of women's singing. It is high pitched and rhythmic but not too melodic, giving it a kind of ethereal, ancient, and pure sound. I find myself wishing that it will go on and on. They encourage me to join them when the women dance and reward my efforts with cheers and hankie-waving. A crowd of women circles me, laughing and teasing, taking turns to dance with me in an almost seductive manner. They all gradually back away, and I dance back to my seat, again on a raised platform.

Each time we leave one church, the members of the previous churches follow so that by the time we reach the Church of the Pentecost, almost the whole village is there. The chief is there waiting on the platform of this fancy cement building, and I am motioned to join him on an adjoining stool. As before, the preacher says a few words and reads a passage from the Bible. There is also dancing, drumming, and singing. By this time, there are several kinds of drums, timpani, and rattles. The women once again dance, and I am encouraged to join. Again I am saluted with rings of women dancing with me, beside me, and at me. The men join, and even the chief. He seems to be in fine spirits as he dances reservedly. There is then a swell of music, drumming, and movement until we are all in a circle holding hands. The preacher, tall in a beautiful brown cloth, says the closing prayer to lively "amens" and foot stomping. At the end of almost every one of the preacher's statements, our Nana stomps his large sandal soundly on the floor and gives a hearty "Amen!" He smiles grandly and looks straight at me with joyful eyes each time he stomps. The preacher finishes his prayer, says what seems to be a benediction, and the service ends.

However, the chief is not finished, so he motions to me to move with him. Someone says they will accompany me back to "my house," so Nana and I walk together toward the door; the crowd, bands, and children all follow. We walk out of the church and down the muddy road with the beating of drums, singing, bells, rattles, cheering children behind. As we approach the house, the chief decides that we should keep going to the small center of town and then turn around and back. So we go to the bottom of the hill, turn around, and slowly make our way back up the hill to the house. We are in step with each other, he in his cloth and I in my wet, muddy gold-embroidered top and trousers. Everyone there bids me an extravagant farewell, and I am escorted into my room.

It is a spectacle, a royal display, and a grand day. Photographs are taken. Everyone dances. There is plenty of food and drink. It is also a visiting day. Members of neighboring villages and villagers who live elsewhere come together to celebrate. Afterward, we visit several other villages, and I am formally greeted by their chiefs. Mr. Baidoo obtains a cassava and corn farm in Abaasa. I meet the Assembly Man for our district, travel to Accra with him to see about electricity for the village, and am told by the paramount chief of the district that I am under him at all times and at all times I am to report to him my whereabouts and my dealings. In actuality, neither I nor the chief is to travel unescorted by a decent entourage, but concessions have to be made to accommodate the exigencies of the day.

CONCLUSION

It is a human being that counts; I call upon gold, it answers not; I call upon cloth, it answers not; it is a human being that counts.

[Akan Proverb]

The people of the village make all of this happen. Sometimes it is said that Africans need to learn to organize, to work together. They need decision-making skills. There are nongovernmental organizations that come to teach them these organizational skills. But for thousands of years, long before the industrial revolution and board rooms and committee meetings, they have been running their villages and their complex intervillage affairs. They keep themselves alive, care for the young and the old, maintain the environment, and settle disputes. They do not just run a company, a club, or an organization; they run entire villages. In my village they still practice slash-and-burn horticulture, and the land is flourishing and rich and continues to bear crops. They have developed a system that is communal and values each individual. No one's skills are denied, belittled, or unused. They cannot afford to rely on one or two or three. Each person is necessary, and they all know it.

Right now my village has no electricity, no lights, no televisions, and a few radios run on batteries. What will happen to them when technology arrives? Someone will get a television set, and others will envy her. Furthermore, these are farmers. They are not used to working for cash. They do not currently need much cash, but they soon will. They will be forced into some other form of work. Jobs are scarce in Ghana, and pay is low. How will they manage?

The newspapers are full of "development." Ghanaians are portrayed as lazy, backward, or poor managers because they do not develop. They are to practice family planning and have only one spouse, to whom they are faithful. There are workshops on how to breast-feed your baby. Mud and thatch houses are considered indecent and proof of your backwardness—you must have one of block and tin. You are to send your children to school and teach them how to be punctual and neat. More and more disputes are being settled in the courts. Some fear for the life of the chiefdom, the traditional courts, the power of the Nana, and the ceremony and regalia. There is not time in "modern" society for all this fanfare. There is not time for hours and hours of discussion.

However, Ghanaians want to be "modern," they want to "develop." They want to join the world market. And why shouldn't they? They are poor, and they struggle every day just to survive. So they see this new way of life as the answer, the only answer, and perhaps it is. But because they live such a different life, a life in which patience is important, in which time will wait, and in which they are secure in their place, they do not see the costs of this new way of life. They do not know what it feels like to be alienated, to suffer from anomie, and to rush around according to a clock. Ghanaians are surrounded by relatives, a clan, villages, and age mates from the time they are born. They have a place in the family, and they never lose it. They are always junior to someone and always senior to someone. They are respectful of those above them and caring of those below them. They feel a sense of belonging, a sense of responsibility, and a sense of importance throughout their lives.

Because they belong and because they also have responsibilities, they have dignity, power, and confidence. Because everyone has his or her place and people are not expected to do what the others are doing, they do not have to measure themselves against each other. They cooperate with each other, and they compete with themselves. Even now, in the churches and in the schools, everyone is a leader sometimes. Americans are often impressed with the confidence and ease with which a young Ghanaian will sing or play a keyboard in the church. It is not traditional music, it is European, and they sing it in a stilted, off-key manner. But they take the microphone in hand, and they confidently belt out the song. They copy something that is not their own, so it is not exactly a duplicate, but they do it just the same.

Some say that in this complicated system of duties, obligations, responsibilities, and entitlement, one loses one's sense of identity. One has to do what other people tell them. It is true, for they cannot do whatever they want to do, and some may suffer from it. Because there are many before you, there are different family needs at different times, and ultimately your father, your uncle, or your grandfather can tell you what to do. He can support you, help you, or override your plans. If you have to wait for your first two siblings to go to university or trade school before you go, then you must do it. This is because you are not an entity unto yourself, but you are a part of something much larger, stronger, older, and more enduring. I have rarely met a young person who does not understand or who does not want to help the younger ones or the older ones, making their special contribution to their people. Their own needs and desires are only important insofar as they fit with the needs and desires of the entire family, clan, or village.

However, you cannot take a clan along with you whenever a new job develops. The village cannot raise the child when the child is not raised in the village. In Akotokyir or Abaasa, if a parent, a grandparent, a sibling, or an aunt leaves, the child's life goes on just the same. The child still has many other siblings (cousins are considered siblings), many aunts and uncles, several different mothers to go to, and different fathers, uncles, grandmothers, and grandfathers. They have their friends, their school, their rituals, and their routines; if the participants change now and then, the child still has his or her own life left intact. Although the children (of whom we will speak more in Chapter 4) may be controlled ultimately by this large network of people, they also are free to run and play unhindered. They are welcome to eat, sleep, or play in many places, not just one, and they are loved, nurtured, and disciplined by everyone around. Therefore they grow up with dignity and with what Maya Angelou has said is the most important thing: courage. They try things. They have the courage to be humble, to care, and to be aware of each other. They have the courage to be themselves.

Often this kind of old fashioned "tribalism" is decried as hindering one's freedom. What if you do not want to marry the one chosen for you? What if you do not want to wait to go to school? But have we confused freedom with narcissism? Does freedom mean that you never have to consider your brother, your mother, or your aunt? Does it mean you have no responsibility? If so, how can we be human? Humans are social animals. My Nana says that to be honored in your own time is something you cannot buy with money. To be honored is to be given dignity, security, and a sense of belonging. The knowledge that you are obliged to think of others frees you because it gives you honor, strength, and courage. It gives you power you do not even have to use.

The boys, as everywhere, want Levi's and Nike sneakers (real leather, not synthetic). They want corduroy trousers, flannel shirts, and nylon running pants. The girls do not want to dress in the traditional kaaba and slit, except out of necessity for funerals, weddings, or church. They want to wear short skirts and high rubber shoes. They want to straighten their hair, lighten their skin, and keep slim figures. Many want Coca-Cola, television, cars, and VCRs. A funeral is not proper any more unless it is accompanied by Western rock music blasting out of giant speakers.

Are they forced to want these things? Can they resist them? Can they blend them with the earlier parts of their history? Or will the old be forgotten in the seeking of the new? Is this really development? Will the people be better off if they have television and Nike shoes? I believe that they will not know what they have lost until they have lost it, and by that time there will be no one left to remind them. There may be stories about the way it used to be in the "olden days." The children will lose their power, their courage, and their core, but because they are so complete now in the cradle of their extended families and villages, they do not know what it will feel like to lose it. They will give it away because they are so sure of it, so comfortable in it, and so safe.

In Ghana, children do not commit suicide or kill their parents. They do not take guns to school, and they do not carry knives. They fight, but mostly verbally. What will become of them?

There is nothing wrong with Ghanaians' decision-making abilities, their organizational skills, or their sense of real democratic behavior. There is nothing wrong with their analytical skills or their willingness to work. Work has forever been the center of their existence. They know about work. They know about walking miles in the hot sun with pans full of rocks on their heads or with firewood piled high. They plant with a cutlass and a digging stick. They water by hand, or they depend on the rain. They dig in the earth with their stick, and they put in each cassava plant one at a time. They get together to weed each other's fields because that is also done by hand. They know how to use the earth without destroying it and how to use the abilities of each other without destroying them because they respect the land and the people.

But what they do not know is this new kind of work, this new kind of democracy. They have not learned yet how to change from respect of land and people to exploitation of land and people. It is like a puzzle they need to put together. They have the pieces, and someone tells them they must do it, but they are not given the complete handbook, the rule book. They do not know the language or the rules. They have been plunged suddenly into a world, of which they understand only parts. They are called foolish, childlike, or illiterate when they do not understand. Their own local sociology is replete with tales of the illiterates. Because of their humility, their courage, and their trust of fellow humans, they want to learn; so they will accept the new ways. Only the very old can see that what the new generations are trying to learn is not really new, is not really necessary, and really will not bring them peace. However, these elders also know that you must change if you need shoes for your child to attend school, if you need a cutlass to use in your field, if your child needs education because the crops are not enough, or if the local dress is not enough. You must learn the new language. My husband says that when he was young, they hardly wore anything—a small cloth or string around their waists, men, women, boys, and girls. He chuckles when he recalls that time. Now they wear jeans and long sleeved shirts and polyester dresses in a climate that is subtropical and relentlessly hot.

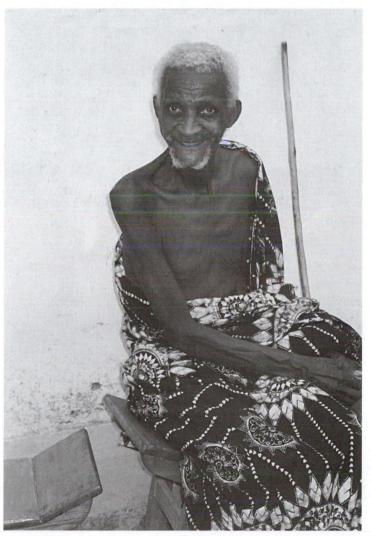

Elder and Healer—Abaasa

How has this come about? Where is it going? Who is in control? What does it mean to have an agency in this context? In the following chapters, I continue to record the process as Baidoo and I see it. We discuss the family; the children; schools; the powerful importance of religion, trading, and commerce; new commodities; the commodification of ethnicity; and the relations between men and women. We record a small part of the lives of a people who live at the edge of a time when their way of life, culture, language, and attitude will surely be lost.

Abaasa children

Nkrumah, Kobina Eight and Nana Mansah III—Royal visit from neighboring Queen Mother

4 / Kinship, Marriage, Family, Clan

The poor kinsman does not lack a resting place.
The beauty of a wife is due to her husband.

PEOPLE TELL ME that the campus of the University of Cape Coast contains within its boundaries five complete villages, but that is hard to imagine. The campus is large and sprawling, winding through farms, clusters of bungalows, woods, and a few academic buildings. There is an "old site" where the main campus had once been. The "new site" is incomplete, is occupied mainly by an unfinished library and a huge concrete science complex, and represents the "new" vision of Kwame Nkrumah for a large, modern, fully equipped university. His inspiration was far-reaching, but the reality can not match it, so the campus remains unfinished. However, the students are compelled to make use of the science buildings and another one built recently, which houses the social sciences, music, and arts. They must take taxis and mini-buses from campus to campus and scurry to make the class before all of the seats are taken and they must stand in the back or outside the window for the lecture. This creates lively activity at each take-off point and across the campuses, but the rest of the grounds remain uncongested by buildings or people most of the time. There are acres and acres of grounds.

Nevertheless, it is difficult to imagine that whole villages actually are contained therein. Where are the people? Why is it not noisier? Why do you feel that, apart from the cluster of buildings on each side of the campus and the old site and new site, you are out somewhere in the middle of the woods? It is tranquil and peaceful, interrupted mostly by the sounds of birds, crickets, frogs, and other forest animals.

I set out to find these villages. This is how I find Akotokyir and Mr. Baidoo. The days from January to July become increasingly hot and dry. The earth becomes parched, the grasses are low and brown, and the red dust from the dirt roads rises up and fills the trees, the houses, the cars, and the air. It is on one of these steamy days, when the sun is high and hot and burns through your clothes and the stillness is palpable, that I arrive at the end of the long farm road at the village of Akotokyir. Somehow it is a surprise. It is not the African village of my imagination. I have been to visit the Fra Fra-speaking Tallensi in the North, and the villages there appear as I expect. They are low clusters of cone-shaped, mud houses, nestled together in a coherent system; they have hand-smoothed, hard-dried mud floors, which are clean, and trees and corn dry on the small, round rooftops. People hunch down, wrapped in colorful Ghanaian cloth, to ease into the low, oval doorways.

However, Akotokyir, as I have come to discover, is more representative of villages in the south and central regions of the country. These villages are all surrounded

University Drive—Cape Coast

by towns or cities and therefore have some of those aspects. Originally, the villages had a symmetry of sorts, and the square or rectangular houses were constructed of mud and wattle, with a thatched roof. Most were organized into compounds with an inner courtyard and rooms around the sides for the many members of the extended family. But more recently, perhaps in the last 20 years, the buildings of preference are made of concrete blocks, roofed with sheets of tin or asbestos in some cases. My informants tell me that the tin sheets and cement were used by early missionaries and other colonial personnel and later became fashionable. A cement house with a tin roof and plenty of fluorescent lights is also a sign of upward mobility and improvement in one's position. It is my contention that the mud and thatch is cooler and better adapted to the climate. It is certainly cheaper and can be repaired with local materials by a group of villagers. However, all Ghanaians with whom I have spoken of the matter assume that the tin and cement are more durable and more comfortable. This is despite the fact that almost all of the tin roofs are held down by a series of large stones, they leak at each point where a nail is driven, and they quickly rust. The cement also crumbles and pits. But because I have only lived in the cement and tin variety and have felt the oven-like concentration of heat in it, I am not an adequate judge of the virtues or drawbacks of thatch and mud. I only long for a structure that does not contain the heat, making the indoor atmosphere stiflingly hot and airless to the point that I feel I might suffocate within the confines of the airless box. But I know that I am missing something. There is a value or an aesthetic that my eye is unable to appreciate. The value and elegance of these structures is taken so for granted, however, by the average Ghanaian, that they are unable to explain to my foreign eye what seems to them obvious.

Thus when I enter, the village stands naked in the dust, against the sun-drenched, clear sky. The trees and underbrush are cut back, as it is in most villages, and there appears to be a litter of houses scattered randomly in various states of repair, some still of mud, some part mud and part cement, and some nicely-secured, complete cement with tin sheets as the roof. A bar (of mud but coated with cement), a thatch roof, and part of the cemetery in front mark the entry to the village. The cemetery looks cheerful and always has a crowd in and around it, sitting on tombstones and talking in groups. As you walk up a slight incline, the sun reflects off the sand, and the buildings take on a hazy, almost unreal quality. It is quiet. The sounds are those of roosters crowing, sheep bleating, and an occasional cry of a baby.

Mr. Baidoo's school is situated halfway up the hill in a prominent position on what could be considered the main street, although it is not a street at all but a path etched out over years of the walkers and the occasional taxi or automobile. The school is constructed in a design common to most of the schools in Ghana. It is a rectangle, painted a cheerful pink, covered with a tin roof, and divided into classrooms that open out onto the sandy yard. Behind the school is the home of the Baidoos. On my first visit to the village, I walk back from a short tour of the sometimes thatch, sometimes cement, sometimes crumbling, and sometimes unfinished houses. Mr. Baidoo seems to appear from nowhere and greets me formally in clear British English. As always, he is dressed professionally in slacks, sandals, and a crisp shirt, which suits Mr. Baidoo's tall, slim, distinguished-looking countenance. He is working on his motorcycle, he says, and he is also, incidentally, the headmaster of the Tuwohofo Holly International School I have just passed. It contains a Kindergarten and grades one through six. Mr. Baidoo started the school himself after a career that spanned

Akotokyir

several years and a few countries; he began at the university in the physics department as a lab assistant, held several other positions, and concluded as a teacher in Nigeria. Back home in Akotokyir, he decided to build a school so that the children, who otherwise had to walk a distance to Abura, more likely would attend and go on to Junior Secondary School and perhaps even to Senior Secondary School.

Since that first meeting, Mr. Baidoo and I spend many hours together in his office, his village, with his family, in church, and at festivals and anniversaries. We discuss everything from the nature of Ghanaian religion, to how to talk to your wife, to how to discipline a wayward teenager, to spirits in Ghanaian tradition, and to his youngest child's new teeth. On one such occasion, we discuss kinship. I feel compelled to call it kinship here, using the broadest category, because the nature of family, marriage, love, friendship, and courtship are all a part of an extended network that is often referred to as the extended family, or a lineage system. It also includes the clan, the entire lineage, and in some instances even several parts of different villages.

The Baidoos are Fante and thus are matrilineal. The majority of the inhabitants of the Cape Coast area are from this group, which is also called a "tribe," linguistic group, or ethnic community. In Ghana there are anywhere from 20 to 50 of these groups. The number varies depending on the authority and how narrowly the groups are defined. The dominant group, however, generally is agreed to be the Akan-speaking group that includes the Fante, Asanti, and Twi. The Akan all speak slightly different forms of the same language. Asanti are the dominant group in the country, composing more than one-half of the population. They reside in large numbers in the upper central region, encompassing the second largest city in the country, Kumasi. In Kumasi the Asanti king reigns, and the old Kingdom of Asanti continues to maintain its keen sense of history, power, and dignity. They are all matrilineal.

In the southern part of the Volta Region are the patrilineal Ewe. The president of the country, J. Jerry Rawlings, represents this group, which is also one of considerable numbers. In the Accra area there are mostly Ga and Adgangbe people who are also matrilineal. In the northern region are numerous patrilineal groups, mainly descended from the Mole-Dagbani groups. These people live in the most arid, flat section of Ghana, where making a living is a challenge. They tend to be the poorest peoples, and sometimes are considered to be more "traditional" and thus less modern and progressive than the other groups. They are heavily Muslim although they share a large number of Catholics with the rest of the country.

Although there are sections where certain groups dominate, all of these groups mingle and occupy the same towns and villages. They intermarry and, for the most part, live respectfully together although there may be preferences within certain families for their offspring to marry into their same religious and clan group.

Baidoo's Story

After our first meeting, Mr. Baidoo and I spend many interview hours and much time in casual conversation. On one such occasion, I meet him in his office, and he explains kinship in Ghana. His immediate family is large, descending from one of the first members and founders of the village. His great-great-grandfather settled with his family in this area, which is close to a healthy river and in the midst of good farm land. They called the village Akotokyir.

Mr. Baidoo writes:

Akotokyir village in the Oguaa Traditional Council was founded some hundreds of years ago by Opanyin Yeboah. The founder had traveled with a group of other Akans and settled temporarily with a chief of Anomabo named Nana Baffoe.

Opanyin Yaboah, who was an industrious farmer, left Anomabo in an effort to look for virgin land where he could cultivate yams and other food crops. He met the Gyaasehen and chief of Kakomdo, who directed him to the west of Kakomdo and south of the River Kakom. Cutting paths through the thick forest, he finally settled near the banks of the river and named his village, "Akatakyiwa," meaning: "I have reserved my words." "Akatakyina" is a kind of black pot used by the palm wine tapper to collect the sweet and foamy liquid from the palm tree. The nature of the pot, its shape and blackened color, do not allow one to see its contents. Hence, the name literally means, "it is difficult to see what is in one's head." He cultivated yams and also sold "nhweba" sticks to people of Cape Coast, who needed them for the ceiling of their rooms.

Nana Yeboah, for the Aboradze clan, was later joined by other friends and relatives. One of such nieces had a grand daughter, Obaapanyin Kokwenua, whose mother was a prominent queen mother, Nana Ama Kyirba, alias Elizabeth Thompson, daughter of a renowned minister, the late J. H. Thompson.

The founder of the village developed an interest and love for Gyaasehen's daughter. The Gyaashehen and his wife, Aba Egyirba of Anana clan, gave their consent to the marriage and consequently Efuwa Abokyi was married to the founder. She lived happily and raised children.

Nana Yeboah accorded his wife with pride and respect and offered more than 140 acres of land in recognition of Efuwa Abokyi's selflessness and devotion. In appreciation of her husband's honour and respect, which was quite unusual, she sought permission and named one of her daughters with the name Kun Pa, meaning "a good husband."

As years rolled by, the founder married a second wife called Obaapanyier Dokee, another member of Anona clan, from the Akroma in the Asebu traditional area. Gradually the name was mispronounced and misspelled "Akatakyiyir" as Western education came. The village is also called Ngyadu by admirers.

There are three clans in the village. These are: Aboradze clan, which is composed of four families with the symbol of the lion under a plantain[;] the Anona clan, composed of three families having the symbol of the Parrot feeding on rich palm fruits[;] and the Twedan clan, that has only one family with the symbol of the leopard. The people of Akotokyir are interwoven. Men and women in these clans are married to one another. It is really difficult to draw one member of any of these clans into disrepute.

Ngyadu is a member of the No. 3 Asafo Company of Intsin in Cape Coast. It is noted for its bravery in wars and leads the No. 3 Asafo Company in all its deliberations. Many men in the past have shown wonderful prowess and have defeated villages and Asafo companies in wars. One of such men was Opanyin Kow Bin of the Anona clan and a descendant of Efuwa Abokyi. Flying birds could be easily brought down with an ordinary yell from the people. These were extraordinary. The people are culturally blessed and maintain a high degree of skills in farming, drumming, and fishing.

This is what Mr. Baidoo writes of the village history. They are an old village and a proud one, but things are changing. The old ways are giving way to the new. The village was taken by the government of Kwame Nkrumah when he had visions of his great new university. The village chief was compensated a small amount, which Mr.

Baidoo says he squandered. The promise was that the village would be moved. This has never happened. Now there is a new government and new ideas. Now the land on which Akotokyir so proudly sits is not the property of the clans but the property of the government of Ghana. Many villagers, however, are not aware of this. Some have even begun to sell the property that they think is that of their forefathers but is, in fact, owned by the government and a part of the university. Someone, Mr. Baidoo tells me, tried to sell a part of their cemetery. That is going too far, he laments.

However, today we are not discussing the land. Today we are discussing the complications of the workings of the family. The old is mixed with the new in a curious blend that is sometimes smooth and natural and is sometimes painful and confusing. Today Mr. Baidoo tells me about some of the pain.

He tells me that when he was a small boy of about 18, his father unexpectedly died. There were nine children belonging to Mr. Baidoo's mother. The father had had other children with other wives, but because the Fante are matrilineal, the children of his own mother are the ones considered hers. All of the groups in Ghana are historically polygamous, as are most West African horticultural groups, and therefore siblings are traditionally many. One's cousins also are considered one's siblings. So when you ask a Ghanaian how many siblings or children he or she has, the answer is not simple. In fact, the question is not exactly relevant. The answer to these questions usually depends on the reasons for asking. One counts their numbers in various ways, depending on the occasion, the questioner, and many other factors.

Mr. Baidoo is telling me a story about himself and the children of his mother and his father. When Mr. Baidoo's father died, they were living in a house that they considered their own and that had belonged to Mr. Baidoo's parents. This house was mud and thatch, and it was composed of rooms situated within the compound of the father. Because the family is matrilineal, when the father died his nephews came to claim the house. Mr. Baidoo's own mother belonged to another clan, as did her children. However, the family had been Christian and seemed to have functioned somewhat as a nuclear family, so the children were shocked when the cousins (the father's sister's sons) came for the house and the belongings. His mother had no recourse because these nephews are traditionally the natural heirs to their deceased uncle's wealth.

Baidoo watched as his mother struggled to rebuild her house and her life to accommodate her still growing family. Now, because he has his own family, he wants to ensure that this will never happen to them. Therefore he has moved away from the family compound and built his own rooms for his own family: father, mother, and six children. He has been forced to leave two of the sons behind in the family quarters, but he works regularly to add extra rooms onto the house and retrieve the two boys. Because the houses are not even a city block from each other, the boys are not really separated from the family. However, Mr. Baidoo would like to be sure that his own children are clearly with him so that they will have claim to the buildings and the land if something should happen to him.

This is a somewhat radical move, but it is one that Ghanaians who can afford it (and especially those who are of the Christian faith) are making increasingly. Originally, the Fante people lived in matrilineal, extended family compounds of the husband's clan. The husband is brought into the household of the wife's father and therefore is not really a part of the lineage. His children belong to the lineage of their mother and therefore are headed by the brother of their mother (their uncle). Mr. Baidoo, in other words, is not technically responsible for the care and maintenance of his own children because they are the responsibility of their own lineage, the lineage of their mother. Mr. Baidoo, then, is responsible for the care and futures of his sisters' children (his nieces and nephews).

However, Mr. Baidoo does not like this idea. He says that he has raised his children, sent them to school, fed them, clothed them, bathed them, and sat with them through sickness and disease, so he should be responsible for their futures. He does what he can for his nephews but believes that his and Mary's biological children should be called his and that they should inherit from him. It is extremely complicated, both in its matrilineal origins and in its juxtaposition with a more Western (some would say "modern"), unilineal, monogamous, nuclear system. In the following section, Mr. Baidoo explains, as well as he can, the original system.

LOVE AND MARRIAGE FANTE STYLE

Courtship

If a young man wants to marry, he informs his elders. He must inform his father, uncle, or another appropriate senior male (usually it is the oldest living male of the lineage of the boy). If the boy does not make such a request within a reasonable period of time, the elders may initiate a match themselves. The same is true for a girl. The girl can inform her elders of a partner interest, or the elders may decide on a suitable match for her.

The boy's father or his uncle then approaches the family of the girl with a bottle of apeteche and maybe a bottle of schnapps. This libation is a knocking fee, the amount needed to open the door. Now the way will be paved to negotiate the union. The age when this occurs varies. Essentially, the most important determinant of marriage readiness is whether or not the boy can provide for his bride the necessities of cloth, farms, and a house or room in the family compound, which will be their home. Both the family of the girl and the family of the boy then spend time investigating the proposed partner. If all goes well, the patriarchs of the two families sit down and agree on a sum of money paid to the family of the girl by the male members of the boy's family on his father's side. The fee varies depending on the status of the girl. For example, if she is unschooled, the fee will be less, and it increases as the level of her education increases. If she comes from a wealthy or especially fine family, is a particularly hard worker, or is known to be a very good girl, the fee may be higher. Ultimately the fee is a matter of negotiation. The boy or the girl can reject the choice of the family. Today, often younger people are choosing their own mates, but this rarely happens without the knowledge and consent of families. Today, Baidoo says, there is the problem of teenage pregnancy when a boy impregnates a girl before he has the ability to care for her. This used to be met with the condemnation of the clan, accompanied by a heavy fine for "stealing" the girl. But as traditions change, modern life makes for less stability in all areas, including marriage and family building.

An interesting aspect of this contractual marriage system is that all individuals who are desirous of a mate acquire one. In our current global market economic system, everything is bought and sold—everything has a price. It is the way of the world. It is understandable, then, that those of us raised within the context of a free market look at relationships in these terms. We "invest" in a relationship. We "waste" or "spend" our time on a desired mate. We expect a return for our money. If my money has been invested in the movie, I want something for the investment. If I "spent" my time with you, you owe me in return. Therefore it is not illogical that we look at the money exchange in our own market terms. The groom's family members are not "buying" a bride for their son; they are showing their respect to the other family, they are solidifying the relationships, they are demonstrating their support for this mutually beneficial union, and they are making a material contribution to the continuation of their joint interests. The union, if so sanctioned, brings together allies and provides larger arenas of potential aid for themselves and future generations. The union is a family affair; it affects large networks of people on both sides. All clan members have a stake in the success of this new marriage. They must indicate their interest and willingness to participate. This is not a decision to be entered into lightly, and it is not left up to the interests or desires of the boy and girl. Therefore it is not left up to a chance meeting, a glance across a crowded room, or a pretty face. There is not the need or desire for one to "sell" oneself to a prospective mate. A girl is not a commodity, packaged and marketed to attract the highest bidder. A boy is not chosen because he looks nice in his Calvin Klein jeans. A girl will not be "left on the shelf" to become an "old maid" if she does not appeal adequately to the current eligible male population. There is a mate for her by virtue of her being a member of a particular lineage. Within the lineage, she has a special position. There are comparable potential mates for her outside the lineage but within a large circle of lineage acquaintances. The elders see to it that an appropriate match is made. She does not have to market herself. She is not a commodity.

Of course this is changing, as is everything, and as Ghana becomes increasingly drawn into the world market, it becomes increasingly subject to the market's rules, values, and expectations. As monogamy and the neolocal nuclear family gain ascendancy, so will individual freedom of choice and, as a result, the need to present oneself in a desirable light. In the old system, individual choice may be sacrificed for the needs of the whole. In the new system, perhaps the needs of the whole are sacrificed for individual choice. In the "modern" system, individual choice is one of the sacrosanct values. Let us see what this means in the context of kinship.

The right to choose a mate means that one must be chosen. To be chosen, one must be desirable. If a family is nuclear (father, mother, and children) and no longer extended, elders are no longer invited to participate, nor are they likely to feel much commitment to the process. Married children are economically independent and physically separate. The choice of a mate resides in the hands of the relevant parties, not in the hands of the elders. Children, in other words, are on their own in making this important decision. Usually it is the boy who chooses the girl. Therefore a girl spends most of her life preparing herself to be desired. Her external "packaging" is critical because the boy is selecting on this basis. Young people are sometimes blind to attributes, such as ability to produce good children, to be a good mother, or to be a hard worker; and given the mobility of contemporary populations, they are unaware of family background. Families, especially those with large fortunes at stake, may make efforts to control their offspring's social settings to ensure a seemly union, but they may be outwitted by the rectitude of personal choice. Without the assurance that a partner will be provided for her, a girl (and to a lesser degree, a boy) in today's world must be instructed very early in the ways to foster selection. This is done through the media, the schools, parents, older siblings, the parish priest, and peers. It is not difficult to conclude, then, that much of the creative energies and economic resources of a young girl and her immediate family might be spent in this endeavor, creating the framework of her existence. One's worth becomes connected to one's success in the market.

However, we are not discussing all of this today. Mr. Baidoo is a confirmed believer in the virtues of monogamy and neolocal post-marital residence. He is aware of the differences between the old system and the new and very much prefers the new. Much of the old, he believes, is still here in the new. He continues telling me about marriage among the Fante. He says that, as in his own case, it is customary for the man to bring his new bride to his own village and sometimes his own compound even though they are matrilineal. His wife, Mary, spent a large part of her young life in Kumasi where her father has farms. She came to live with Baidoo in his room in the family compound.

Baidoo says that courtship and marriage rites today are more "polished" but are essentially the same. The husband still is required to provide for the wife in marriage and still must contribute baby items with each birth. Today, however, instead of cloth for wrapping the baby, he may provide a small bed or mattress, and instead of baby rags, he will purchase nappies (diapers) made for the purpose. The marriage ceremony may be accompanied by a religious one in many instances. In Baidoo's case he was married 13 years before they had a church ceremony despite the fact that they are staunch Catholics. It takes time to prepare yourself for such a ceremony, he says.

Traditionally women have carried their babies wrapped in cloth on their backs and nurse them on demand. Most often, they continue to do so. However, as with most things, this too is changing. Some young mothers want to wear Western-style attire that makes nursing difficult and that does not adapt itself (as well as a traditional Kaaba and slit) to wrapping the child in matching cloth to lie snugly on the mother's back. I am often struck with how quiet and alert the babies seem, I tell Baidoo. On the tro tros, taxis, in church, or on the street, almost every woman seems to have a baby tied on her back. Little brown feet poke out on the sides of a woman, almost as a part of her dress. But you rarely hear them cry.

One day I am in a church where most of the women are attired in Western dresses and hold the babies on their laps. I am reminded of the whimpering and jostling in the arms and frantic rearranging of mother and child, which prevails in public places in other parts of the world. As a result, parents are discouraged from including young children, necessitating the expensive and often unsatisfactory use of babysitters. In Ghana, babies go where their mothers go, and they, for the most part, go there happily. Ensconced in their wrap close to their mother, they constantly are rocked by the movement of her body and able to be pulled quickly around to decorously nurse under the same wrapping cloth, after which they are once again placed on mother's back. This allows mother to walk, work, dance, and greet friends without juggling a fretful baby, worrying about the babysitter, or missing out on work or play. I take bus trips of several hours, unaware of the presence of a child until the bus stops, mothers pop up from their seats, and I see the little round heads at their backs. I also am astonished to find that an infant I think is around 4 or 5 months old has really only been on the earth for 4 weeks. Often these tiny infants peer straight into your eyes, either with businesslike intensity or smiling glee. There is evidence to suggest that the motion of hefting the infant onto the back several times a day, along with the constant stimulation and eye-level gazing, put some African babies developmentally ahead of their European and American counterparts (Tronick 1987). I mention something of this to Baidoo, who is not surprised.

There clearly is a conflict between admiring the old and enjoying past traditions and wanting to be a part of the new, the "modern," and the better developed. Must "modern" Ghanaian women put their babies in a play pen, crib, or stroller when they work or go out to socialize? As soon as they are able to abandon fetching firewood for cooking or water for drinking and as soon as they are relieved of their farming and trading occupations, will they take their babies from their backs and their breasts and follow the models of their Western sisters? It makes sense, I think, and Baidoo agrees. Ghanaians traditionally are somewhat communal and cooperative inside family compounds, clans, tribes, and villages. They have to cooperate and work together. They know their neighbors, their relations, and their village mates, and they have known them for generations and look forward to knowing them for generations in the future. In horticultural and pastoral societies, even agricultural ones, this form of close, companionable, family-oriented society is necessary for survival. Children take care of their old parents when there are no nursing homes and social security; older siblings are responsible for younger ones; and sons, nephews, daughters, and nieces must learn to take over land and village maintenance when the elders go. Most spaces in villages are public spaces where people cook and bathe outdoors, use public toilets, and merge concepts of public and private space. In this setting where work and play and learning and domesticity are not so easily discernible one from the other, babies, children, old folks, and young folks participate together in the ebb and flow of the cycles of birth, marriage, death, and life.

Within the contemporary free market economy, it is true that this kind of life is not the norm. Space, time, categories of activities, and categories of people are kept separate in neat categories. Work is done outside the home, usually miles or sometimes hours away. Individual families have their individual houses, and children have their individual rooms and beds. At least this is the norm, the model, and the desired form. Individual family members increasingly enjoy their individual television, computer, and telephone, which accompany the individual room and individual bed. Entertainment is designated for adults, children, or families and, as such, requires divisions of place and personnel. It is also true that this kind of individuality (private ownership of increasingly individualized and specialized commodities) prepares the individual for individual competition and fuels the fires of capitalist consumption and thus growth and prosperity. Baby is prepared for this life from the moment she or he leaves the hospital, cocooned not in her mothers arms or in her cloth on her back, but in a sanitary, easy-to-clean, vinyl baby chair, strapped safely in the car. Thus baby is whisked from womb to hospital basket to car to one's own baby bed in one's own room. It must be a rude awakening for baby, but it invariably prepares the way for a developing sense of the world and one's place in it.

This scenario is so foreign, however, to someone even as sophisticated as Baidoo, that it is hardly worth the mention. Nevertheless, if such a scenario were possible, it is my view that Ghanaians generally would agree to its virtue. Like many aspects of cultural change occasioned by the production of products for profit, in other words capitalism, the loss of a human adaptation will not be felt until the adaptation is no longer adaptive. In other words, we may find that it is adaptive for human infants to feel the strength and support of the continuous contact and interaction with other humans as they grow, so as to effectively maximize the physical, emotional, maturational, cognitive and social equipment with which they have been endowed. However, the absence of this adaptation is not felt. We are told, with some alarm and some admiration for the wonders of science, that babies who do not nurse do not do as well on I.Q. tests (or maybe other more relevant life tests). We find that babies who lie on their backs behind closed doors do not sit up, crawl, or walk as quickly as do their African back-born sisters (Tronick et al 1987). There is evidence, science tells us, that babies who do not "bond" with their mothers, do not bond with others later, may become sociopathic, without feelings of guilt or remorse, may not be social. Furthermore, maybe mothers who do not "bond" early with their infant may be more prone to abuse them or ignore abuse of them by others. "Latch-key" children, we are told, have problems in school and with peers, and infants who do not crawl may not read. Divorce has effects on children, which are yet to be understood and which are exacerbated by the persistence of the nuclear family because extended family is not available to care for children in a parent's place.

But what do we tell a Ghanaian parent? Should they forgo jobs in offices to be with their children more often? Should they carry their babies on their backs and go to their fields, the products of which bring them little compensation in a competitive world market? Should they continue to breast-feed their infants and not take jobs that do not allow them to keep their babies? Should we say that to have a room of one's own, a television of one's own, and a telephone of one's own should be privileges of American children but not of Ghanaian children?

SUMMARY

We discuss the previous questions in following chapters. Here we summarize our discussion by reminding ourselves that kinship in Ghana traditionally is unilineal. The Fante are matrilineal with patrilocal postmarital residence. Northerners are mostly patrilineal, as are the Ewe. Although it is possible to intermarry between groups, it is more common for Fante to marry Fante, Asante Asante, and Ewe Ewe. Among all groups, the traditions are that marriage partners are chosen by the respective families, the bride resides with the family of the groom, polygamy is the norm, and children are many.

With the coming of Christianity and what is considered to be modernity, marriages increasingly are monogamous and result in fewer children. To work, new families may move away from the clan to a city or town some miles away.

This does not preclude the pervasive, much-discussed, extramarital sexual activities of large numbers of both male and female members of Ghanaian society. Partly because of the tradition of polygamy and partly because of what some call sexism, this practice of outside sexual relationships is most common among men. It is a theme discussed again and again by all members of society in my acquaintance and is taken up in the section in which we consider gender relations more explicitly.

For this day Baidoo and I are finished with our discussion. I pack up my tape player and notebook and walk out of his office into the last rays of sun. In the kitchen/bathroom of the Baidoo compound, Mary is sitting on the floor over a hot coal pot, cooking the evening meal. Her niece's 11-year-old daughter helps her. Small, barefoot boys are playing football with an orange, and women and girls walk with bundles of firewood and water buckets on their heads. With their babies securely on their backs, mothers walk back from their fields. Children run after me and shout as I leave the village, making my way home.

The Family is a Complicated Thing

One wall shells our homes:
Tells the world we share
One compound, pebbled, yet safe;
Living on a common ground
Of being:
Living with, and not against;
Praying at a common stool:
Our experiences, our school!

(A. Kayper-Mensah 1976, 17)

He positions himself against the door, looking slight, serious, and gentle, and reminding me of Christ. His hands are spread across the door, and his head tilts to the side, looking steadily and solemnly at his father. He does not move or change expression for at least one half hour. The father and son never exchange a word. Nkrumah has come with me to the village of his second wife. She has left the room of Nkrumah's "father" (in Western terms, his uncle), who replaced his own father as head of the family at his death. Her mission is to find their daughter, Margaret, now 18, so we can discuss her employment. In the meantime, George, the 13-year-old boy, is summoned by his father. On entering the room, the boy positions himself against the door, waiting for his father's attention. Mother leaves the room, leaving Nkrumah, his son, and me alone. None of us speak.

The boy looks so sweet, delicate, and fragile. I cannot help wonder at the lack of attention his father shows him. He has not seen this son for perhaps months. I think he should have something to say to the boy. But both boy and father avoid observing each other, and no words seem possible. I would leave to allow them privacy, but I know that this is not possible, so I stay and sit quietly. They could speak Fante, which, because my skills are limited, affords them privacy. But there is not a word, not a smile, nor a gesture of recognition.

I sit wondering at the relationship. This boy and girl are Nkrumah's two youngest children by his first wife. He tells me that she is one of two wives he had when he went to Nigeria for work. When he returned, both wives had left him. He then was encouraged to take another wife because he was alone. He assures me that this was not because he desired several wives or because he approves of philandering or even polygamy, but because circumstances necessitate changes in wives. He seems to be embarrassed. It seems to be a past he prefers to forget. Both wives have returned to their home villages with the children although Nkrumah takes different children at different times to live with him in the village.

The new wife is about 26, Nkrumah about 40. The girl was recommended to him as a good and responsible young woman whose father is an important member of a local Pentecostal church. Nkrumah obtained permission from her father, paid the bride price, and brought her to his village. He says that the new wife must by all means come to his village to live, and now she must attend the church where he is the pastor. This is only correct for a wife, he says. He does not actually marry these women in the church or by civil law although he believes, he tells me, in monogamy, faithfulness, and church marriage. But, being a poor man with few resources, he is forced to make alliances as well as he can. His current wife has not gone to school, works on his farm, and is expecting their fifth child. As is the case with many Ghanaians, it is difficult to know exactly how many children and wives he has. Children, wives, brothers, sisters, mothers, uncles, and aunts keep emerging as relationships develop. No one seems exactly forthcoming with this information, so the full extent of one's relatives unfolds as one's acquaintance deepens. Whether a woman is a wife, a mother is a mother, an uncle is a father, an aunt is a mother, or a nephew is a son depends, to some extent, on the context. The families are large and multilayered, always ensuring a large network of people dependent on each other.

I think about all of this as we wait. It feels almost as if we are holding our breath. I know that this child has been staying away from school, creating tensions in the family. Shouldn't the father chastise the child? Shouldn't he question him? Doesn't he want to discuss the problem with the son? Doesn't he want to show interest, concern, or fatherly prerogative?

When the mother returns, she has a baby, a grandchild, on her back and Margaret in tow. Margaret greets us shyly, averting her eyes. She sits, looking shy and intimidated although robust and pretty in a black and white European-style dress. She still wears her hair in the close-clipped style of a school girl and wears tiny dots of gold in her ears and no other adornments. Other men join us. The boy continues his solemn vigil at the door but is soon asked to sit. Everyone then begins to talk. Nkrumah's former wife speaks calmly but with animation. It seems that they have problems with both the boy and girl. The boy is not attending school, and the girl, having finished Junior Secondary School, has no place to go. Uncles and the grandfather are there. In the end it is determined that the boy has been sacked from school because he has not paid the required school fees, which is not an unusual occurrence. The mother has no money, so they are depending on Nkrumah to help. He says that he will do what he can. He has no suggestions for the daughter. Maybe they will look for a husband for her, but Nkrumah would like for her to continue in school. However, Senior Secondary School costs money, and no one seems to know from where this money would come.

After more discussion, mother and children are dismissed. Nkrumah and his children never exchange words. This is the village of his father, he says. He likes it very much. Although he is really related to his mother's village, Nim, he tells me that he and his younger brother, Kobina, have special feelings for the village of their father. His mother's village is a larger village with more conveniences, closer to Cape Coast. We travel there on many occasions and we are met with great ceremony by the chief, his linguists, elders, and the family of Nkrumah.

Nim—More Family Complexity

A person is not a palm tree that he (or she) should be self complete.

On one occasion, Nkrumah, his 4-year-old son, his mother, his younger brother, two of the chief's council and I set off from Abaasa on a late Sunday morning. We are to meet with the chief on some matters and also consult with Nkrumah's kin regarding a misunderstanding between family members here in Nim and those residing in Abaasa. Although often on a Sunday men dress in the traditional cloth, on this day the men of Abaasa are in European attire. Both myself and Nkrumah's mother, however, have on the usual Kaaba and long slit that is worn by women of the village most of the time and by all women on most Sundays. The two men sit in the back of my pickup truck while Nkrumah, his son, and his mother sit with me in the front. We drive down the rutted dirt road, which is dry and dusty today, to the main paved road into town. After driving in the dry, sunny heat about 3 miles, we turn off onto another rutted and dusty road leading the 3 or so miles to Nmwoa. All along the way, people are walking. They are carrying babies on their backs; water, fruit, or wood on their heads; and Bibles in their hands. There is a decidedly special feeling about a Sunday. The men are in beautiful cloths, dress slacks and shirts, or sometimes in suits and ties. The women wear colorful, puffy-sleeved Kaabas with long slim slits, which are more dressy than they might wear during the week, and their heads are tied in intricate, elaborate, and creative splashes of matching cloth. The boys are often decked out in proper shoes, trousers, and dress shirts. The girls wear sweet, frilly, lacy dresses (usually modestly long) with puffy sleeves and old-fashioned sashes tied in extravagant bows in the back. They wear the mandatory earrings, definitively identifying their female gender, and their heads are adorned with bonnets, ribbons, or colorful hair ornaments. Unlike their mothers, the girls are attired mostly in Western-style dresses, especially for church and other special occasions. Small boys likewise wear Western-style trousers or knickers if they are under or around 12 or 13 years of age. They do not don the elegant cloth of their fathers until they are in their twenties. The activity is lively as folks stroll down the dusty dirt road, talking and laughing, and children romp excitedly as they mark a special interruption of the week's ordinary activities.

We bump along the road, passing several villages until at last we reach our own. Parking alongside a grounded road grater, we are approached immediately by a throng of men and women, old and young, who come to confront the unusual sight of a white woman driving a truck full of Ghanaians. They are curious, surprised, interested, and generally pleased. In their usual friendly and accepting manner, they are willing to welcome this strange group into their midst as long as they can participate. We get out of the truck and are trailed by the crowd, who are talking quietly, watching, waving, and smiling. We enter the courtyard of the auntie who is to sit with us as we begin to arbitrate the feud. The chief waylays us. He is on his way out of the village back to his job as a school teacher in a town some miles away. He has left behind his elaborate cloth, gold, and chief's sandals, and he now looks very much the school teacher in his tan political suit. He is distressed that we have missed each other during our previous visits and quickly invites us to his palace so that he can greet us briefly and establish another date for a real visit.

Off we go with our large entourage to the chief's palace. I am already beginning to sag under the piercing sun. I totter in mincing, slit-constrained steps on my little high-heeled shoes between the stones, sand, and ups and downs of the rocky path to the house, and I recall that our real business has not begun yet. I have an enormous amount of energy by most standards, but I continuously marvel at the energy these folks have for traveling around in the scorching tropical heat for endless hours and enduring various forms of social interaction while fueled by little more than calabashes of apateche and palm wine. I always carry with me a thermos of water and think that I would perish if not for this cool repast now and then.

We slowly caravan our way into the palace, which is a room with three walls and opens onto a courtyard (behind which is a chamber one assumes is that of the chief). The lean-to style palace is made of cement blocks, with a cement floor and a tin roof typical of "modern" building in Ghana. It replaces the older mud and thatch that is still a part of the village landscape. The chief's stool has been removed, so someone brings a chair for the chief to use as he faces us for our conversation. Other chairs and benches form a rectangle facing the chief and his linguist. I am given a chair with arms, much like that of the chief, and the rest are seated around on benches. By now the group consists only of the elders, linguists, and chief's councilmen of both villages. This means that I am the only woman present. Women and children sometimes pass through the courtyard, but they do not participate in our congregation. Drinks are brought out and put on a small table before me—a bottle of beer, a Guinness, two Cokes and a malta. In another bottle that is filled with what looks to my untutored eye like sticks, roots, and herbs is the locally made apateche. I have brought a bottle of Schnapps that Nkrumah presents to the chief with a few words. Although this chief speaks excellent English, he waits to speak to me until all of the formalities are completed in Fante. This means that we are welcomed by his linguist and asked for our mission. Our linguist (today it is Nkrumah), responds with a greeting to the chief, his linguist, and the elders and a recitation of our mission. This is usually done in some detail, explaining the circumstances of our last meeting, our travels today, and our intentions for future discussions. Sometimes there is discussion regarding our trials while attempting to reach them, what has happened before, or what we are here to discuss. Sometimes this invokes laughter, sometimes sympathy, sometimes distress, and often all.

After appropriate greetings by both parties, we partake of our refreshment. This is done slowly and ceremoniously. Only after this do we begin to talk. The chief apologizes for the brevity and informality of the meeting. We will meet again soon. He is interested in many issues concerning our two villages. We discuss teaching, children in Ghana, the education system, and his pending golden jubilee celebration of his 25 years as chief of this village. The others chat and joke around us. We are ready to leave. Nkrumah asks permission to leave, and the chief grants the request through his linguist. We rise, extend good wishes to all, and again parade out of the room, into the courtyard, and down the stubbly path in the direction of Auntie's house.

We stop to see Nkrumah's grandmother on the way and to greet his senior mother. After this is done and appropriate respect is paid to other relatives in the house, we finally arrive at the house of Auntie. When we arrive, she is in the courtyard pounding palm nuts into palm oil. Others keep her company and supply her with the hard red fruit. We immediately go inside where awaiting us are a cousin, Nkrumah's brother Kobina, someone else I do not know, Nkrumah's mother, and his baby son. We all take our seats. The baby immediately attaches himself to his father's lap, and Nkrumah indulgently unwraps a piece of bread, which the child chews happily. This meeting seems to be somewhat in progress, and Nkrumah just jumps in. The child wiggles in his father's arms as he gestures and enters the verbal fray. Everyone is talking at once. They are clearly agitated. Sometimes they address their comments to me, and every now and then Nkrumah says, "Wait, Nana, I am coming." This is a common expression that, depending on the context, means: "I will get to you," "I am going," "I will be right back," "Wait," or "I will be right with you."

The story has been unfolding over the weeks. Now I get bits and pieces to fit together the problem. It seems that some weeks before, Kobina had been to a funeral in Nim where he verbally insulted relatives living in the village. The family members then declared that no member of the family from Abassa is welcome in Nim. This means that Nkrumah, his mother, his children, and other siblings are unwelcome in Nim, the village where brothers, sisters, uncles, and aunts reside. Nkrumah says that his brother had a bit too much apateche and was wrong in what he had done. He is not pleased to receive this censure for the misdeeds of his brother.

I was told of the trouble weeks before but had observed no animosity between the brothers in the interim. We sat together on many occasions, the brothers speaking and joking together, with no obvious indication of the family problem they were experiencing. This is typical. There is a time reserved for settling the problem. In the meantime, life goes on, and there is no interruption in their relationships. It seems to me that this is a sensible arrangement. The brothers each play important roles in the village and the family. They see each other every day. The village is small, the family close. It would be tense and difficult if they disturb the flow of activities and events by openly feuding. How much better to know that the issue will be resolved, that there will be help in resolving it, and that their relationship, in the meantime, remains intact. This appears to militate against months and maybe even years of stored up resentments, anger, and frustration. People in many cultures, especially American, have a tendency to value directness ("letting it all hang out") and complain about the Ghanaian evasiveness and indirectness. But in a context in which almost all relationships are personal and in which physical and social mobility is limited, privacy is achieved only through discretion in speech and action. This method of dealing with family disturbances ensures continuity and social ease and provides a formal apparatus for personal grievances.

I am having trouble keeping track of the issues, the players, and even the residences of the different parties. There are senior aunties, senior brothers, uncles, and brothers, and they all seem to live in different villages and all have different amounts of influence. I try to keep up with it all, but they all talk and argue so fast and furiously that Nkrumah has little time to fill me in, and I cannot always follow the allusions to kinship and place. However, they continue to direct their conversation to me, in Fante as if I understand not only the language but also the complexities of the family relationships. From previous experiences and conversations, I know that if I knew the language better, I of course would understand more completely. However, even if I understood Fante better, it would take me a lifetime to really understand who everyone is, whose father is whose, where they each reside, where they call home, whose mother is whose, who is related, and in what ways and how they all relate to the individuals and the problem involved. Nkrumah gives me a different rendition of the kinship complexities than his brother, the offending party. This is because, although they are called brothers, they do not have the same status in the family, and therefore they have different sets of relatives and different family responsibilities.

Hence, I do not interrupt the discussion with questions. Eventually they turn to me. Nkrumah explains that Kobina needs to beg his auntie's forgiveness so that the Abaasa members of the family can resume usual family relations with the Nim family members. This fact seems clear and indisputable. However, the cousin is not convinced of Kobina's humility or of his recognition of culpability. With this pronouncement, there ensues a spate of charged words. Kobina is then asked to leave the room. Again Nkrumah turns to me to advise me of my role. I need to prevail on the younger brother to get down on his knees and beg the forgiveness of Auntie. Even though he is not properly contrite, he will have to make this gesture, and it seems possible that he is ready to do so with a word from me.

I am filled at that moment with a sense of terrible responsibility and ignorant presumption. This has gone too far, I think. There must be a mistake. This man is a member of this long lineage, an African, and a Ghanaian. This is a man whose language I don't even speak and in whose country I am still, after all this time, a visitor. How can they really believe that this strong, grown man will listen to me? Yet, here they are, waiting anxiously for me. I have only a second to think. How can I refuse my duty? Can I show them that I do not deserve the title they have so graciously and earnestly bestowed on me? Can I let them think that their own queen mother, in whom they take such pride, will let them down in another village, in front of a relative?

I rally myself and indicate to all present that I understand my task and am ready to perform it. They call Kobina back. Everything is quiet. They all look to me. I pull myself up, muster as much dignity as a short, pale American can command, and, looking at Kobina, explain as well as I can what seems to be necessary for us both. Without a moment's hesitation, he drops to his knees, turns toward his auntie (who is still furiously pounding her large pestle into the wooden mortar), places one hand cupped into the other in the obligatory position of supplication, and begs her forgiveness. It is a stunning, touching moment. Auntie stops her pounding, looks into the eyes of her grown-up nephew, and without expression softly murmurs something in Fante. He stands. At the same moment she stands and looks at him hard. They do not smile, they do not embrace, but everyone recognizes that the job is done. Kobina sits back down in his seat; Auntie sits on her low stool, takes the mortar in between her legs, and returns to work; the room bursts into easy, relaxed conversation. Nkrumah's baby boy is asleep on his father's knees. Only the baby's mother smiles. We are now ready to leave. However, as we exit the house, Kwame informs me that the issue must still be heard by the senior brother (whom I wrongly thought was the elder brother in Abaasa). This will be done later, he says, and I feel a great pang of relief.

There seems to be plenty of time for this, and we have done enough for one day. It is getting late. It will be dark before I drive the family back to Abaasa and return to my own bungalow. Furthermore, tomorrow is Monday—a day filled with more work, more conversations, and more family complications. None of our day's activities have included any of Nkrumah's wives or children, past or present. On none of our travels does his wife accompany us. The business does not include her. These are not her affairs, and this is not her family. Her family resides in a whole set of different villages, has entirely different sets of problems, and includes an entirely different set of uncles, mothers, brothers, and aunties. This thought leads me to the contemplate the relationship between men and women in a kinship system that is unilineal, matrilineal, and potentially polygamous.

GENDER

Women in Ghana traditionally and commonly occupy different spaces and live in different worlds than men. They come together as an economic unit, a procreative unit, and a social unit. They do not come together necessarily as friends, companions, soul mates, or partners, although they can. The Daily Graphic (February 26, 1999) reports that, according to data compiled by the International Food Policy Research Institute (IFPRI), women in Africa produce approximately 90 percent of the work of processing food crops and providing household water and fuel wood, 80 percent of food storage and transport, 90 percent of hoeing and weeding, and 60 percent of harvesting and marketing. This unequal workload is reinforced by comparable inequalities in education and paid employment in which women suffer in comparison with men. There is also an enormous difference in health according to gender. Although both men and women suffer from a variety of health problems, women's maternal mortality rates in Sub Saharan Africa are the highest in the world with between 600 and 1500 maternal deaths for every 100,000 births. Although

Kwame Nkrumah chats in village

Africa accounts for 20 percent of the world's births, it accounts for 40 percent of the world's maternal deaths.

Although men I have met agree that women's and men's spheres are different but equal, the above statistics paint a different picture—one that is more consistent with my experience and that of other women. Their lives are different but decidedly not equal. Because women and men lead such independent lives, there does seem to be a certain amount of freedom and female support absent in some places where men and women are expected to be each other's best and only friend and lover. Nevertheless, as the previously mentioned profile suggests, the lives of most women are limited and circumscribed by the health and social contingencies of everyday existence. For the most part, as is often true for people everywhere, men and women see themselves as participating in the reproduction of their society as they each fulfill their different roles. The fact that the roles, rules, and obligations are gender-specific typically is not emphasized more than the fact that they are also age-specific. It is considered respectful to recognize a woman's child-bearing function just as it is respectful to recognize the function of one's elder.

Boys and girls in the cities, in the villages, and on the university campus, are all expected to marry. After marriage they have children if they are able. Whether or not these roles are completely natural and desirable usually is not contemplated. Whether or not these roles are complementary also is not usually a part of conscious consideration. In an earlier time, when we were all horticulturists or fishers, there is evidence to suggest that the roles were, in fact, complementary and equally valued. We must not, however, forget

Woman resting—Abaasa

that men are the chiefs, the chief's linguists, and the elders of the tribe or village, and therefore many important decisions are always made by men. I am always reminded, however, that there is the queen mother who is the mother of all—the real head of the family, the clan, and the village—and she has great power.

However, today the pressures of the industrial global economy causes the division of labor to be marked by increased division of the domestic and public spheres, the necessity to incorporate into an increasingly competitive market economy, and the ability of men to earn more than women in that market. Men are considered the main wage earners and heads of the household while women's shares of domestic tasks increase. Pressure on the family increases as the need for cash increases; this necessitates the migration of men for the purpose of employment, which leaves women with more of the burdens of domestic and child-rearing tasks and continued farming and fishing responsibilities. Women and men both suffer under the strains of incorporation into the industrialized world. There are new demands, new needs, and new requirements. As is usual in this transition, women's and men's roles and relationships are redefined and reconfigured along previously constructed gender lines yet accommodate contemporary gender constructs. Men and women daily enact an intricate dance, renegotiating their duties, their relative status, and their relationships.

The Market—A Woman's Place

The market at the center of Cape Coast is a place familiar to everyone in the central region of Ghana. Although individuals may shop regularly in their village markets, they almost always have some occasion to be in the Kotokaruba market in central Cape Coast during the course of the year. It is a woman's place. Women are the sellers, the buyers, and the shoppers. Cape Coast was originally only a market, a stopping-off place for produce, and buyers and sellers, so it is the true center of the town—dominating it and usurping any other center. It is a triangle with octopus-like tentacles stretching out from its center. Each of the tentacles, like its triangular shaped body, contains little nodes of small market spots. Some of the spots are tiny one-room stores, some are heaps of goods on the road, some are little improvised stalls, some are traveling carts, and some are shops carried on the heads and shoulders or umbrellas of merchants. Outside the body of the market, traders are men, women, and children selling everything including: toilet paper, bread, hardware, clothes, kitchen utensils, plumbing, medicines, electronics, sandals, cloth, and used imported clothing. They sell everything that anyone would ever need and, sometimes it seems, anything that an industrious trader can obtain from anywhere in the world.

Inside the triangle, the body of the market beast, the merchants are almost entirely women. They mostly sell food and cloth, but they also sell some of everything else. They sit all day in their stalls, and they chat, eat, mind their babies, fix hair, sew, sleep, dance, sing, and talk to their customers, who are also almost exclusively women. Once in a while a woman turns over her small stall to a nephew, uncle, or son, and once in a while a man comes in to shop, but by and large it is a place for women.

I frequent the market as much as my heavy schedule allows. The women have fun with me when I visit. They make fun of my hair (it is very short) and my Fante (it is very bad). Sometimes they scold me for my dress (it is not queen mother-like), and sometimes they comment on my weight. But for all their joking, teasing, and chastising, they are never mean. They love to laugh, to play, and to hear me stumble through my clumsy Fanti. They also like to hug me, touch me, and fuss over me. Although public touching, hugging, or kissing of men (even husbands) is decidedly out, they are free to display such gestures of affection with each other. They hug, offer cheeks (not lips) for kissing, and particularly seem to like touching my hair, my skin, and my body. I am significantly different to stimulate curiosity and am old enough and foreign enough to safely satisfy that curiosity.

When I enter the market, there is quite a commotion—a diversion that I sense is enough to add a bit of excitement to their day. All of them have husbands and children, or will have them, but you would not know it from the activities of the women. I sit down to talk to my old friend and seamstress, Jane. She takes me aside in a conspiratorial fashion to disclose a piece of information. Her youngest daughter needs school fees, and Jane has no money. Her only son is to bring her money from Accra, but he has not done so yet. She also tells me that the Methodist church is having its harvest and can I donate to it; that her migraine was bad the last few days, and she needs medication; and that she wants to sew me a special Kaaba and slit so that I can attend church with her. Life has many trials, most of which are connected to her lack of money, but it also contains pleasures. There are funerals to attend, weddings, church activities, new babies, and opportunities for her children. The women plan and plot and borrow here and there to sustain all of these activities. Sometimes they receive help from their men, but usually they do not. "Men," says Jane to me, "are all evil. They are just evil." She says this with vehemence, and her friend Theresa, the queen mother of the market, nods her head vigorously in agreement. As is true of women in many places, mothers support the social system by encouraging their children to marry, even though they are marriage's worst critics. There is nothing else to do but to marry and to provide children, but each generation seems to need to learn anew that children are a burden and men tend to go their own way.

The women in the market are strong, smart, savvy, and independent. They travel to buy, they set the prices, they collect the money, and they take care of their children. Yet, they are perceived and sometimes perceive themselves as weaker, dumber, and more dependent than their male counterparts. But Jane and Theresa are quite clear. Whatever illusions they may have had about men in their youth, they have them no longer. They carry on without them in the hope that they can educate their children and provide for them a better life.

Love, Ghanaian Style—Kissing in Public

Odo Nnyew Fie Kwan (Love never loses its way home).

What calls, pulling you
Towards it, lights a path
For your homing feet.
Love, they say will surely draw you
Blind yet safely to her hearth
Where our limbs will meet.

(Adinkra poem in A. Kayper-Mensah 1976, 15)

Pounding foo foo in Kotokuraba market

A friend, Peter, tells me that when his brother Mr. Mensah returned to Ghana for a visit, there was a problem between him and his African-American wife over kissing in public. It seems, my friend explains, that the wife became upset with the husband because he refused to kiss her in public. Peter says that of course it is not a part of Ghanaian culture to kiss in public. In fact, kissing is not very important at all. I have heard suggestions here and there that some Ghanaians are offended by their partners' interest in kissing. Of course we in America consider kissing close to universal, if not instinctive. Peter tells me that this custom seems peculiar to him. What is it for? Mashing lips together! It can even be dangerous. That is why, he says, laughing, you white people have such thin lips. You are always mashing them together.

Jane sewing in market

So what is the big fuss all about? As I think more about it, I come to the conclusion that, in all likelihood, the problem is not about kissing in public or kissing at all. Peter is the youngest of five and his brother the eldest, very much his senior. Furthermore, Peter is not a child. The couple presumably have been married for a long time, and therefore she has had plenty of her husband's kisses, both public and private. No, the problem is about paying attention. It is about profound cultural differences. I speculate that the wife was not complaining about the kissing. She was complaining that he did not pay respectful attention to her when they were in public. They live in Canada, so both are outsiders without extended family and friend ties. Over the years they probably have depended on each other. They have been each other's support and each other's family. The husband, freed from the binds of kinship and cultural expectations, was able to be a husband in the Western, nuclear, monogamous family style. That is, he does things with his wife; they go out together, they share dinners and movies and the theater, and maybe they take long leisurely hand-holding walks.

However, they decided to visit Ghana—his home, his culture, a different culture. Americans believe that they are culturally aware, are interested in cross-cultural exploration, and love other ways of life. But, as most of us learn, culture is not simply a geographic difference, a way of dress, a cuisine, or dances and music. A culture is how people live, how they breathe, how they love, how they die, how they cry, how they feel pain, how they laugh, how they think, and most of all, how they live inside families. In Ghana, social rules and customs are followed rigidly, and family responsibilities are powerful. A friend of mine from Zaire says that people think that because he is not married and has no children, he is alone and his money must go far. But, he says, an African is never alone. The family, the age mates, and the ties are always there.

So in Ghana, this Canadian and Ghanaian was now confronted with all of these ties, all of this family. Ghana is a small country, and Cape Coast is a small town. Everyone knows your business, everyone feels they can get into it, and almost everyone is your family. In Ghana, a man is not supposed to be "bound at the hip," as some describe American marriages. Men are expected to lead their own lives. They are not to cater too much to the wife. Men's and women's lives are somewhat separate. She has her friends and relatives, and he has his. He goes out at night with friends, relatives, or girlfriends. She stays in the house or visits her relatives.

When Mr. and Mrs. Mensah arrived in Ghana, Mrs. Mensah thought that her relationship with her husband would stay the same, despite the change in culture. I speculate, using this woman I do not know as a model, that she imagined she would enjoy the new culture, food, clothes, sounds, smells, music, dance, and even her relatives with the same husband she had in Canada. But when they got here, he was swept up into the kin network and peer network that would not and could not allow them the same relationship. If kissing, hugging, sharing, and moving about together have been their language of love, then in its absence, was the love also gone? Was the relationship changed? Did he care more about his family, his friends, and his "old boys" than he cared about her?

He, on the other hand, had no real choice. Because he was back in his home with his very large and complicated family relations, he had to conform to their expectations. Had he paid too much attention to the wife, he would have been chastised, counseled, and maybe even charged. When he visited friends and family, it was not expected that he always do so with the wife. He would need to visit certain specific members of the family to pay them respect and to visit certain classmates, his "brothers." It might have been disrespectful on certain occasions to have visited with the wife, especially a foreign one whose family is not known and who has no place in any of the kin networks. What was he to do? To actually *kiss* on the street, to show affection in public, and to show concern and interest specifically in the wife would have been met with serious disapproval, perhaps manly chiding and even family censure. At the very least, there would have been profound pressure on him to marginalize his wife and her needs and to observe the proper traditional modes of comportment.

If they had each had the right training and the ability to be objective, to observe it all, and to understand it as a temporary condition necessitated by the culture, they could have managed, even perhaps enjoyed, the new roles they were forced to acquire. But because most people are not in a position to take such a culturally critical or culturally relative stance, it probably caused confusion, pain, insecurity, disruption, and even doubt about the nature and content of their relationship. Thus it expressed itself in the guise of an argument about kissing in public. The complaint seems minor, perhaps even frivolous, but it is a complaint of great magnitude. The fact that Peter can remember and recount this incident after many years suggests that it was an issue worthy of note by the family and of much greater magnitude than the missing public kiss might suggest.

In reflecting on this story, it strikes me as a useful illustration of the depth of cultural tradition, its power over its members, and the significance of the differences when one gets beyond the level of enjoying a "cross-cultural" dance, meal, or musical evening. The nature of the relations between men and women in Ghana is understood more completely by seeing them in this intimate example. What is the nature of love? Is it holding hands, sharing a kiss, walking hand in hand, returning each night to the arms of each other, and putting aside all other relationships? What is the nature of the relationship between a husband and wife? Is it a partnership? Is it an economic unit? Is it a procreative unit? Is it the culmination of the desires of a man and a woman, or is it the reproduction of family units rendered by a union of two different families? Are we ever free to decide? Or are our decisions already culturally determined? Is the marital unit erotic or merely functional? Is love something enduring and something untouched by cultural proscriptions? Or is it conditional and contextual? If we love in one culture, will that love translate to another? Can the meaning of "wife" in one culture translate to another culture without changing its meaning, its structure, and its boundaries?

I do not know how this relationship survived this coming home, but I know that it was shaken, just as I know that all of the relationships I see here between Ghanaians and someone from another culture are shaken. It is difficult, sometimes impossible, for the Western mind to grasp the complexities and nuances of the very essence of what it is to be human in Ghanaian culture. I believe the fundamental differences (often obscured by a similar language, similar manners) result in "culture shock." It is shock at the ways in which the new culture challenges the fundamental assumptions of one's painstakingly acquired culture. How can love be so different? How can the nature of the family be so different? How can the symbols of family, of love, and of relationships be so different? Does that mean that they are always relative? Does it mean that our own sense of things is not the "real" sense of things? What then is the "truth?" Is there one? Have we been fooled all this time? Are we trapped by our culture into believing that which can so easily change form and substance? It is a shock when we think we know at least some truths—such as the joys and pleasures of kissing, the husband and wife enjoying a life of shared experiences, or the superiority of honesty in the marriage bed. When these basic truths are challenged, it shocks us to the core.

If our Ghanaian returnee husband had been able to see all of this and explain it to his wife, and if had the wife known all this, she might have been reassured. Or perhaps the understanding might not have spared them. At least this knowledge would have eased some of the pain that they both surely suffered.

Big Men

This leads to the topic of Big Men. The object of life, it appears, is to be a Big Man. A Big Man has a Big Stomach, Big House, Big Car, plenty of gold adorning his body, plenty of women and Big Stereo Speakers. I had a weekend full of Big Men, and I am so tired of them. Women cannot be Big Women. They can only acquire Big Men. I was aware this weekend that I will never win in this world of the competition of Big Men. I think the problem is that I do not know the culture well enough (which is true) and that I do not know the rules of the game. Then it suddenly occurs to me that I have never known the rules and that it is the same game. It is a man's game, and I was never taught to play. I was never meant to play. However, these days I am forced to play with the Big Men. I think that I have escaped this game, but I discover that it has followed me. Because I am a professor, an anthropologist, and a queen mother, I am forced into a man's world. Because I want to use my mind, to be challenged, to do the fun things, and to be in the world, and because I refuse to stay in the house, I am forced into the world of men. Of course, I am an interloper. As queen mother, I am supposed to have power. I choose the chief and I am over all, I am repeatedly told. But I know that this is not really true. It is still the chief, whether I choose him or not, who runs the village. It is the chief to whom they all show obeisance. It is the elders, the chief's council, the sub chiefs, and the linguists, who are respected, are admired, and are feared. I am, once again, only decoration. I am the only woman I ever encounter in my many trips to my village and the many trips I make to other villages. I know the women are there. They come to honor me when I am sitting with the elders in the chief's palace. I meet the various mothers and, sometimes, sisters; but they do not sit with me during long hours of discussion and negotiation. I sit alone with *men*.

However, I do not have the same feeling when I am sitting in the villages with the men, as queen mother, as I do sitting with the new Big Men. The ones who wear gold chains, suits, and ties and drive fancy cars. The ones who are chief executives, assemblymen, professors, or especially high government officials. I believe this is a new form of male supremacy. The old one, the African one, is strong, clear, and irrevocable; but, somehow, the old form seems more gentle and more palatable. It is absent of this thing the small boys here covet and call "macho." The new form is macho. The new form requires the status, the house, the cars, and the women.

I am to meet with the assembly man to work out our money problem. Earlier, he had taken money from me under false pretenses and never returned it. I was surprised and offended. The total was quite a lot of money, but more than that, I felt cheated and betrayed by him. We are to meet at the home of the chief executive, Mr. Frank, on a Sunday morning at 10:00. This is highly unusual. Everyone I know goes to church on Sunday. No business is transacted on Sunday. I think he does this on purpose. I do not know for sure, but it seems like he does it to separate himself from the old and the parochial. He is more cosmopolitan and more modern. He does not have to stick to conventions. Or perhaps he thought I would come alone. I can only speculate on his motives for such a social faux paux on his part.

I ride up to Abaasa early. I have to be accompanied to the house. I wear a proper, modest Kaaba and slit and appropriate, dainty high-heeled shoes. I am tired before I begin. The night before, I was in the company of two Big Men at a dinner party of the Old Boys and Old Girls of St. Augustine's Secondary School for boys and Holy Child, its sister school. I did not get home until after 1 a.m. The day before, Friday, I chaired an all-day symposium sponsored by the sociology students. I was, of course, the only woman on the dais and the only woman who spoke. These are a different kind of

Big Men. They are more subtle. The gold is subtly born in a modest watch. But they are Big Men just the same. I am a token.

I force my tired old body into my tight slit and drive my truck through the mud on the rain-drenched road to Abaasa. There I am greeted by Nkrumah who is prepared, but we have to wait for a few people, look in on the man with the broken leg who is now being treated by a local healer (who looks about 100), collect my friend with the bad leg who will be dropped at another village to see his local healer, and wait for the chairman to dress. After all of this is accomplished, we jump into my truck, and off we go. We are about eight by this time. Then several are dropped in different places, leaving only me and four escorts.

We drive the considerable distance on the other side of Cape Coast to the rather large village of Abura Dunkwa. The chief executive's house is just outside the village, on the main road. It is not difficult to find. It is large, built on a slight rise, and enclosed by a tall fence, and the door is guarded by a sleepy-eyed, bored-looking young man. We enter his compound. It consists of a large main house, a smaller house, and significant grounds. The main house is built much like a traditional compound, but of cement and tin roof. In front of the main hall (or sitting room) is a large veranda. Behind are several rooms surrounding a courtyard. A woman is pounding foo foo to the sounds of a wailing toddler.

We are greeted cordially by a stout man in knickers and with a bare, hairy chest and belly. He seats us all on the veranda and says that we are waiting for the arrival of the assembly man in question and the assistant to the chief executive. Mr. Frank is attending a funeral, he informs us. His assistant is presiding. After informing us of his recent automobile accident, he leaves us. We wait. He returns and says that his driver is out with the car but that another man will soon return and will be sent to find the missing assembly man, Ben Clarke, and the assistant, whose name is not revealed. We wait some more. In the meantime, there is much activity in and around the house, including the delivery of very bare, new-looking speakers. We hear them reverberating from the hall.

After about a 2-hour wait, the assistant finally is deposited in our midst. There is no sign of Clarke. Information from the wife indicates that he went to Accra the day before and has not returned yet. After some discussion, I agree grudgingly to another meeting date with Clarke. Because this is the third or fourth effort to gain an audience with the man, I am not anxious to pursue him further. This has already taken my day—a day I badly need for other pursuits.

Mr. Frank has already donned his lovely black and white cloth and charged out of the yard with a similarly clad woman, in his recent model Land Cruiser. We leave to return the assistant to his house and try to retrieve some of the day. The assistant wants to travel to Winneba to see his family but has been made to stay for our visit. Neither of us is too cheerful about this time, but he is a thoughtful, sanguine man, who is gracious and polite despite the inconvenience and failure of the occasion.

Then we are saved. Before we reach the house, along comes Clarke, masterfully at the helm of a small bus. When he sees us, he stops, hops out, and cheerfully greets us in his black corduroy trousers, black t-shirt, and gold chain. He is just returning from a funeral in Accra, he breathlessly reports.

We all meet at the crumbling, old government house of the poor assistant, who immediately rallies and hosts us by bringing extra chairs and cold water. It is customary for a host to offer something, at least water. Frank has either forgotten, ignored, or deliberately refused us this common courtesy. In fact, a man of his stature would usually offer more than water, at least minerals, and maybe even beer or gin. But the assistant is trying to be cooperative and does his best to do the right thing.

The conversation begins badly and ends badly. Until it is over, I do not realize that I will never be able to win. Clarke did commit to pay back the money he denied absconding from me. It is a large sum that I cannot afford to lose. But more than that, I am angry with his method. He is a public official, I reason to myself and hopelessly to the others, and as such he should not betray the public trust. I am the public, and I, as queen mother of Abaasa, am also a member of his constituency. How can he do such a thing and not at least be reprimanded? How can he take money from someone who is generous to both himself and to one of his own villages? Why doesn't anyone seem to care? Shouldn't he at least be censured? Instead, my village elders are begging me to forgive him and forgive the debt. The chief executive, who is his boss, turns the entire matter over to his poor assistant; the assistant is helpless to do a thing. In the end, I lose my temper and my dignity. I feel in the wrong when I know that I have been wronged. He seems exonerated while I feel like a troublemaker, a whiner, and a petty, mean-spirited, stingy woman.

I chastise myself in the end for handling the situation badly. I am not used to feeling this way. I usually manage such situations quite well. Decidedly, this situation was handled poorly. Perhaps I should gracefully let the matter drop? Should I generously let go the money matter? But it is a lot of money and everyone knows the man is a scoundrel. Should I be quiet and let the elders sort it out? But the elders are pleading for my forgiveness.

It takes me some time to realize that all of these people are men and that all of them take care of each other. Usually a woman would not be in this situation at all because usually women do not have control of such resources or their lives. This is when I begin to realize that I handled this situation poorly because I do not know the culture or understand the rules. This is also when I begin to realize that, once again, it is not the Ghanaian culture that I do not understand but the male culture that I refuse to understand. Even if I understand and play by their rules, I will not win because I can never be a Big Man. I can be a rich, white American, a professor, a queen mother, a traveler of the world, a mother, and a competent member of society, but I am still a woman. I still lose.

I may get my money. I may not. However, I know that I lose a great deal more than the money in the process. I am made a fool of by this man whom everyone knows is a scoundrel. I should know better. I should never have trusted him. But if I don't accuse him, no one knows he is a scoundrel and that he is not to be trusted. "Here is a rat. There is a thief in your midst, and he is corrupt," I cry. But no one hears me. Then I outline his offenses. I am offensive for having exposed him. I say that my village has not supported me. They want me to forgive him when everyone knows that he is in the wrong. Furthermore, now I am even more offensive because I told the assistant something negative about my village. I suggest that they are not behind me all the way. Now I have caused a mess. I have made a public display. I have taken up time. "But this is how corruption works," I persist. Doesn't anyone care? There is corruption in the country. Everyone is always complaining about it. The Big Men keep skimming off the top, and the little men get nothing. Resources are not equitably distributed. The small villages and the little people never get their share. "Can't you see?" I object. "This is where it begins." There is embarrassed silence. They all already know it. They do not want to hear it, and certainly it should not be recognized in public. I didn't understand and was lost in the heat of the moment, but now I understand. We are all to keep quiet. No one will help us if we speak up. In fact, maybe we will be silenced if we persist in seeing these things and keep opening our mouths.

I learn my lesson again. Yaro always says to me, "Women are women, and men are men. It will never be any different." He has lived in many houses and has seen people living as husbands, wives, children, and families from all parts of the world. Whether they are American, African, German, or Danish, he tells me, it is the same. Women like money, he says, and they will deceive you if you are not careful, especially Fante women. In fact, although Sabonzee has two wives and numerous liaisons, he never eats the food of any women other than his wife. This can be dangerous. Yaro and Sabonzee are from the North; they are not Fante. However, this view of women is not theirs alone. Women are often depicted as menacing. In popular television dramas, the story often revolves around an unfaithful wife, a seductress, a cunning money grabber, or even a murderess. She is out to cheat a man, to humiliate him, to toy with his affections, and to control him. Women are not to be trusted. In daily conversations, this theme is often repeated. Women will try to control you, will betray you, will poison your food, and will make a fool of you. The tro tros and taxis have sayings and scriptures emblazoned on them. One of them says "FEAR WOMAN" across the front.

Unless one subscribes to the "anatomy is destiny" analysis of male and female qualities, it seems that both men and women are capable of a range of behaviors, characteristics, and attitudes. Their manifestations differ depending on the social, economic, political, and psychological environment of which the individual is a part. In the context of advanced industrial capitalism, the market defines relationships. In both the case of Big Men and of Cunning Women, one of the motivating forces is cash—who has it, who wants it, and how to get it. Ghana shares with her Sub-Saharan African neighbors the status of "third world" in a global economy dominated by the powerful, capital-heavy "first world." As Ghana increasingly is drawn into this unequal world economy, women are economically marginalized for historical, political, and economic reasons. Money not only brings status and power, but in these times it also ensures survival. Therefore those who have it want to keep it, and those who do not want to get it and thus are always suspect. Because the capital flow in Ghana is among the lowest in the world, wages stand at a low, and costs move at a brisk upward pace, the gaps between life and death and starvation and survival are very narrow. A piece of cloth, a piece of jewelry, a meal, and a few coins can be enough to keep a woman and her children going for another day. With an infant mortality rate of 84 percent, a life expectancy rate of 55, a morbidity rate of 13 percent, inadequate health care, one of the highest rates of AIDS in the world, and perennial killers such as malaria, typhoid, and cholera, survival is not taken for granted.

This was not always the case in Ghana. There was a time when there was plenty for everyone to eat, everyone had a place, and everyone had a job. There was a time when babies were born with the help of a midwife and when no family went without the help of the local healer. Women and men were chosen for each other, and they had as many children as they wanted. There was a certain organic logic to the family relations and their relations with other families, the clan, the village, and the earth. One of the old men in Abaasa puts it this way: "When I was young, there was plenty for everyone. All of this land [he makes a wide circle with his hands, denoting the land all around the village] belonged to us. We wore our cloth, we did not wear shoes, we did not go to school. We farmed the land, and everyone had something to eat. I had one wife. We lived together our whole lives. Our children learned from us. They learned to farm."

5 / Children

Nothing is as painful as when one dies without leaving a child behind.

Absence does not bring up a child.

WILLIAM

Gentle character is that which enables the rope of life to stay unbroken in one's hands.

WILLIAM IS STANDING at the door, a large pan filled with cabbages and carrots on his head. He is a short, stocky boy with a broad, open grin. He wants us to buy the vegetables from his family garden. He barely speaks English but is not apologetic and not deterred from his purpose. He is one of nine children living with his mother and ailing father in Akotokyir. Although he is short and looks much younger, he is 16 years old; however, he is still referred to as a "small boy" and is still in Junior High School. For 2 years he has come to the house regularly, selling while he slowly and laboriously completes the remaining 2 years of middle school. He shows me his farm where they grow cabbage, carrots, tomatoes, peppers, cassava, and sometimes maize. During the dry season all of the children carry water on their heads from the nearby stream to keep the little farm alive. William (who is not called Kwesi or Kofi, but William) knows all about the farm. He knows when to plant, how to plant, which crops should have which kind of attention, and how and when to water. He is interested in commercial fertilizers. He says that they will increase the farm's yield and they can sell more. He is proud of his knowledge, confident, and optimistic.

His family lives on one end of the village in a small yard circumscribed by a short rectangular cement room, a mud and thatch building, and a defunct mud and thatch bar. The father suffers from an illness unknown to the family that seems to be taking away his life before their eyes. He is skinny and frail and barely able to speak because he coughs and chokes so frequently. His cousin, Ato Baidoo, says he suffers from too much smoking and drinking, but probably now also has tuberculosis. The extended family does not have much to do with him. They think he has been a failure, has neglected the family for drink, and cannot control his bad ways.

But Arthur Baidoo greets me with a charming smile and a dignified and gracious welcome. He ran the bar, he says, until he became too ill. Now he is seeing the doctor and trying to recover. Until then the children try to keep the farm and his wife makes kenky (fermented corn balls), which the girls sell in Cape Coast. He has built the new tin-roofed cement room for the family, although he continues to sleep in the mud and thatch kitchen because, he says, it is cooler. In the daytime, he rests on the hard-packed, cleanly swept dirt of the yard on a mat. The Baidoo children are all well-behaved, obedient, and respectful. Their mother is a beautiful woman who looks like a young girl. She does not speak English. Mr. Baidoo says that he has only this one wife, that all of the children are his, with his name, despite their matrilineal family system, and that he intends that his land and house will be left only to them. William is the eldest and is earnest, hard working, helpful to his parents, thoughtful of his siblings, and filled with schemes and plans and hopes for the future.

Today he comes to me with a sheet of paper. He holds it out proudly for me to read. It is the results of his exams taken at the end of Junior Secondary School (JSS). The schools are based on the British examination system. Children pass onto the next level by virtue of the marks on their final exams. William's marks are poor. His uncle looked at them and scoffed, dismissing them as hopeless; nothing could be done with those marks. William thinks differently. He seems unmoved by the scores themselves or comments by others. He tells me that he plans to go on to Senior Secondary School (SSS). The marks are clearly not high enough for this, however, so he will go to a technical school. He has some ideas. When they write the examinations, they submit three schools they hope to attend. He says he put down Asuansi for his first choice. It is a technical school, he says. I haven't heard of it but he convinces me to take him to see whether or not he has been accepted. He says that if they are accepted their names will be listed on a board at the school. I am skeptical. You mean to tell me that each child must go to each school and check a list to see whether or not he or she can attend? Yes, this is the way it is. I reluctantly agree to take him and we set out on a holiday afternoon, a Thursday.

He has told me that the school is one of the Cape Coast schools and, although this encompasses a fairly large area, I assume that, in the car, it cannot be more than 15 or 20 minutes. He directs me down the road, out of town, and onto the road going to Accra. After some distance, we turn. Then we turn again. We are now driving in the forest, passing only an occasional village. It has been more than a half hour. We will be there soon, says William, encouragingly. After driving for about an hour and a half, through towns, villages, forest, and up a long winding hill, we arrive at the large campus of Asuansi, the technical school. It is now late in the afternoon and has begun to rain. The landscape is beautiful; the buildings are old and institutional-looking. We arrive at a building that shows signs of life, and inquire. It is the home of the headmaster, but this is a holiday. No marks are posted and he is decidedly not in the mood for visitors. I apologize profusely, as William maintains a respectful silence, and I quickly mumble out our mission. He grudgingly invites us in, chastising us grumpily for not knowing that our behavior is highly irregular, that we should of course know that no marks would be posted today, and we sit. I get information about the school: fees, dates, procedures, and so on; then he asks about the boy's scores. When we tell him, he, too, acts amused and disgusted. These scores will never do. How can the boy expect to get into a school with such scores, he queries us both. I say something in his defense and he agrees that there might be a place in the arts course because not too many boys want that course. William is to return next Monday. We thank him and take our leave.

Out on the dusty, bumpy road, with the long ride ahead of us and the day waning, I am filled with a limp fatigue. This seems hopeless. What can we do? There is no money, the fees may as well have been a million dollars for such a family, the boy's marks are bad, and he has no other obvious redeeming qualities. He has always been a rather dull, plodding, stolid, sincere kind of child with little winsomeness or personal charm. Now, with no money, no connections, no grades, and no talent, what can he do? I cannot imagine myself making this trip again soon, with lectures, writing, reading, meetings, village obligations, and social responsibilities facing me.

But William has no such thoughts. He does not seem discouraged in the least. He says that he will take a tro tro there on Monday and see to it that he gets into the arts program. Are you good at art? I question him. Oh yes, he replies confidently, his eyes aglow with enthusiasm. If I could only help him with the fees, he continues. We theoretically borrow from here and there until we come up with the resources. Suddenly his mind is busy anticipating this new life.

On Monday, William returns to the school, and he does get in. I am shocked and filled with admiration. In the next few months, he busily prepares. He comes to me, he goes to other Americans he has befriended, his mother borrows from a money lender, and he calls on friends or relatives for some small contribution. Finally, the day comes for him to go. He approaches me several times to ask if I will take him. His mother and father greet me warmly when I arrive to take their son. He has to take his mattress, food, coal pot, and a suitcase (which he borrowed) packed with two new uniforms and a few other items: pencils, pens, paper, pots, and pans. Somehow we load all this into my car; his parents say that God will bless me and smile and wave as we head out of town on the long journey to his new school. William has cut his hair, borrowed new black jeans, and wears a white long-sleeved shirt buttoned to the neck. The worn collar is dark around the edges and it hasn't been ironed, but William is grinning happily; the effect is an air of pride and care in his appearance for this important day.

When we arrive in Asuansi, we are met by a young man, Mr. Akron, who says he works for the agricultural extension department; he also supervises the dormitory that is used to house boys who cannot afford to board across the street at the school. He will show us where William will stay, but before we go in, he wants to take William's coal pot. William protests. He wants his coal pot. Mr. Akron explains to me that none of the boys uses coal. They all cook over open fires in the yard and collect their own fire wood. They can't afford to buy coal, he tells me. This makes sense to me. William cannot even afford the fees or rice to bring, so how would he buy coal? Akron says that all of the boys do fine cooking over the fire, and if William has coal it will cause trouble. But William is still protesting. I am confused. He has struggled so hard, put up with so much to get here. Why is the coal pot such an issue? My mother bought me a new pot, he finally tells us. She told me that I was not to get it all blackened because it is new. If he cooks with wood the pot will become black. William is not budging. We are still outside the dormitory. What to do? Akron and I look at each other. Akron says, never mind, leave it to me. William will be fine. We will work it out. Let us just go in now. William gives a bit. I suggest that perhaps they have an old pot at home and they can exchange. William seems pleased. I will send his brother Mark to him with his mother's old pot and he will collect the new one from William. We go into the building.

It is a large room, like a barn but made of cement. It is clean but unadorned. Around the edges of the room are piles of foam mattresses, each about four inches thick. There is an ironing board at one end of the room, a few tables and benches, and, at the other end, a small black and white television set connected to an automobile battery. There is no electricity in the building but sometimes they can watch television with the battery. They wash and iron their own uniforms, cook their own food, and do their studies. Mr. Akron says that the boys behave well. He does not allow any trouble and most of the time there is none. There are about fifteen boys in the hall with a junior and a senior prefect in a separate room to make sure the boys behave. At night they all take their mats down and lay them side by side on the floor. They each have a trunk for their clothes.

William seems content with this arrangement. His mother has already come with him to pay and make arrangements. I leave him there with Mr. Akron, his suitcase, foam pad, and coal pot, promising to visit in a few weeks time. This is my mother, he proudly proclaims to Mr. Akron.

After William has completed only one year at the school, his father dies. William has never done well, but he never becomes discouraged. Even after his father's death, he is not discouraged. When the school term is completed, he always comes by my house on his way to his own. He has made me a huge sculpture from a tree and always comes to see how it is doing. He used the section of the tree that stands about five feet high, because it resembled a human figure and he wanted to turn it into a work of art for me. He begged me for paint money, for varnish money, for money for brushes. I was reluctant because, from my point of view, this was the last thing either of us needed: a large tree-like human, painted brown, with gold studs on its painted hat, and long, tangled limb-arms that was going to cost us money. Didn't he need paper? Food? Pens? Transportation money? Tuition? But he would not be dissuaded. After months of discussion, he extracted the money from me and we hauled it back, hanging out the windows and trunk of my car, into my sitting room where it continues to reign.

Today before he reaches my house, someone offers condolences on the death of his father. William did not know until now that his father had died. It is Friday and he is told that the wake keeping will be next Friday and the funeral on the following Saturday. He is stunned, but calm. After all, his father has been very ill. He goes home to face his mother and the ordeal of funeral preparation.

A few days later, William is at my door, looking red-eyed and sweaty. He says that he has not been sleeping much. He is trying to arrange the wake and funeral. He needs money for drinks, food, and music for the 3 days of funeral activities and the funeral. He tells me he heard his mother weeping late into the night because she has no money for the funeral and the family will be disgraced. As the eldest son, he feels responsible.

Somehow during that week William manages to obtain the requisite sound system, drinks, and food. When I arrive for the funeral, he greets me in dressy Western attire; music is blasting out of a huge stereo system as he offers me a beer. There is the usual dancing and weeping; somehow the family has managed to save face this time. Saving face, creating a sculpture to present as a gift, making a party, wearing

William's mother—Akotokyir

the attire of the day, these are what make up our lives, no matter how humble the gift, how small the party, how tawdry the dress. Sometimes we may be tempted to say, "How can you be worried about a party, a sculpture, or a pair of Levi's, when you don't even have anything to eat?" But when I watch children like William, I know we cannot ask that question.

William does not make it back to school. He tells me he will continue. Soon after he comes to my house. He has a job now in the new guest house in Akotokyir as a bar man. He has brought his boss to meet his "mother." They are wearing ties.

Author at funeral of William's father

CHILDREN'S STORIES

The decline and fall of a nation begins in its homes.

William amazes me, as do many of the children I meet. Most of us who travel to Ghana are overwhelmed by the poverty we see. Most of the streets are unpaved, human waste flows down the sides of the roads in gutters, and the city streets are littered with refuse. Prices go up every day, the Cedi goes down, and wages are low. There is electricity in Aktokyir, but not in Abaasa. Most people find it hard to eat more than one meal a day. People cook over open fires or in charcoal pots outside and most save their only pair of shoes or rubber slippers for church on Sunday.

However, the children are joyful. They shout to us foreigners, black and white alike, "Brunyi, Brunyi. How are you. I am fine, thank you." They laugh and sing as they walk along, carrying themselves with pride and dignity. Often I hear children singing all alone, unselfconsciously, as they walk. In the villages, the first people you meet are usually the children. They are running and playing and shouting, kicking balls or oranges, swinging sticks, or pushing small, hand-made cars. They usually wear very little and play without shoes. Sometimes they creat a football field in the sand and children as young as four or five play. Two- and three-year-olds toddle freely, knowing that older siblings, aunties, and grandmothers will be there if there is trouble. They look proud, confident, and happy.

I ask the children of Mr. Baidoo's primary school to write and draw about themselves, their families, and their village. Their work confirms my visual impressions. The children tell about the pride they have in their village and families. They are also a valuable source of information about the nature of their lives. They do not feel poor or disadvantaged or afraid. They seem to feel protected, and they are proud and happy about who they are and how they live. They write honestly about their world. The following are some samples of the children's writing. They are typical of what all of the children said. The children who wrote these essays are all between the ages of 10 and 13. Listen to their voices.

Children's Voices

Gloria: The name of my school is Ahaha. The people in my family are six. The children in my family are four. The names are, Efua, Kwaku, Adwoa and Kwame. The name of my mother is Ama and my father's name is Martin. I am the elder child in my family. My mother's work is trader. My father's work is farmer. My mother sells so many things like: cassava, tomatoes, pepper and gaary. The children in my family all go to school. The people in my family all go to church. In my family they eat three times a day. My father grows so many things like: cocoa yam, cassava, pepper and tomatoes. In my family my father is the head of my family. My sister's work is dressmaker. My brother's work is mason. My family is beautiful. My family has a toilet. My family has a lot of money. In my family there is a lot of cocoa. There are a lot of taboos in my family. My family has pipes (for water). I love my family because there is not quarreling. My family is located at Akotokyir. In my family the boys are handsome and the girls are beautiful.

Ashley: The name of my family is Ado Batwa. Batwa is a good family. The leader of Batwa is Nana Kwasi. Nana Kwasi is a good man. He sees our children very well. The children all go to school. The sons in the family are three and the daughters are two. The name of my mother is Araba. The name of the oldest child is Kofi Abaka. The school Abaka goes to is Tuwohoful School. He is in J.S.S. He is twenty-one years old. Kofi Abaka is a very good boy. We are in Akotokyir. Akotokyir is a big village. We worship God. We worship on Sunday. Sunday we go to church at 8:30. In my family we clean our compound. Nana Kwasi is in Accra. He is electricity driver. He is forty years old and the wife is thirty-eight years old. The people in my family are twenty-five. Every day our mother prepares good food to eat. Kofi Abaka is a great boy. My father loves Abaka more than the others because he is a smart boy. I love my family.

Mark: The name of my neighborhood is Akotokyir. There is plenty of work in my village. Some of my neighborhood people do work at the University. My uncle also does work at the University. Some people boil kenky and some of them sell things at the market. There is a big river when we are not happy we go there and swim. After that when it is Sunday our fathers and mothers do communal labour. At the same day we also sweep around the village.

And they are building the house of toilet. When some year come we go to Cape Coast and celebrate Efutu Afehe. There are Asofoma they also go to Cape Coast. There are four churches in my village. There is also a big river at my village. When some year we come we go there and catch some fish. There is no chief in my village.

There is one school at my village. And they make cultural at my village and my village is very beautiful. And there are two clans in my village. These clans are Anona and Aboreze and these two clans are good clans so everybody like that clan. There are big big trees at my village. It is nice village. It is beautiful village. It is freedom village. So everybody like to visit that village. There are 10,000 people in my village. We have okyeame but we don't have a chief. And all the people in my village are Christian.

Margaret: The name of my neighbourhood is Akotokyir. It is a village near the University bungalows. It is very big. It is far from Cape Coast to Akotokyir. It is in the Central Region and it is in the Cape Coast District. Some of the important personalities in my village are the chief and his elders. When it is Sunday all the people in my village went to do the communal labour. The men in my village, some of them are farmers and some of them are officers and typists. And the women too are farmers and traders. Some of them sell rice, kenky and bread.

The people in my village is about two thousand. We have a river behind our village. When it flows all children and women go to the river side and wash. After washing they swim in the river very happily. There are five churches in my village. These are Catholic, Moslem, Pentecostal, Methodist and Twelve Apostles. When it is Sunday, all the children in my village go to church. We have a school in my village. The name of the school is Tuwohofo Holly International. It was established by Mr. A. Ato Baidoo. There are seven clans in my village but normally some of the most two clans people in it is called Anona and Aboreze, the Tiger and the Parrot. There are some of the old men and women in my village.

There are some of a big land around our village. Some new people have come and brought some and built their houses and among or join us. We have a statue at the station of my village. Sometime the men in my village go to the cemetery to clear the land. We have a shrine in our village. When it is Wednesday, people come there to worship God.

Anthony: The name of my neighborhood is Akotokyir. My neighbourhood has the chief and his elders. There is a lot of taboos in my neighbourhood. The women are farmers. The men are also farmers companies. In my neighbourhood we don't like dogs because of gods. My neighbourhood is near Kakomodo, Ankafor, Kwaprow and Abura. In my neighbourhood there is one school and six churches. And some gods worship the day they go to worship gods is Tuesdays and Wednesdays. In my neighbourhood they grow vegetables and tree crops. My neighbourhood is about 3,969 years. The people in my neighbourhood is 5342 people. The chief and his elders and the people of the neighbourhood built a toilet. This toilet is added into two, men's one and the women's one. The personality people are the chief, elders and neighborhood. The poles of my neighbourhood are not strongest because they are poor.

Joyce: The name of my village is Akotokyir. I stay at Akotokyir village. The people of my village is about five hundred people in that village. Some of the women in that village are traders and farming and some mans work at offices and others are farming. There are some churches in the village. The chief and his elders they describe to do something for the village how our village may be fine. For some days the women go and catch the fish in the river.

The chief and his people think that when they go and catch fish in the river the river will destroy. So that if they don't have any water to drink they stop the people who want to catch the fish in the river. And the chief and his elders told the people that the pipe has come in this village. They have something like toilet and other things. They made a law that every Sunday everybody should go and do the communal labour after going to church. We have a school in that village and they told people to pay taxes to help the school.

Charles: I stay at University bungalow. In our bungalow we have a lot of playing things like football and etc. Every person have his own house. Many white men stay there. The place the white men like is Chalet. I live at wooden bungalow. Many people over there work at offices. Others were drivers. Many women help their husbands in their work. Some of them sell something to support their husbands. Other men farm. We have a children church and adult church. It is called University Residents Church and we have children's classes. We have people who do not come from the bungalows who sell some fish. Some people of Kwaprow work at the bungalow. In the rain season many people plant corn. In my house we have planted some vegetables like onion and others. I go to school at Tuwohofo –Holly International School. I am in class. . . . In our bungalow we don't have a place where we sell things like garden eggs and others. So when we want to go buy some things we go to Kwaprow or town. If you want to go to town, you take a car.

Peter: Abura is the name of my village. It is near Oguaa. It is a big village. Abura is a village that have second good road. The name of the chief at Abura is Nana Adai the II. The people of Abura is about six hundred thousand. There are many houses at Abura. Some houses are built with blocks and others are built with hard clay with a good iron sheet. There are two public parks. There are many people at Abura. Some are Gas, Ewes, Fantes, Sisala, and so on. There are many provision stores and their names, some are Abura Kings Way, God is my Helper, Praise God Enterprise, Thy will be Done, and so on.

WILLIAM

I have been working all day, so by 8 p.m. on a Saturday evening I decide to take a walk and go visit William at the Pakap Hotel in Akotokyir where he works. He has asked several times for me to come see him and to visit his mother in the village. I think it adds to his prestige to have such a "distinguished white lady" visit. Adwoa is sitting around me as usual, asking questions, chatting, joking, and generally getting in the way, so I say that she can accompany me. She is thrilled. I say she needs to wear something at least moderately presentable so she leaps up and heads for the door to change into her jeans and a t-shirt. Usually she prefers a dress but also usually does not have a clean one, so the jeans will have to do. Before she gets out the door, she darts back and says that we need to get Kwame to escort us. "Kwame?" I am incredulous.

Why Kwame? He never accompanies us anywhere, and we may be late, and I don't know him very well. "He is a man," she says, "and we are two girls. We can't walk alone. We need Kwame." I want to laugh, but I control myself. Kwame is barely thirteen, but he looks six. He is half a head shorter than Adwoa, a mild mannered, soft-spoken little guy, juxtaposed in my mind against the loud, tomboyish, bold Adwoa. But Adwoa is insistent. Her big brothers, Kwesi and Kojo are both out; besides, they are getting past the age at which accompanying a woman and little girl on a Saturday night can be considered anything but a punishment; so, in Adwoa's mind, Kwame is it. I relent. "Just tell him to wear something that can go inside a restaurant," I call as she darts exuberantly out the door.

In 2 minutes the two of them are standing eagerly in the courtyard. Kwame has been washed and brushed. He wears a nice cotton long-sleeved shirt over a clean white t-shirt and tiny tailored trousers, which are too short and too tight, but neat and pressed. I am touched by his little neat dress-up trousers, rubber slippers, and confident, proud self. We are off, tiny Kwame, the man, in the lead.

It is a dark night. There is only a sliver of a moon and no street lights. The only sounds are the crickets and frogs and the beating of distant drums. It is two weeks before Christmas, but there is no sign of a pending holiday. The dirt road is mostly deserted and at this hour it is still sultry. The children giggle and chatter, switching back and forth between Fante and English. Adwoa feigns fear and Kwame remains brave. They have an easy companionship. Although Adwoa is obviously developing into a young lady, there is nothing of sexual innuendo or awkwardness about their exchange. They are like young children, enjoying the evening, the surprise outing, and the companionship.

When we get to the hotel it is, as I expected, empty. Empty, that is, of all but its employees. William is happy to see me, and greets us all formally and solemnly. He is, however, distressed. He had planned to visit me tomorrow, he says. This is the most discouraged I have ever seen him. He is worried about the family and about himself. He says that if he had known that the world would be like this he might have asked not to come. Yesterday he wept, he says. He doesn't know what to do. His mother makes kenky to sell, but is now ill and cannot work. Mark, his junior brother, has "brought forth," he tells me in confidence, with some shame. Mark is about 18 years old. I try not to reveal my shock. It is hard to believe that this quiet, small, seemingly young boy could possibly have become a father. Worse, he has no income, no home, and no family to support him. He is now an apprentice to a welder. There is no pay and he is expected to pay a fee and to feed himself. William continues that the girlfriend had come to his mother with the baby because the baby was sick and needed medicine. William says that he gave his last 2,000 Cedis, then wondered where they would get the money for food.

William feels as though he has lost his childhood. He keeps saying that he is only a "small boy" and he has all these problems. He is working at the hotel but the owner has not paid them for several months. When he does get paid, he receives 60,000 Cedis for the month, which is as much as some teachers get paid, and is equivalent, at this time, to about $20 U.S. With prices for all goods going up each day and school fees to pay, it is impossible to live on this amount. The family kitchen has lost its roof, there is no refrigerator or music for the bar, all of the children are in school, and the mother is suffering from some unknown stomach ailment. As determined and brave and optimistic as William is, these circumstances are finally almost too much. I feel overwhelmed and can do nothing more than sympathize with the boy. He has struggled so hard, worked so hard, tried so hard. What is he to do?

I offer some small support, give some words of encouragement, and say I will return. Then Adwoa, Kwame, and I set out again into the dark night for the walk home. This time we walk quietly. The children have had a mineral and they are tired and happy. I think as we walk about all of the Williams I know. I think of all the young men and women who have no jobs, no schools to attend, no options. I often wonder what keeps them going. They are young and strong and smart, but there is no work and there are not enough schools. Yet they go on. They find something to do. They help support and care for their families. They become discouraged, but mostly they stay optimistic, patient, and hopeful.

ADWOA

The Story Book

Adwoa is a strikingly beautiful child of twelve. She is poised, demure, tomboyish, witty, funny, and absolutely without guile. She is completely at home in her thin, blossoming body, whether using it for work or play or lolling on the floor. Her teacher told her that her face is like a smile. She was puzzled by this. When some-one slips and cannot help exclaim, "But no one told me she is a beauty," the words seem to have no meaning. Sometimes she scrutinizes her face in the mirror, trying to figure out why people think she is beautiful. She twists her face, smiles, frowns, and then gives up, saying she cannot see it. Once she asked me why I like her so much. "Why does everyone like me?" I told her what a little friend of mine once told me: "You are smart, pretty, and nice, so why wouldn't people like you?" She seemed satisfied, although not completely; but she was visibly pleased.

Despite her beauty, however, she is a terribly bad student. She is in class five in elementary school, but she cannot read or write anything other than Margaret, her school name, and she cannot draw or do any mathematics beyond simple counting. She is not sure about her colors. The headmistress says that there are too many children in the class, and she has not found what she likes yet so she won't learn. The teacher and her siblings say that she is lazy. At the end of the day when I ask her if she went to school, she usually answers in the affirmative. When I ask her, did she learn anything, she says firmly, "No! You know I cannot read or write so how can I learn anything?" So she sits every day in her neat brown jumper and yellow blouse, listening to things she does not understand. The doctor says she is retarded. He has a name for it. It occurred in utero. But she does not seem retarded and in many ways behaves like any child her age. The teacher at the special school she attends says that she is a fine, bright girl, but has a learning disability. They don't know what it is.

The interesting thing is that the family thinks she is a bit slow because of con-vulsions she had as a small child. Her father believes that if she goes to school every day at the "good" University Primary School, she will eventually learn. She knows better, but he and her older siblings will beat her if she does not go, so she goes. No one has ever mentioned the word retarded to her; no one has ever told her that she is a "special needs" child; no one has told her that she will probably never learn to read or write. Next year she should go to JSS. She will sit some more, and they will tell her that she is lazy, or not so clever, or recalcitrant, but these attitudes are common in children and usually solved through beating or berating, but not by labeling. Her father always says that all of his children are clever. None of them does well in school, but that does not dissuade him from his stand. So the family expects her to behave like a 12-year-old girl with a few weak areas. They are profoundly protective of her and seldom make her do much more than wash her eating bowl and wash her home clothes. So Margaret goes merrily along, happy, charming, and beautiful.

She sleeps in the boys' quarters of my bungalow. It is a small, square, cement room she shares with her two brothers and her sister. They have two twin beds and a table. When they have something to eat they cook with charcoal on an outside coal pot, and they share the bathroom and shower stall with a large family that occupies the other room. Their father sleeps in the University Guest House, where he is in charge. He serves parties who stay in the guest house and those who come for meals. He also sometimes serves the Vice Chancellor or other members of the faculty. His wife died 10 years ago, when Margaret was 2, and, in particularly un-Ghanaian style, has not married since. He visits them once or twice a day, gives them money for food some days, and tries to pay their school fees. They borrow or are given clothes by visitors or caring friends. Anything else is considered by their father to be an unnecessary frill and therefore not a consideration. Playthings, story books, soccer balls, dolls, toffees, and biscuits are all in this category.

So I, being an American who is trained to believe that children will perish without such things, have provided Margaret and her sister and brothers with many of these items, for better or worse. They get ice cream when I come home from my lectures, soft drinks for a special treat, popcorn we make, and playthings when I return from a visit to Accra. The most important of these, which seem to me to be necessities, to their father, extravagances, are story books, which Adwoa loves but of course cannot read. The ones she chooses are at a very basic level, generally aimed at children of between 3 and 5 years. I try to read them to her but, more often than not, cannot find the time. This evening I am reading in bed when Adwoa comes in with her latest book. She is pouring over it so I say I will read it to her. Sitting cozily on a bed with a mama, reading a book or telling a story, is something she does not know about, but she is absolutely delighted. How can I not read to her more often? She is bubbling over with happiness and determinedly appreciative in ways that make me feel alternatively awed, guilty about my own petty complaints, and self-critical for not doing more.

So this night, we are both happy, sitting on the bed to enjoy a book before bedtime. It is the story of *The Snow-White Pigeon*. We begin. First comes the title of the book. Adwoa does not know about snow, because they have none in Ghana. But she knows about white so I tell her that snow is white, at least most of the time. It is also cold. Next comes the pigeon. What is a pigeon? she asks. A bird, I say, like a chicken. Is the chicken cold too, she says? No, it is white like snow is white. So now the title is *The White Chicken* which seems to do pretty well. Then we begin the story: Once upon a time there was a little girl named Isabel. But the picture looks like a boy. Why is Isabel a boy? It is not a boy, it is a girl, I say, trying to get on with the story. Then it says that she was very fond (what is fond?) of birds and animals. She even had a tortoise once. This makes little sense to Adwoa, because in Ghana birds and animals are used only for eating or protection. A tortoise is hardly ever seen, but it would also be good food. But the child loved these creatures, although I can't explain why, and she longs for a pet. What is a pet? A pet is an animal you keep, usually in your house. Birds are in the trees and even cats and dogs are not allowed in the house. Animals are dirty and full of fleas and are another mouth to feed. How can this be, she says? She has cats, but they stay outside and hunt and have no names. I used to ask her what she named her kitten. She said solemnly that it had no name. The next day I asked her again and she repeated slowly, as if I were a small child, it HAS NO NAME! The next day I asked if she had named the cat yet. She looked me right in the eye, loudly enunciated in an exaggerated way, NO NAME! After a while it became a joke between us as she adamantly stuck to the proper form of Ghanaian cat care, and I tried to prod her into the American.

We try to carry on with the story. One day a snow-white pigeon came into the yard. Isabel, who wears no earrings or dress and has choppy, messy hair, but who is supposed to be a girl anyway, hugs the pigeon and exclaims to her mother what a beautiful bird it is and that she wants it for herself. Does she want to eat the chicken? No, she wants it for a pet. Why would she want a chicken for a pet? Because it is beautiful. At this, Adwoa just twists up her face and indicates that we may as well go on. So the story went on in this fashion, the whole premise lost on Adwoa because there are no such thing as pets in her life, a chicken is definitely not a pet, animals are not cuddly and sweet and cute and especially not a plain old white bird. Pretty soon the bird was hurt and Isabel took care of it, even doing jobs to feed it. Adwoa does jobs to feed herself. The story ends with the pigeon laying an egg, hatching a little baby white pigeon that stayed with Isabel and was loved and also named. It's name was Snow White, of course.

It took us a very long time to get through this tiny book. We both felt dissatisfied, but Adwoa was glad for the story, however unclear it was. This was the first of many such frustrating storybook-reading sessions. We have tried the Ghanaian ones, but they are mostly about boys and Adwoa is drawn to pictures of girls, especially princesses and queens. So far, we have not found an entirely successful story, although the brightly colored pictures continue to hold great allure.

The Last Day of School

Adwoa has been bothering me now for about 2 weeks. It is almost time for school term to end, and on the last day they have festivities. She used to feel ashamed because she had nothing to take to the party, and therefore watched as other children ate yam and chicken and rice, drank refresh from a small box, or even brought a mineral. Now she has me, so she begins early, making sure that I will provide adequately. I am a reluctant and therefore underattentive surrogate mother for the child, so I am not always paying close attention. She is used to this, however, and it does not dampen her spirits. Each day she lists the different items she plans to take on the last day. Each day the list gets longer and the items more extravagant. She wants chicken and biscuits and refresh and tampico juice and rice. Sometimes she adds bread, sometimes an egg. She likes to plan how she will take the feast and what the other children will say about it. They will say that now she is a rich girl. Now she has a "white lady" to take care of her, so she can have anything she wants.

LEARNING TO BECOME A PERSON

Childhood is a time of learning how to become a person. It is the time of primary socialization into a new culture. Each culture has its own requirements to be learned.

Confidence

> It is a human being that counts; I call upon gold, it answers not; I call upon cloth, it answers not; it is a human being that counts.

These children are hopeful, cheerful, optimistic, even exuberant. In the face of what appears to most outsiders as impossible circumstances, they retain an enormous sense of power, of confidence, of self. Unlike the stories told by the children of Hyde Park in Chicago (Waldman 1993), these children color in bright colors and they talk about their neighborhoods in loving terms. Whereas the children in Hyde Park see their world, to a large extent, as frightening and dangerous, the Ghanaian children see their world as safe and pretty and clean. William's perseverance and good humor, despite the obstacles and despite his occasional low spirits, is typical of the children and young people I have met. Despite difficult conditions, the children are proud and carry themselves with a sense of entitlement that they never seem to lose. They belong. They are a part of a large network of people and places and activities that provide for them a supportive, consistent, safe environment in which they can practice how to be an adult member of society. The rules, the roles, and the rights and responsibilities are clear. Children can feel safe and secure in the knowledge that they are cared for and protected. They have chores to do, and they are always to be available to run errands for their seniors. They may not eat many times in a day, but they know that sometime during the day, someone will provide them with something to eat. They do their jobs, they are obedient to their elders, and the rest is up to the family, the household, and the community. If they are in school, they must "learn" hard, but they are not expected to do anything else. If they do not behave, they will be caned or in some other way reprimanded. If they fail to go to school, they are treated likewise at home. It is all very clear and most adult members of the society help to enforce the same rules wherever the child goes.

In the villages and the towns children are everywhere. From the tiniest tot, to the biggest teenager, they are out roaming freely about. They play football with an orange or make wooden cars and run them around with a bamboo stick, or push a tire, or just run and squeal and play children's games. As is true of most places in the world, after they reach 5 or 6, the boys are freer to roam and play than the girls. At this age, they separate to a large extent: the boys play football or with wheeled toys and the girls play a clapping and jumping game to a rhyming song. Girls are expected to relieve their mothers and carry younger siblings, so they often must play their games with their small charges bouncing on their backs. Girls also help in the house and carry water and wood.

Because most of village life takes place out-of-doors, the children have ample opportunity to observe the behavior of their elders. There is a broad range of different styles of behavior and different adaptations to the society and thus different models for proper cultural behavior. As is described by others (Brogger 1992), most of life takes place outside in a public space. The room is a place for sleeping and, sometimes, entertaining mostly adult male relatives. Bathing, toileting, teeth brushing, cooking, lounging, and often daytime sleeping are done outside. Thus children grow up in the public eye, receiving attention from a variety of adults and children.

Just as every child has his or her chores and every child has adult protection, so also does every child have responsibilities. There is a clear hierarchy in which seniors are responsible for juniors, and juniors must obey seniors, so that at all moments most children are both junior to some and senior to others. In this way, everyone is in some way responsible for someone else and everyone must be obedient to others. One of my Ghanaian colleagues told me that the reason the children are so good is that the system is so authoritarian. The rules are clear and the punishment is equally clear. Although children are beaten by their elders, it is rare to see this occur. Mostly the children fear the cane so much, and know the rules so well, that a caning is not often necessary. They are treated with respect, but they are only pampered in early infancy. From around 5 years of age on, they are expected to do their work, go to school, be respectful, and obey their elders. There is not a child I have known, from tiny tot to my University students, who does not know how to behave toward the elders. The most Westernized university students, on entering the palace of a chief, will know to remove their shoes, divert their eyes, bow in a supplicating manner, and greet the chief appropriately.

However, as is evident from William, Adwoa, Kwame, and the others in the examples we have seen, obedience and respect does not mean loss of self. On the contrary, the fact that they know the rules, know their place, are respectful and in turn are respected, seems to give them freedom to be themselves. Within this safe, secure context, they are able to define themselves. They may not eat more than one meal a day or have many suits of clothes or more than an orange for a soccer ball, but they know who they are. We can see in the stories above that they are proud of their families, they are proud of their village, and they are proud of themselves. They seem to have a sense that they are in control. Even though the society, the elders, the family control them, they are also in control. Each child is free to develop his- or herself within the confines of a structured, but stable, frame. Every child, of course, is not the same, and every family is not the same, but the extended family in small villages with deep roots provides a safe cradle to hold the growing child. Someone said to me that Ghanaian children run and play and chase like any other children, but they hardly ever cry, they are obedient, and their mothers are not screaming at them all of the time. What accounts for this difference? Americans and Europeans are very loud. Ghanaians, in general, are quieter. Children are taught to lower their voices almost to a whisper when speaking to adults. They don't need to cry, they don't need to be screamed at, because they know their limits, the rules are clear, the entire village is their home, and all the seniors are in concert about expectations.

In the village, the chief, the elders, and the queen mother take care of the people, the adults take care of the children, and the children take care of each other. They have not yet come fully into the competitive market arena and therefore still watch out for each other. In advanced capitalism, it is necessary to be competitive, and highly industrialized societies teach this to their children well. Here in the village, where life is slower and quieter, the children can still cooperate.

Education—Differences are Accepted

The fingers of the hand are not equal in length.

Knowledge is like a baobab tree; no one person can embrace it with both arms.

Just as children are socialized at home in the family, they are also socialized in school. The schools are still primarily modeled after the British system, although many are gradually changing to the American system. Classes are large and crowded. Children in uniforms sit several to a seat in rows of wooden desks. Textbooks are few. They are mostly either of the West African variety or are from America or Britain.

Education is considered the key to everything. Most parents want their children to go to school. Mr. Baidoo's school is run from the fees of the village parents. He continuously struggles because parents find it difficult to pay. The fee is minimal, 2,000 Cedis (approx. $.75 U.S. per term). Technically, education is free for all children to the tertiary level. However, there are small fees for various items and families must provide books, exercise books, uniforms, and anything else required of the student. Parents who have more money can send their children to private schools, often Catholic schools, which are more prestigious and where the children receive more attention. Until the late 1980s, Ghanaian schools were based entirely on the British system, with 6 years of primary school, followed by Junior Secondary School for 4 years. If a student made good enough scores on standardized examinations, he or she went on to Senior Secondary School for 5 years to obtain the ordinary certificate when they passed the *O* level exams. If one qualified, he or she could then go on to work for 2 more years toward the A level, or advanced certificate. After this arduous 17 years, a student might hope to go on to the University; this was only possible if he or she both passed the examinations with high enough scores and was accepted at the University. University studies could take 3 or 4 years to complete, depending on the program.

There has been a shift in the system, which now more closely resembles an American-style calendar and curriculum than the British form. This means that students now begin with kindergarten one and progress to kindergarten two before beginning primary one. After primary six, they then proceed to Junior Secondary School for another 3 years. If they pass the examinations, they travel to Senior Secondary School for 3 years. From Senior Secondary School, they go straight to the university if they qualify. A very small percentage of the population gets this far and qualifies for the university. This new education system has been supported by the World Bank and the International Monetary Fund (IMF) as a more economic and efficient way to provide at least a basic education for more people. The U.S. Agency for International Development (USAID) has supported this program and has supplied funds targeted particularly at the primary level.

As funds and attention have focused on the primary level, and as the country is, in general, emphasizing the legitimacy and importance of the private sector, responsibility for education is likewise shifting from public to private responsibility. Therefore small fees for primary school children and increasing fees for those in secondary and tertiary institutions, is considered to be an important step in the development of a financially independent and educationally advanced Ghana. Although the virtue of such educational policy may be embraced by the population in general, the reality of increasingly higher fees, increased competition for limited slots, and the pressures from the job market make providing an education for their children a constant struggle for many parents. Children are admonished to "learn hard" to climb the educational ladder and reward their parents' efforts, and parents spend a large portion of their limited incomes on uniforms, school equipment, and fees, and spend their limited time and emotional energy regretting such expenses. To get a child into Senior Secondary School usually requires not only money and high scores on standardized examinations, but the pressure of priests, teachers, businessmen, bronyis and/or significant, well-placed dashes (bribes).

As is the case in most parts of the world, the quality of this early education varies throughout the country. In many regions, and particularly in rural areas, teachers are scarce, materials are limited, and children often walk long distances to attend school. The buildings are often in poor repair and children are crowded into limited desks, three or four children sharing a single desk. Teachers' pay is low, and many are either poorly qualified, disinterested, or both, which makes for a less than perfect learning environment.

Tertiary education has been supported by the government, providing all of the living expenses, tuition, books, and fees since the time of Kwame Nkrumah. With increasing economic pressures, however, private responsibility for education at this level is rising, as are tensions among students, faculty, the government, and parents.

In Akotokyir, Mr. Baidoo struggles daily to keep his primary school functioning and to develop his Junior Secondary School. He likes the idea of keeping the children in the village so that they do not have to walk long distances and so that the community can support their progress. However, many villagers earn barely enough to survive and the school suffers. Nonetheless, the voices of the children heard in the previous essays demonstrate to us that the children are proud of their school and happy to go there and learn.

Learning is not easy here. The classrooms are crowded, equipment is limited, books are almost nonexistent, teachers are poorly paid, and the children are usually hungry. Children are expected to sit in rows, listen to the teacher, and repeat what the teacher says. They are taught in English, but English is not the first language for most of them. Tardiness, sloppiness, spontaneous activity, noise, moving about, and challenging the teachers are all actively discouraged. If a child engages in any of these, he or she will be caned. Caning in school is considered to be a part of learning, as old and revered as the institution itself. If a child is not learning, he or she is being stubborn or difficult, and thus must be disciplined. There are other forms of discipline, such as standing on one foot in the front of the classroom, kneeling on a rough surface, or standing with arms outstretched. But the long, thin, cylindrical stick used for caning is found on any market street and forms a recognized part of the teacher's tool kit. The Ghanaians I know are not aware of another system. Because the schools were originally Colonial schools, and therefore British, it is reasonable to assume that the learning format is thus derivative.

Originally, Ghanaian children learned how to hoe, to plant, to cook, or to wash clothes as they lived life in the context of the village. They were socialized in the home, in the community, and in the fields. When the need to learn English, to read English books, to do math problems, and to learn different skills arose, suddenly there was a need for children to dress in a uniform, wear shoes, and leave their homes for a special place called a schoolroom. The schools were designed, in architecture as well as ideology, to replicate those of the colonial masters. Much has been written about colonial education, which we do not need to reiterate here (Marable 1983; Memmi 1965; Davidson 1992; Freire 1981; Fanon 1967). Arguments can be made for the school system's virtues and its vices.

What seems obvious today is that there is an educational system in place that was designed to be British, is becoming increasingly American, and that does not function optimally as either. It cannot. There are not enough resources. It is therefore difficult for an outsider such as myself to understand exactly for what the average child from Akotokyir or Abaasa is being educated. Most of them will not go to Secondary School, and even fewer will go on to University. If you ask the children and the parents, they are not sure either. They are being educated so that they will have a better life than their parents. How the lessons they painstakingly learn in their school will translate into this better life is not exactly clear. Nonetheless, just as William struggles to acquire as much as he can, so the other children struggle. While their British and American colleagues fill their heads with internet and cyberspace and cover their bodies with techno-sneakers and micro-fiber jeans, the children of Akotokyir sit in the same mud classrooms with the same brown uniforms as were left by their now Jet Age British ancestors. Their parents are still carrying wood on their heads for a fire, hauling water from the stream, and clearing the fields with a single cutlass. The children sit in their neat brown jumpers and knickers and hard-earned shoes, learning from old, weathered, outdated books about math, physics, geography, and neoclassical economics. If they don't learn it, they are beaten, so they try.

Children are socialized and educated to fit into their culture. The culture determines how to educate the young. What does it mean if a child in Akotokyir is educated in a manner appropriate for a different culture? For a long gone culture? Are they educated for the Britain of the 1960s? They no longer yearn to be farmers or long for the trials of the sea. Just as in America and other parts of the world, working with one's hands, hard manual labor, is seen as undesirable, as something to leave behind. In answer to the question, "What do you want to be when you grow up?" the answers are about money. They want a job so they can make money. The models are of farmers, fishermen, traders, an occasional teacher, as the stories above tell us. In capitalism, everyone is free to be an entrepreneur. The business program at the University is the most sought after. To do business is to make money and to make money is to acquire what is necessary and what is desired in life. Everyone understands the concept of the entrepreneur. Everyone is an entrepreneur. Everyone wants to sell cloth, fish, or vegetables in a shop or on the street or from the head.

In all cultures, the old teach the young how to survive. Whatever the name for it, survival is what is necessary; cultural survival and personal survival. Once, elders in Akotokyir and Abaasa taught the young how to hunt, how to gather, how to plant maize and cassava and yam. They taught them how to find food. Today, they are also taught to find food, but the food is bought, not harvested. It is not that food cannot be harvested, but that food harvested is not the only food, or the best food, or the desired food. Now, the food includes packaged foods, foreign foods. Then there are the foods of the mind (education), foods for the soul (religion), foods for the body (sex and pleasure), and foods for the spirit (music, tapes). There are modern foods (soaps, hair products, toothpastes, videos, televisions, radios, cars, cameras, watches, plastics, and we could go on). These new foods, new needs, cannot be acquired through foraging or fishing or sowing. New foods require new methods. New foods are obtained with MONEY.

Money is both the means and the end. Even the smallest child understands that money is the key to survival. Survival today is not solely dependent on food, but on formal Western-style education, dress, and status. The culture teaches the child the value of money and what it can buy. Schools systematically and consistently teach the children about how to value what it is necessary to value in the contemporary world: striving, dominance, power, money, education, control, authority, and all of the markings of Western culture. Perhaps the most important thing a child learns in school today is what is important in the eyes of the world and how to have it. What it teaches is the desire to achieve success within the context of a world political economy. However, what most of us succeed in acquiring is not so much the success, but the trappings. We sport Nike sneakers, Calvin Klein t-shirts, Levi's jeans, BMWs, or big fancy houses, not knowing that we have only succeeded in emulating what we think is successful, what appears to be the top. Sociologists have long known that the markers of class are set by the ruling classes and emulated by others until they become common, and then the markers change (Goffman 1974). So, for example, the ruling classes adopted a casual shirt with the design of an alligator, called Izod. Soon, the middle classes were sporting the shirt, so the upper classes shifted to Polo. Now I see the little alligator cropping up on men in the villages as a discarded relic of the bourgeoisie. The striving, the clambering after symbols, is what keeps the system alive and moving, and the rules have not eluded the people of Ghana.

So today are we all preparing our young for a world culture? How can the schools in Ghana teach the children about how to be Ghanaian? What does this mean? How can the school books and uniforms and blackboards and pictures translate? If we are training, educating for global survival, for the global race toward progress, toward Rostow's stage of High Mass Consumption, isn't the race lopsided? How can anyone catch up? How will Ghana "take off?" Are we training our children to desire that which they will never have? The traditions of a long ago Ghana are considered over, outmoded, good only for the theater stage. But what of the new one?

It seems cruel to beat children to make them conform to a system within which they will only minimally succeed. It seems too reminiscent of the colonial masters; maybe this is only a remnant and will go with time. The colonial stick has been transferred to the colonized mind of the teacher. Have the teachers taken up the colonial mantel? In their desire to compete, their need to survive, has the servant taken up the tools of the master? There seems little choice. The old is no longer possible, so the new must thrive. These people who once grew their own food, tended their own gardens, ruled their own land, raised their own young, now must change. Change is necessary and inevitable. What lessons are these children learning in the process of this change?

Race and Gender: Learning Where You Belong

If you trample on another's right to seek your own, you will be disappointed in the end.
[Gyeke: 191]

Race   "Bronyi, Bronyi - How are you? I am fine, thank you," the children chant wherever I go. It means, "White person, how are you?" and it is meant to be a friendly greeting. But most Brunyis are offended. How can you call me "white person?" It is demeaning. It is undignified. It dehumanizes me, makes me into a category, into a thing. But the children, as well as the adults, use it lovingly; they think it is a compliment. It is an honor to be "white." The word is also extended to all foreigners, whether of African or European decent. "White" and "foreign" are merged in the minds of the people. This kind of foreignness, equated with whiteness, is considered a blessing. People have told me that the children are happy to see such newcomers because it means that they are close to God. There is a story about how when folks used to go to church, if they saw a white person along the way, they needn't bother to go to church, because they had already seen God.

We only have to look to colonial history to understand the origins of such ideas, a history by now all too familiar to us. It is a history of European expansion, slavery, colonization, and the painful, sometimes bloody, decolonization. It is a history of expropriation of lands, proletarianization of people, and religious and secular proselytizing. However this period is theorized, it has left in its wake a colonial legacy of vast import. It has left an impression on the land and in the minds and the hearts of the people. A part of this legacy is what we have come to call racism. In Akotokyir or Abaasa or in my University classrooms, racism is an unidentified, unarticulated, but ever-present reality. It is a reality demonstrated in the straightening of women's hair, in the reverence held for whiteness, in the dress, in the almost universal unflagging belief in the wisdom and superiority of what is unselfconsciously called bronyi. It is a belief so entrenched in the psyche of the people that it replicates the laws of nature or of God. God or nature has created different human beings with different attributes, different talents, different responsibilities. It is not the antagonistic, hostile racism of America or Europe, but a more subtle, underlying, formal racism.

There is a story in Ghana about a family of mice and a family of cats. The mice children and the cat children, on first entering the outside world, played together. When the cat children arrived home to greet their parents, they told of the fun they had with the mice children. The cat parents were horrified and told their children, "Don't you know that you are to eat the mice? The mice are your food. Next time you see them, you are to catch them so that we can eat them." The mice children likewise told their parents of their day, and, likewise, were admonished. "Don't you know that the cat is your enemy? You are the prey of the cat. Next time you see the cat children, you must run away and hide, lest they eat you for lunch." The next day, when the cat children saw the mice children, they began to chase, and the mice children began to run. And so they learned who they were.

The story reminds me of the film series, *Africa,* in which Basil Davidson talks to the headmaster of a colonial-established Methodist school. The headmaster tells the story of the chameleon and the fly. The chameleon is capable of changing color and thus can creep slowly up on its prey. Then the chameleon will open its mouth and quick as a wink, flick the fly away, down its throat. We are the fly, he says, and you are the chameleon.

These stories, of course, refer to colonial times, to the time when Africa, with its people and land and gold and diamonds and oil, were snatched up into the mouth of European expansion. It refers to that time when Africans were taken to the Americas as slaves to work on the plantations of the New World, when Africans were considered backward and childlike and savage and of a separate race, a unique species, different from that of the European. We say that these times have passed. We know now that we are all one species, that "race" is a social and political, not biological, category, and that all *Homo sapiens* share a common heritage. However, just as there remains the colonial legacy in the poor infrastructure, the foreign ownership of land and resources, inadequate industry, destructive reliance on imported necessities, and an arcane educational system, there, too, remains the colonial legacy of racism. It is a racism that persists in elevating one perceived race above others. It is a racism that does not recognize the equality of all human beings. It is a racism that makes appear immutable that which is, in fact, mutable and socially determined. It is a racism that divides groups of people, that undermines the talents of certain groups, that highlights difference. It is a racism that elevates phenotype to the status of genotype, making melanin, hair texture, and facial structure the determinant of the contents of one's heart and mind.

Too much has been written about race and racism to require review here (Montague 1974; Harris 1980; Berreman 1981; Fanon 1967; Magubane 1981; Ake 1981; Jenkins 1997; Lundgren 1997; Bowles 1976; Gould 1981 to name a few). But what we have learned from each other and what I have learned from the Fante, is that it will be a long while before we are free from the devastating and limiting influences of a racism hewn in the fire of colonialism and refined in its aftermath. This racism affects every part of every child's day. It is like the "thing with no name" that Naipahl's Popo is always trying to create. It is a "thing with no name," but a thing that moves and breathes and lives. The children are not actively taught it. It is in the air. It is there as they watch their mothers and sisters straighten their hair and lighten their skin with cream. It is there when the men discuss "the black man" and how he will cheat and do wrong. It is there in the billboards and the magazines in which images of prosperity and beauty are identified with white, American, and European. It is even there in the churches, where Jesus still has long flowing locks and his disciples peer out at us from blue eyes framed in porcelain faces.

It is not that the children learn racial hatred. They learn simply that "black" people are different from "white" people, and that the difference is not just one of degree, but one of kind. In school, at home, and in the community, they learn that black people have a long way to go before they will be where white people are, which is where they all want to be. Yet this knowledge does not seem to dampen their spirits or deter them from their lively exuberance. As I leave the village of Akotokyir to the chanting of "Bronyi, bronyi," I am amazed by the remarkably sturdy, confident little beings, so eager and innocent and, most of all, so trusting.

Gender   Teaching a child to be a woman or a man is one of the first priorities of socializing the young. In every culture we have encountered, gender roles are distinct and clearly defined. From infancy, Fante children learn how to behave as a boy or a girl. Girls do domestic work; boys do everything else. Gender, however, is a complicated issue in Ghana. Although men are considered to be the strong ones, the knowledgeable ones, women work on the farms, do the trading, and are strong and independent.

Because the Fante are matrilineal, a unilineal system, the affairs of women are kept separate from those of the men. Children are members of their mother's lineage, thus excluding men from the "family" of the mothers and their children. This is a double-edged sword, however, especially in these times when the bilineal, nuclear, monogamous family is becoming fashionable. Fathers are technically responsible for their sister's children and, therefore, exempt from responsibility for their wife's children (their biological offspring). However, as we saw earlier, many fathers claim responsibility for their biological children in preference over their nieces and nephews. This tension sometimes catches children in the middle. The fathers' responsibilities may be unclear, but those of the mother are primarily focused on her children. She will therefore almost always engage in some form of income-generating activity and will control her own income and property. The reality is that the women are strong, competent, in charge, and hard working, but the ideology is that they are weak and dependent and that the men are in charge. Children learn both the reality and the ideology. Men have political power and decision-making clout, but women but do most of the domestic work, most of the work in the fields, most of the trading, and much of the income generation for herself and her children. Men contribute to the support of their children when they can, but they also contribute to the support of their own lineage group.

As I watch the women and girls in Akotokyir and Abaasa, I cannot help but think of Zora Neale Hurston's words, "Women are the mules of the world." When I go to the village, the women are there, but it is the men with whom I meet and plan and

Ready for anything—on top of the world—Cape Coast

discuss. Women and children sit outside or on the periphery, observing and support-ing, but not actively involved.

There is nothing particularly unique in the ways male and female are defined. The African, the colonial, and the contemporary have combined to create a situation in which men have most of the power and women do much of the work. But because women have control of their own resources, to a large extent, and because they are mostly in the company of other women, there is a kind of autonomy and power the women seem to maintain, despite this lopsided gender arrangement. So both the boys and girls carry themselves with a kind of power and assurance that is gender specific, but shared.

When you lift up a child, you bring it down gently.

A Fante child is a unique and special blessing. Without them, you are not a full Fante adult. They are your legacy, your connection to the future. They are a special link in the cycle of life. Without them your life is meaningless. If you raise them properly and help them to do well in the future, they will care for you well in your old age. Theirs is not the child-rearing of Freud or Dr. Spock. Theirs is the child-rearing of common sense and tradition. God provides you with the children you are meant to have and with the guidance to provide for them and bring them up to adulthood. If you follow God's guidance and provide what you can, you have done your job. You have contributed to your lineage, your clan, and your village, and you have done well.

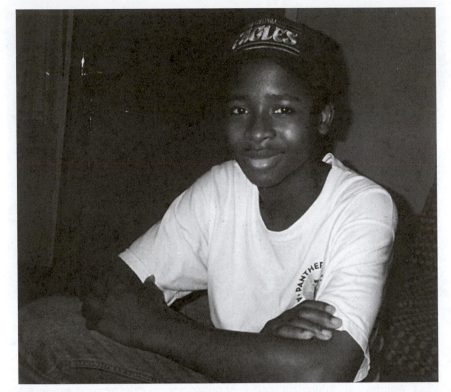

Assistant Kwesi

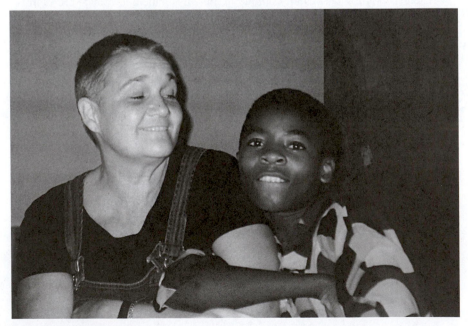

Author and young friend

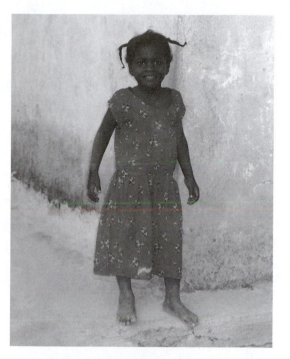

Abaasa child

Babytender—Abaasa

6 / Religion

All human beings are children of God.

Goodness is the prime characteristic of God.

Because God does not like evil, he gave each person a name.

IT IS MARCH, the dry season. It always seems that March is the hottest month. It is as if the universe begins to boil up after the rains in October or November; the earth dries up and the heat builds and boils, until by March it is a raging hot cauldron. The land is parched and dry, the dust blows, grasses are brown and scorched, and it is sometimes so hot you think you cannot breathe. When it is so intense and hot and dry that you feel the earth must explode, it begins to gradually cool down until, finally, the cooling, healing, life-giving rains come. It starts with some small rains in May, then in July the nights and early mornings are finally almost chilly and the rains are heavy; by Christmas they have usually ended again.

This year, I have to remind myself, is not as bad as it was that year when the rains did not come, and the people stood in lines all through the towns and villages, buckets on their heads and in their hands, waiting for water trucks or a trickle from a pipe. That year, we stood in lines until the wee hours of the morning for water. The University reservoir was drained, the village bore holes were drained, the rivers were dry, and students were sent home from the University and from boarding schools. I couldn't imagine how people without cars and without large containers ever survived that year. It was said that many did not. Without the water, the electricity did not work either, so I marked papers by candlelight, without the aid of the now ubiquitous ceiling fan. That was a desperate year. This year the rains came, there is usually water, and my fan soothes me at night, so I remind myself that it is not so bad. It is hot, just the same.

On this hot March Sunday, I drive to Abaasa to officiate at a service of the African Faiths church. There are four churches in Abaasa: the Twelve Apostles, New Apostolic, Church of the Pentecost, and African Faith. There are Muslims, Catholics, and other Protestants in the village, but they must attend church in nearby Efutu or Cape Coast. All of the churches use the Bible as their scriptural guide, they all have male preachers, and they all pray to the same God. The Apostolic Church, headed by Nkrumah, does not use drums, and the members do not dance. The African Faiths Church uses many drums and rattles, and they do dance. Mr. Nkrumah said that he grew up in the Catholic Church and attended their schools. They did not dance or use drums at that time. However, now they do, and Nkrumah thinks it is because the Pentecostal churches will take all of the people if the other churches do not change. Africans like the drumming and dancing, he said, so they will go to those churches, but he prefers to sing from a hymnal and to use only a Casio electric piano, if possible; no drums and no dancing. He officiates in a white shirt, tie, and black slacks, not in robes or traditional cloth.

The announcement said that the service was to begin at 9:30 a.m. sharp, but my people tell me that I can arrive around 10:30 or 11:00. When I arrive at 11:15, people are milling around, organizing, and still in their home clothes. Mr. Nkrumah is still in his white shirt and black tie from his service. Mr. Adams, who is the preacher of the Church of the Pentecost, has traveled to Pedu, where they are having their own revival. People have come to Abaasa from all around, so the little village is teeming with activity. I wait in my temporary palace until they finally come for me around 1:30. I am dressed in my queen mother sandals and cloth. We are accompanied on our walk to the outdoor church area by drummers. As we walk slowly down the road, crowds of men, women, and children greet us enthusiastically.

We enter the village center, where bamboo poles covered with palm fronds provide a three-sided arcade, under which worshippers wait on benches. At the front of the space several rows of seats are arranged for dignitaries. I am escorted to a place of honor on the side, a large, velvet-covered chair. Drummers and dancers accompany us, with the help of rattles and singers. The music is beautiful, a kind of melodic chanting. At the head of the arena are the priests, men, and women dressed in white, with a swath of red around the waist and across the chest. They look to me very much like Catholic priests.

I was asked before the service if I would serve as chairman. I, of course, said I would be honored. After we are seated and the music subsides, a young priest graciously welcomes me in English, explains the program to me, provides me with a hand-written schedule of events, and proceeds. From the schedule, I determine that the official title of the church is the United Faith Tabernacle Church. Villagers refer to it as African Faiths because it is considered to be more traditionally African than others. There is a prayer in Fante and, once again, music. Most of the worshippers are women, many with babies on their backs and small children by their sides. Most of the dignitaries are men. The women are dressed beautifully in Kaabas and slits, many in blue and white with white on their heads. There are several drummers, all men, and many men who carry rattles made of gourds wrapped in beads. As the drumming continues, the congregants dance in the center of the arena and down to the front, where a priest places his hand on their heads in a spirit of blessing.

Several speeches are made by the dignitaries, who are introduced with a great deal of fanfare. I am then asked to officially open the service with a speech. They provide a translator. I have already been prompted by Nkrumah as to what to say, so I say it quickly. It amounts to much thanks, gratitude, and encouragement for their Christian efforts. I recognize most of the community leaders in attendance. Regardless of different religious affiliations, they respect each other and like to support the different churches.

By now it is close to 4:00. There is more dancing and singing to the beat of the drums and rhythm of the rattles. Everyone dances, young and old, men and women. It looks as if the service will go on for hours. Children are watching from the sides, women are selling bread and ground nuts. The sermon has not yet begun when Nkrumah leans over to tell me that I need to give them my collection envelope and say I need to leave. He was given instructions from somewhere that we would not stay. I do as I am told; Nkrumah makes polite gestures and we are off, accompanied by the drummers and rattles. We are thus accompanied until I reach the house where we meet again before my final departure. The drummers are given a small sum of money and sent back to the meeting, which will probably continue until dusk.

RELIGION: OPIATE OR LIBERATION?

I am doing the good [thing], so that my way to the world of spirits might not be blocked.

[Proverb - Gyekye: 190]

Gye Nyame - Except God (I fear no one except God)

Adinkra Symbol (A. Kayper-Mensah: 1976)

It has been said to me that if you want to understand Ghanaians, you must understand their religion. Ghanaians *are* religion, I am told. It is a part of all of life, leaving no room for the separation of the secular from the profane. You do not have to be in Ghana long to realize the validity of such a statement. Kwame Gyekye (1996:3) begins his work on African Cultural Values with a chapter on religion because, he says, "Religion—the awareness of the existence of some ultimate, supreme being who is the origin and sustainer of this universe and the establishment of constant ties with this being—influences, in a comprehensive way, the thoughts and actions of the African people."

God gives life and God gives sustenance. God is everywhere. God is good. God is the provider. God is just. But if God is so good and so powerful how is it that God can allow so much suffering, so much poverty, so much cruelty? Sometimes I look around me and I want to shout, "Oh, God, my God, why hast thou forsaken these people?" Where is the fairness? Where is the justice? Where is the goodness? I ask this of Father Paul, my friend who is a Catholic priest. How do you believe in such a God? I ask. He says that it is not God who allows these things to happen. People choose. It is the choices they make. They have not chosen God. They choose to do the wrong thing. They do not make prudent choices. They run after the wrong things. They run after women, after cars, after houses. They choose to spend their money on apeteche instead of on charcoal to boil their water, and they become sick and can't work.

According to Gyekye, in African religions, evil occurs, not because of God, but because of lesser deities or human will (Gyekye 1997: 12). Lesser deities can possess either good or evil or both, and therefore can use magical forces to author evil in the world. But, as Father Paul has told me many times, it is the free will of humans that causes the real problems. Humans are possessed of free will so that they can exercise it either for good or evil. It is their evil choices that get them into trouble and cause the pain and problems we see.

Houses of Worship

It is Sunday morning. I am in church because that is where everyone is on Sunday mornings, except for the Muslims, the few Hindus, and the Seventh Day Adventists. The church is Anglican, but it is not unlike others of its type. This one is an old church built in the days of colonial Anglicans. It is big and modestly ornate, with stained glass windows in the front, dark wood on the ceiling, dark wooden pews, and a tall wooden dais that raises the priest high above his people. It is bigger and more elaborate than the churches they build today. As in Catholic churches, the pictures at the "stations of the cross" are in place in anticipation of the coming of Easter, when the crucifixion of Christ will be re-enacted and the photos ceremoniously removed. The photos are, again in typical style, reminiscent of the European Renaissance in period and rendering, with figures that are creamy in skin tone and have light, flowing hair. There is the usual large wooden crucifix at the alter, along with candles and incense. Fans overhead quietly hum accompaniment to the amplified music of the small band and the choir's Casio. The band, with its huge black speakers, is in the front, and the choir, replete in mauve and black robes, sings from behind the congregation in the upstairs balcony. The band has contemporary, rock-band-like drums; the older, more traditional types, along with gourd rattles, sometimes accompany the upstairs choir.

The people are dressed in a combination of dressy, fancy Ghanaian, and Western garments. Most of the women today are in the traditional Kaaba and slit. Because it is also a Thanksgiving service for a deceased member of the church whose funeral was yesterday, many of the congregants wear black and white, red, or black. Many of the men also wear the traditional long flowing cloth, but others wear Western suits and ties or dressy slacks and a Sunday shirt. Children are clearly in their best dresses, small suits, small Kaaba and slits, or knickers. They wear shoes, not the usual rubber slippers.

The music begins and the congregation stands. After the music, there is a prayer. The priest then arrives, wearing a long mauve surplice over his white cassock. He puts on his spectacles, puts his papers on the pulpit, and begins. He speaks in English and seems to be reading the sermon. He is speaking today about the different roles we all can play in the Church and in Christian life. The sermon is rather formal and without much emotion, but it is short and dignified. He exhorts all to find our place, to do our part, to feel that we have something to offer, whatever it is. He uses examples such as teacher, choir leader, singer, usher. After the completion of the English sermon, he removes the spectacles, comes away from the pulpit, and gives another brief homily in Fante. This one is much more lively and spirited. The people laugh, the priest smiles, and he moves about in a somewhat spontaneous and less formal fashion. The church is crowded. Children can be heard noisily chatting in the back and fans are rhythmically swaying in people's hands as the priest warms to his subject. He does not go on for long, however; then there is a prayer, some more music, and the usual two offerings. Offerings often take quite a lot of time, but they create a physical and emotional break, as people sing and dance down the aisles to the accompaniment of the choir's music and the beating of the drums. Many dance freely as they make their way to the front of the church; others walk sedately. Babies usually bounce contentedly on their mothers' backs, but today they are frequently in the arms of an elder.

People have said that the religious ritual used to be much more sedate and Western, with very little of the African because it was so frowned on by the early missionaries. It is only recently, in the past 20 or 30 years, that this dancing and drumming and clapping has been reintroduced into the Ghanaian Christian church service. At the moment, churches appear to mix the old and the new in a kind of peaceful coexistence. Despite this mixture, however, most churches are quite conservative in style as well as message. The choir, the decor, the symbols, the music, the clergy, and the messages all stay quite close to the formula of most Christian denominations around the world, although there is considerable room for individual innovation.

The essence of the religious messages, however, are quite simple and consistent and do not deviate a great deal from traditional African religious doctrine. They extol the virtues of God and encourage followers to observe the life of Christ and use it as an example. They should strive to live virtuous and modest lives and to avoid the evil temptations of elicit sex, lying, cheating, and especially placing undo emphasis on material things. They are prevailed on to live simply, dress simply, work steadfastly, and be faithful caretakers of their families. Many scholars have spent a great deal of time discussing African religions (Eboyi-Anza 1997; Evans-Pritchard 1937; Gyekye 1996; Malefijt 1968; Uchendu 1965; Radcliffe-Brown 1952; Malinowski 1954; Little 1954 to name only a few) so I will not reiterate their work here. However, just as it was for those who went before them (Gyekye 1996), it is difficult for almost any Ghanaian to imagine a life without God. Almost everyone, in all walks of life, believes in some God. They may not particularly care which God it is and they usually will not try to convince you that theirs is best, but some God is essential. We are all God's children, and as such we have certain responsibilities to that God, to ourselves, and to each other. Sometimes I argue with my friend, Father Paul. I tell him that his God is a God of the West, that it is an imported God. He does not yield. His God has always been here, he says. It is the God that was here in Africa and is in the people. Whether you believe in God or not, God is there inside you, he insists.

This is consistent with views of scholars who say that the concept of God as a supreme being and the creator of all, residing in all people, is a particularly African concept (Gyekye 1996; Eboyi-Anza 1997). I protest to my priest that their God is European, is not really African, that it is a white God, and that images of Jesus are white images. Even your dress, I say, is a European cassock for priests in Italy. Jesus did not come from Europe, he says. Jesus came from the Middle East. We can't help it if his word was taken to Europe and then brought back to us by missionaries. And the dress, he says. What is a dress? It is external, a convention. But the words of Jesus, which are the truths of God, are African. Don't take our God from us.

According to Eboyi-Anza, the Fante people (as one of the Akan groups), believe that human beings are made of the father, who gives the spirit or personality; the mother, who is the blood; and God, who is the soul. When a person dies, the three parts of the person become one and change into a ghost. Ghosts are either good or bad depending on the life they have lived on earth. If they have lived a good, kind, generous, and honest life on earth, they will successfully travel to a place much like the Christian concept of heaven. If they have lived an unrighteous or evil life, they will not be able to make the long difficult journey and will live forever in a place much like the Christianity's hell (Eboyi-Anza 1997).

The service ends. The music is in the background as priests and altar boys slowly process up the aisle carrying crosses and Bibles, the symbols of their religion. Drums keep the rhythm, and the congregation sways slightly before dispersing into the midday sun. As I leave the church I feel refreshed, cleansed, as do the other congregants, I am sure. The church service marks a break in the day-to-day toils of life. It has been a meditative time, a time to dress in special clothes, to set aside daily cares, to join with others in the praise of a higher power. It is comforting and helps give order to what is often an otherwise orderless, chaotic, perhaps even meaningless world. People meet their friends, chat about their lives, and plan to meet again. There will be other activities throughout the week and the people can look forward to these times. Later in the week there will be prayer service and choir practice, and perhaps the women's groups, men's groups, and young people's groups will meet. There will be funerals and weddings and engagement parties. There will be special fund raising services and meetings to plan church activities. All of these activities give meaning and order to people's lives. They break up the days and weeks and months and years. They provide reasons to gather, to celebrate, to work, to play. In all of these times, cultural values, norms, and rules will be imparted. Children will learn about what it is that their culture expects of them. They will join their fellows to pray and sing, but they are learning important cultural messages.

I recently attended a wedding. It was a large, extravagant affair. It resembled other church weddings I have attended. The church was decorated with every kind of symbolic item. Because the ceremony was in a church, there were the usual candles, crucifix, and statues. In addition, there were balloons, banners strung across the ceiling, ribbons and bows, extra candles, real and artificial flowers, and an archway at the front that was painted white and covered with flowers and balloons. The color scheme seemed to be mauve and white, so much of the decor was done in these colors, although other pastels were represented in the balloons, ribbons, and flowers. The bride was dressed in a long, white lace gown with a long veil attached to a diamond-style tiara. The groom was dressed in a dark suit and white shirt and had a boutonniere of mauve and white. There were flower girls and maids of honor and best men and a tiny little ring bearer. These young people were all dressed in lace and satin and ruffles and suits, all of which matched the other adornments.

The congregation was dressed in their Sunday finest. They filled the church and were flowing onto the arcade outside. There were many young people and small children. Some were in Western dress with large, beribboned hats, some had golden or silver Kaabas and slits, some of the men were in extra fancy cloths, some had dark tailored suits, white shirts, and ties. Some of the congregants wore the colors of the wedding, either in dress or accessory. The children sat obediently in starched and stiff new dresses and suits and smartly done hair. The women's hair was done in some fashions I had never seen before. It was braided and twisted and waved and piled high on the head, or left long and straight.

It was truly a celebratory atmosphere. The church had a new look, clean and colorful, as did the people within its walls. It was as if all were there with a new look to celebrate this new life. The bride and groom were in clothing they had never worn before and will probably never wear again, signifying their new status as a married unit. The mood was exuberant and festive. It was a time for rejoicing, a time of renewal.

There were several priests, all of whom took part in the service, all blessing the new union. Father Paul was glowing when his turn came to speak. He seemed his happy self, in a festive mood. But his message was serious. This is a serious union. It must be taken seriously. A man, he said, should think of his family as he thinks of his work. Many men, he said, think of the wife and children as second to their jobs. The jobs get most of their time. People laughed as he suggested that sometimes a man spends so much time at his work that he does not even remember he has a home. The wife, the home, should be the most important. Husbands and wives must respect each other and treat each other well to keep the family together. It is only in the family that the children learn what they must do. The family is the place where the children are raised and it must be a place where the children learn the right things. He went on to say that this marriage is blessed by God, that no other marriage should take its place. Likewise, the family is a creation of God and should never be neglected. It is only inside this blessed marriage that the family should be formed and only this family can provide the proper environment within which to raise a child.

He played with the audience lightly, but the message was serious and sober. Children and young people would clearly get the message. He said that only in marriage should there be children (or sex), that only one kind of marriage (a Christian, God-centered one) is blessed by God and approved of by the church, and that once you have this marriage and these children, you have a family blessed by God and the church. At this moment, the bride looked like a princess and the groom, beaming on her, like a prince. Who would not want to be that princess? Who could not admire that prince? The prince and princess then moved to their place under the flower and balloon-laden arbor, and were blessed once again by yet another priest. He offered similar words of support; he had them repeat the wedding vows to love, honor, and obey each other until death; and he slipped the rings on their fingers. The groom removed the veil gently from the bride's face, gave her a long, loving look, and embraced her to the roar of the excited crowd. There was no kiss—in Ghana a public kiss would be most indiscreet—but the hug caused pandemonium. The people stood up and waved hankies and shouted and clapped and laughed and hissed. It was the perfect climax to a brilliantly orchestrated celebration of the beauty and joy of Christian wedded bliss. Anyone, young or old, who was there to witness the event, could not help but be moved and inspired by the entire event.

Religion serves as a powerful vehicle for conveying cultural messages about marriage, family, and God. For Ghanaians, these are the foundations on which all of the rest of society rests. Without them life would be without form, without meaning. All Ghanaians are born into a family, all will contribute to that family, and all come from God. For them, liberation also comes from God. A deep, real belief in God will eradicate poverty, eliminate greed and envy, and truly free the land and the people. Only God can make life on this earth bearable and life after this one possible. Gye Nyame, a popular symbol, means only God or unless God. Only God knows where we come from and where we are going and only God can lead us.

Thus the answer to my constant query: why so much poverty? Why such visible signs of racism? These are not dilemmas for most Ghanaians. These are human problems, human foibles, signs of human frailty, and lack of proper allegiance to God. If all people practiced their religious teachings and followed the ways of God, these problems on earth would not exist on earth. One day God will reign and we all will be free: free from evil and free from harm. This belief sustains the people, gives them strength and hope and courage, through extraordinarily difficult times.

New Priests: Father Emil counseling a parishioner

Old Priests: Chief of Nim and elders waiting for libation

7 / Change

A person cutting a path does not know that the part behind him is crooked.

IT IS THAT time of year again. It is the time when the queen mother is carried. It has been 2 years, and the people of Abaasa want a celebration. It should be done at least every other year. We begin the preparation once again. The t-shirts have to be made. This time I ask no questions. Schnapps is required to invite the chiefs of neighboring villages. Money needs to be raised for rice, fish, fu fu, drinks, and music. We travel to Nim to see about the brass band. They agree to play for no fee, but they need apeteche, chop, and 30 blue t-shirts. We agree and thank them kindly for the offer.

This year we build our own paloquine so that we do not have to borrow. We bring the expert from a neighboring village. He does not have the use of his legs but walks from village to village on his hands padded with children's shoes. He is the expert. He purchases the cane in Takoradi and then weaves the long, sled-like conveyance. We seal the agreement with apeteche and a prayer, and he begins. He is a schoolteacher, so he finishes in March during the long vacation. When he finishes, he calls the people of Abaasa, who collect it in the night so that no one sees it leave the village. Before it leaves, the chief of the village must be given Schnapps. Schnapps is taken, a taxi is hired, and the men from Abaasa successfully transfer the new paloquine to the house of my husband. There arises another issue. The cane is covered with foam and then covered with a kind of upholstery fabric, which is expensive. After this, the whole thing is covered in a new Kente cloth, another expense. The expenses are mounting. We travel to the next village, deep into the forest, where we find the paloquine expert at his school. I do not know what kind of cloth to buy, so he says that if I give him the money he will go to town, purchase it, and then travel to Abaasa, where he will work in the night to complete the job. We agree. The Paloquine costs almost a half a million Cedis. This is without the umbrella, which the umbrella maker makes for us for 300,000.00 Cedis (which we can pay later). We agree to complete the project and let the man make the umbrella. It seems like a huge expense to me, but the village plans to have it forever, so I guess it is okay.

Now we need the "locking fee" for the sound system. The sound system is used for 2 days and provides entertainment for the entire village. It costs 100,000 Cedis per day. After the sound system is locked, Nkrumah comes to my house with a bag full of envelopes. He says that the village has decided to have a "harvest" in conjunction with the carrying. For this event, we need to give people envelopes in which they place a donation. They have brought 140 envelopes. They tell me to print on the envelope and to use my own words. My own words turn out to be unclear because I do not know what to say. So, after some consultation and much running around, I manage to print the envelopes in a satisfactory manner. I have some problem with the envelopes because I am not sure what a harvest is. It is usually done at churches and seems to me like a euphemism for a money-raising affair. It entails people bringing items to donate and having them auctioned off. I think it has to do with harvest time because it usually involves the sale of food stuffs that are recently harvested. It seems to have lost its original meaning and now can be used for any special occasion at which items are auctioned.

The people of the village are building a house for the queen mother. They are eager to have it completed in time for the celebration. On Tuesdays, when they do their communal labor, they work on it. The women carry sand from the river in pans on their heads. The sand is mixed with water and cement and then molded into blocks by Mr. Nkrumah and his helpers. The land is cleared and the men dig the foundation by hand. Now they need wood for the roof, roofing sheets of tin, roofing nails, and more cement. I buy more roofing sheets. Last month, they cost 14,000 Cedis for one. Now, one is 18,000 Cedis. Cement that was 15,000 Cedis per bag last month is now 19,000 Cedis and continues to climb. I try to have the building made of local mud and thatch, but that will not do. A queen mother cannot stay in such a house. I hoped that eventually the house would become a clinic or, perhaps, a real palace for the chief. However, I now know that in all likelihood this will not happen. If I go, it probably will be locked up and kept forever for Nana.

Nkrumah comes to me today. There are other items of business to discuss. His uncle's wife died in Nim, and he wants me to attend the funeral. I will send along money instead because I have a prior engagement. Nkrumah will send my regrets. The man selling the Kente cloth will come Wednesday for the rest of the money. It is a lot of money. Where will it come from? Then there is the matter of the sheep. They do not have one in the village, so they must look in nearby villages. The price is higher. Recently the price of oil has gone up. This affected petrol costs and household fuel costs, which affect the price of everything. We complain bitterly to each other about this situation. Although everything costs more, the local produce, cloth, and charcoal does not bring a higher price because people's pay remains the same. Although Nkrumah and his neighbors pay more for everything that is transported, they are not able to sell their own charcoal, citrus, and maize for more because they sell to local markets where the people have no money. So, what about the sheep? I give him 100,000 Cedis and hope that it is enough. Then we discuss the invitations to the Member of Parliament (MP), the chief executive, and the assembly man; the printing of the program; and the announcement on the radio. Each of these items requires money, and we discuss what can be done or "how far we will go." When business is over, Nkrumah leaves. I will return to the village on Tuesday when we will carry on.

Nkrumah goes down the path. He is dressed in his best black trousers and tan long-sleeved shirt. He is drenched with sweat. His leg still bothers him, but he never complains. We don't mention it anymore because we both know that nothing can be done about it, and Nkrumah does not want it to affect his activities. He is the one who delivers messages, keeps up contacts, and facilitates relations between me and the village. He seems to like this role, and he is good at it, so bad leg or not, he will do it.

Life continues in Abaasa at its slow and steady pace. The electric poles are still standing with no wire. However, we have been told that Abaasa will be included in the next round of the Self Help Electricity Program (SHEP). Roofing sheets are delivered to the village by the MP with the promise of cement next month for the finishing of the public toilet and refurbishing of the community building. We now have our own paloquine, complete with umbrella and new Kente. There have been several new babies born into the village. One is a fat baby boy named Nana Mansah III after the queen mother. The man with the broken leg is walking now, and Mr. Mohammad is recuperating from his hospitalization in his brother's nearby village.

It is the rainy season. The road to Abaasa is muddy and slippery and the rain pounds the mud into ever-larger holes and gullies. It is green and lush and feels cooler even though it continues to be hot. Flowers line the road they share with the birds. The flowers are purple, yellow, and a deep, velvety red. The birds are deep blue, black, and yellow; are small and large; and have long, graceful tails. It is glorious as I travel up the road once again during this Easter season of spiritual renewal. I can feel the spirit of new life, new hope, and beginnings as I revel in the splendor of the green forest dotted with the bright hues of flowers and birds. As usual, children greet me: "Nana Mansah, how are you? Welcome." I come today to tie up loose ends and to bring t-shirts and programs for the celebration. Even before I reach Nkrumah, people tell me that Nana has arrived. The chief is in the village. It has been 2 years. There is an air of excitement and expectation.

Nkrumah, little brother, the chairman, Adams, the young nephew of the chief, and I traveled the 120 kilometers to Kumasi to find the chief. We found him recuperating from an eye ailment. He promised to come in time for the carrying, and now he is here. His eyes are fine, and he seems full of life and vigor. I greet him in my husband's house (he is the chief's brother). They are discussing business with other family members. He is in the wide, velvet knickers typically worn by chiefs under their cloth. This time he has no cloth, only a Western-style knit shirt with a collar. He wears his chief sandals on his feet. He greets me enthusiastically, and we adjourn to our usual meeting place to complete the reunion. There seems to be some tension. Mr. Quashie is there from Takoradi (he is another brother of the chief). My friend, the retired merchant marine, whose broad travels and good English give him a sense of superiority over the villagers and a proprietary, almost conspiratorial, relationship with me, seems in good spirits today. The tension I frequently notice between him and Nkrumah seems particularly high. However, it is controlled. They all begin to speak. They greet me, tell me all is well in their village, and ask my mission. They give the chief and me a beer.

The chief is distracted. They begin to speak in animated fashion. Nkrumah, his brother, and Adams are somewhat solemn and quiet. Quashie and the chief speak. The chief feels my house should have been built more quickly. It should have been built before my carrying so that I and my people can comfortably reside in the village during the festivities. The chief has been gone for 2 years. The village has worked hard during that time to fix the road, make the toilet, build my house, secure electric poles, repair the old bore hole, and fix the huge, heavy electric poles into the ground. This has happened amid constant illnesses, trips to hospitals, births and deaths, clearing of land, planting, harvesting, firing wood for the production of charcoal, selling, and providing daily subsistence, water, firewood, and clean clothing. Is the chief chastising the people for not having finished this important project? Does he focus on the house to deflect from his own delinquency? Is he conscious that he is doing it, or does it come as a natural protective strategy? I will never know, but my people appear chastised, and I feel for them. They have tried hard. They have worked together and struggled together these last 2 years. He has not been here. He has not contributed. But now he says that he will work on the house beginning tomorrow. This is Good Friday, a holiday. The shops are closed. The bank is closed. They only have four bags of cement left. They need more. They also need door hinges and locks. I cannot get them until Tuesday, after Easter Monday, when the town again opens up. Right now the town is quiet. People are visiting, worshipping, and traveling. It is Easter. It is a major holiday, and its importance is superseded barely by the other major Christian festival, Christmas. Will he work during the Easter holiday?

Nana Mensah is determined. He will use the existing cement and begin work tomorrow. He smiles broadly, gestures, and speaks in animated fashion. It will be done. I agree to try to get the necessary items tomorrow. If it is impossible, I will get them by Tuesday when the banks and shops are open for business. I begin a new semester of classes on Tuesday, but the urgency of this matter overshadows my professorial duties. There is more animated discussion. Mr. Quashie is anxious to leave. He seems to have lost some of his village patience in his travels and has acquired the habit of impatience known to most Westerners. We adjourn. I will come back as soon as possible with the necessary materials to complete the building project. The chief is excited and energized. My people and the councilmen are quiet.

AKOTOKYIR

Akotokyir has a new chief. He is a young man whose qualifications are under question by Baidoo and his brothers. He is supposed to be of bad character and has caused problems regarding land in the village. Land problems are legion now in Ghana. There is stool land, ancestral land, privately owned land, and government land. Traditional ancestral and stool lands are handed down from generation to generation without the legal constraints initiated after the Colonial period. Claims are being made on the land from all directions, causing misunderstandings and sometimes leading to armed conflict. In Akotokyir the new chief thinks that he can get some extra cash through the sale of lands he is claiming belong to the stool. He threatens the Baidoos, the Catholic church, and William. Someone begins building on the land behind William's house, saying that the land was sold to them by the chief. I remember that before his death, William's father told me that all this land belongs to his children and that they would inherit it. I remember thinking at the time that all the land really belongs to the University, which means that it is all government land.

William will not let the matter drop. Someone is beginning to build on his land. He dresses up in his black jeans and white shirt and goes to the police. They direct him to the paramount chief. Baidoo and others have already been there, so the paramount chief knows about the situation. William will need to return. In the meantime, the people have stopped their building. William is relieved.

The Baidoos have a small shop in their yard where they sell ice, ice cream, bread, canned milk, and a few household items. Mary spends most of her days there now. Baidoo is working on a way to return to the United States. His one brief trip to South Carolina whetted his appetite for America. He wants at least one of his boys to study there. America is where there are opportunities. Kobina tells me that the young want to leave. They want to explore. They want to use computers and the other exciting technology that they are denied here.

Mr. Baidoo tells me that the chief in his village is destooled. He is too difficult. Others say he smokes marijuana, sells lotto, and quarrels with his fellow villagers. They took the problem to the paramount chief who resides in Cape Coast. The family and the queen mother were consulted. Everyone agreed that he should go. Finally it came to a head one evening when the village was assembled for something having to do with electric poles. The chief behaved badly, and his relatives tried to reason with him, but finally, when nothing worked, they wrestled him to the ground, removed his sandals, and beat him over the head. If a chief is ever beaten in such a fashion, with his own sandals on the head, he is automatically destooled. He is publicly disgraced and dethroned in a way that can never be repaired.

The village and the relatives are relieved, according to Mr. Baidoo. Better to be without a chief, as unsettling as that is, than to have a bad one. Mr. Baidoo is now confident and happy about his future and continues to build for his family and the future of the village. His house is getting bigger, and he is just about finished building his Junior Secondary School. He needs a few more blocks and a few more roofing sheets. However, with the rising cost of the cement, wood, and roofing sheets, his work is now more challenging. Theresa, his only daughter, finishes teacher training school this year, and Kobina is in his last year at the Science and Technology University in Kumasi. Martin finished at the fine private Senior Secondary School, St. Augustine's, and is teaching for his father while he waits his turn to enter the University. The three youngest boys are in school, playing football, listening to music, and seeing their friends. The baby, Vincent, is now 8 years old and, according to his mother, only interested in football. He recently began playing a game with soda bottle tops, at which he is very good. He tells his mother that the game helps him to strategize in football.

William is still working at the Pakup Hotel but does not get paid regularly, so he is looking for other work. Recently his manager lost his wife, and everything came to a stand still while they made funeral preparations. The funeral rites are completed now, and William is back on the job. His mother is making kenky for the girls to sell because her health is improved. Mr. Baidoo's small brother with the baby is back with his master learning the welding trade. Michael, the next boy, is learning to become a plumber. The other children are struggling through school. William is trying to reopen his father's bar.

TRADITION AND MODERNIZATION

On March 6, 2000, Ghanaians celebrated the 43rd anniversary of the Republic of Ghana. In 1957 the first prime minister of Ghana, Kwame Nkrumah, said that this hard-won independence would mean nothing without the full liberation of all of Africa. He was joined in this sentiment by illustrious colleagues, such as Amalcar Cabral, Walter Rodney, Nelson Mandela, W.E.B. DuBois, Fidel Castro, and Jomo Kenyata. However, the dream is yet to become a reality. Now in Ghana the children—William, Charles, Kwesi, Adwoa, Afua, and the Baidoo children—have a different dream. They dream of computers, cars, Nike sneakers, and Levi's jeans. They plan to have only one spouse, carry their babies in their arms, and hope their children will wear Pampers. Money is what everyone thinks of when they think of liberation. All human relationships are measured in money. When I say this to people, either they are surprised or retort, "Isn't this the case in America?"

Money and time are the two key issues that, since the onset of the Industrial Revolution, have altered our lives on this earth irrevocably. Modernity is a tricky business. Ideology is powerful. If you are not modern, then you must be backward, and if you are backward, you are traditional—maybe even "primitive" and heathen. If you are modern, you are more European; if you are backward, you are less European. If you are not progressive, you may be primitive. Primitive is vaguely, if not overtly, connected with Africa and blackness in the same way that modernity is connected with whiteness and Europe and America. We think we have left our racist past behind us. But even the tiniest child in Ghana, who calls out "bronyi, bronyi," knows what is associated with whiteness and what is associated with blackness. Progress does not simply mean better; it means becoming monogamous, becoming Christian, getting the baby off your back, feeding it with a bottle, wearing a white wedding dress for your marriage ceremony, straightening your hair, building with cement blocks instead of mud and thatch, eating with a spoon, wearing jeans, using computers, and driving fast cars.

The schools and churches are complicit in this upward march toward modernity and progress. They teach the children that to succeed they must adopt these new ways. They must obey time, wear shoes, pray to a white Jesus, engage in monogamous marriage, and live prudent, God-fearing, modest, hard-working lives. Weber wrote of The Protestant Ethic and the Spirit of Capitalism in his famous opus. He said, "A rationalized capitalistic enterprise implies two things: a disciplined labor force and the regularized investment of capital" (Weber 1930, xi). At the turn of the 20th century, theorists were concerned about the effects of this new capitalism. Here we are at the beginning of a new millennium. Are we still forcing some into Weber's "iron cage," where we are all forced to live increasingly bureaucratic lives in which "spontaneous enjoyment" is expunged?

Many argue that Ghanaians are free to choose, that they make their own decisions, and that they are choosing the "iron cage." This is a long argument, but what is clear is that in the safe haven of Ghanaian social and family life, the virtues of modernity far outweigh their hazards. It still appears as if one can have this technology with its virtues and without its sacrifices—sacrifices of time, energy, and personhood that capitalist production implies. Gyekye says, "The cultivation of a scientific and technological outlook is imperative if Africa is to participate significantly in the modern world." (Gyekye 1996, 174) However, he believes that this scientific outlook can be encouraged and achieved within the context of a modified traditional Ghanaian/African cultural context. If we look at the recent efforts among young Americans to reclaim roots, find ancestors, and connect with long-lost ethnic

Selling food and asbestos

identities, we might be tempted to say that history has demonstrated Gyekye's conviction. He, nevertheless, says that many of the values and practices of traditional Africa can be accommodated into "the scheme of African modernity, even if they must undergo some refinement and pruning to become fully harmonious with the spirit of modern culture and to function most satisfactorily within that culture." (Gyekye 1969, 174)

No one knows what the future holds. An Akan proverb says:

> A person cutting a path does not know that the part that has been cleared behind him is crooked.

(Gyekye 1996, 167)

Only those who come later will be able to look back and see that the path the ancestors have cut to move ahead is crooked. The ancestors are not always correct, so the path should be open to constant modification. Nonetheless, a path must be made so that people can follow, and it is certain that the Fante are clearing that path with great passion, great hope, great faith, and great charity.

THE CARRYING

The day finally arrives for the carrying. The night before, Adwoa, Afua, and I arrive at the village at about 7:00 p.m. It is a dark night, and deep into the forest, it seems even darker. A few lanterns glow from open windows, but mostly it is very dark and still. The village looks the same. Only a canopy of palm branches, held up by bamboo poles and forming a covered arena, indicates a festival. Women are quietly cooking over open fires or coal pots, children are carrying the last bit of water, and men and older children are quietly chatting under the moonless sky.

We are escorted to our house, the one-room sitting room/bedroom that is now also used as a chief's palace. This is our home for the next 2 days. After sitting for a while, Nkrumah says that we will go to see the chief if I can make it in the dark. Of course I can make it, so we start out. The girls are asked to stay behind. As I stumble over rocks and gullies in the road, making my way tentatively to the chief's palace, I am struck by the reality of life without lights. Because it is always dark by 6:30 p.m. and because Abaasans do not have money for torches, kerosene, or candles, a great deal of life takes place in the dark. There are no movie theaters, no arcades, no stores, no malls, no cafes or real bars, and few televisions and radios. People are forced to invent their own entertainment, and their lives are simplified. The next village is miles away, they do not have cars, and few even have bicycles. So when they come in from the farm, they have plenty of time—time to talk, to cook, to eat, to play games, to tell stories, and to just sit. They are not rushing through the evening meal to jump into their cars to go somewhere. It is no wonder that they are so eager for electricity. The darkness and quiet are palpable. However, once again I cannot help but ponder the enormous change that they will experience when it comes. I cannot help but wonder whether they know what this change really means.

We arrive at the chief's palace. Except for me, everyone takes off his or her shoes as is appropriate when greeting a chief. I have learned that I must not. As I am led to my stool, the chief greets me enthusiastically. He smiles a huge smile, pumps my hand up and down many times, and murmurs hearty greetings. We all sit—I on my pillow-covered stool, he on his stool, and the rest on chairs around the periphery of the room. The room is the same as it was 2 years ago. Only the items on the small table have changed. There are a comb, a tin of shoe polish, and some matches. The chief is a humble and sincere man. He does not have pretenses. His palace is small, simple, and spare. We greet formally and state our mission. The chief welcomes me warmly, they tell me, and is happy to see me. However, it is too dark in his room, so I must return to my lodgings, and he will meet us there. So out we all go, back into the dark night and down the sandy hill to where we have just come. I am not sure about this shift because his room does not seem any darker than mine, and we have already stumbled through the dark to get there. However, no one says anything, and I do not ask.

The chief soon arrives. We have beer and minerals and chat for a short time, after which they all take their leave. Adwoa, Afua, and I are alone in the room with a lantern, and it is so hot. There is no breeze, and the little rectangular, tin-roofed, cement, airless room holds the heat like the oven that I always claim it is. The music system is now turned on and plays the loud, popular music all night and until the end of the celebration on Sunday. We have gone to great expense to obtain it, the accompanying generator, and petrol. However, we are not allowed to attend the dancing. Nana must not be seen at public events of this sort. By 10:00 p.m., after singing a few hymns by way of entertainment, we settle down to sleep until we are awakened early in the morning to prepare for the big event. Adwoa and I share the same bed, and when I awake to the blasting of the music at 3:00 a.m., my pillow is soaked. It is so hot, I feel I will suffocate, and I wonder again at this terrible ironic cruelty. How do people stand to live like this? It is not as if they do not suffer. As soon as they can, they get a fan. Some, mostly in the cities, even have air-conditioning. But why? I go out into the night air, and it is cool and clear and smells sweet. How were people tricked into thinking that they should build with concrete and tin (or asbestos)? How did they come to admire these houses? If they can, they trade the soft glow of the lantern for the assaultive glare of fluorescent tubes. Poor people all over the "third world" are living in these hot, airless, unattractive little houses because they are modern—they are a sign of prosperity, advancement, and privilege. As I drift into a fitful sleep, I wish that I would not have these thoughts.

Morning comes and Mr. Nkrumah is cheerfully at our door. I am escorted to my outdoor shower and bucket of water. He assures me that all is going well and that I need only to wait in our room for the ladies to call me to dress me. We wait and wait and wait. There is a "harvest" at 8:00 a.m., and I am to be carried at 1:00 p.m. By 11:00 a.m. nothing has happened, and they have forgotten to feed us. Soon we are told that all is well and are given our morning tea. People begin to arrive, and my friends and colleagues are graciously escorted to my room for refreshment. Huge

Queen Mother celebration

Queen Mother celebration

piles of food are brought to me by 12:00. It is rice, stew, fu fu, soup, and yam. It is shared among the guests, and there is lively chatter accompanying the eating and drinking. Everyone wonders about the harvest, but we are assured that it will be successful. The harvest is a euphemism for a fund raiser, usually done by the churches. Unfortunately, it is not successful.

Soon the women hustle me off to the church where I am dressed. I should be taken to the river and washed clean, but out of concession for my foreignness, I suspect, they once again take me to a space indoors. Once again, I am stripped and adorned with gold, kente, beads, and a headband. Once again Mrs. Baidoo is there to assist. This time, however, instead of being taken straight to the palanquine, I am taken to a sacred spot in the woods where they pour libation and pray to the gods. After the prayers and libation, I am put into the palanquine with my two little girls, and we are hoisted into the air. The brass band is there, and the people cheer, shout, and run after me as we wind our way through the village. Mr. Nkrumah admonishes me to dance well because there are many dignitaries there, but I am afraid that I disappoint him. Nevertheless, the crowd is wild. They always tell me afterward that I dance well and that the dress and the dance are exactly like a real African, but I really don't believe them. In true Ghanaian style, they are generous and kind and overlook deficiencies. I am always grateful to them because, in all honesty, I feel very foolish. I always do what they tell me and try to appear as if it is natural, but I cannot help but feel like an impostor. In some ways I know that I am an impostor, but they never treat me like one. They treat me like the real thing.

Afterward I am told that the celebration was a huge success. The village loves me, the chief loves me, and they are all such nice, kind people. "Oh, your village people are so kind," my friends say. The chief could be jealous, or he could ridicule. Instead, in his speech he says such kind things about this foreign Nana. I am gratified to hear these words. The celebration is extremely expensive and took a great deal of time and energy to prepare. Often I wonder if it is the right thing. Why spend so much money when the village is so poor? But then I remember that it is an important ritual, and rituals are what makes life meaningful for people. Ritual is what holds us together. It is what teaches us about ourselves and reconfirms that which we already know about ourselves. It makes us feel like one people, like we have a connection with the past and the future, and it teaches our young who they are. Without the rituals, people begin to feel disconnected and purposeless, as if life has no meaning. Without rituals, we forget who we are. These people are people with history. They live their history every day, and they revive it at times like this. Each time they carry their chief, they retell the story of who they are. They evoke the ancestors, they remember the past. They repeat the drama that they have enacted from their beginnings. They give me mashed yam and boiled eggs, which are put to my lips three times and then thrown to the winds. They take the yam and the eggs to the sacred place where they are food for the gods. I wear the rings, necklaces, bracelets, and leg beads that they have used for all the Nanas before me. They use the same kind of palanquine, umbrella, and kente that they always have used. They blow the horn of a cow, and the carriers of the paloquine wrap their cloth in a way only the palanquine bearers wrap.

Even though Mr. Yaro says that this celebration is the "light" version, it serves its purpose. It unites the people into one people once again. It says that they all come from the same ancestors, that they have one chief and one queen mother, and that they are a people. They have a rich and deep history, they have an important present, and they have a future. In the future, their children and grandchildren will re-enact this same drama, and their lives will have continuity and meaning. The village will carry on, even when those present today do not. The ritual reaffirms the importance of the village, the people in the face of the frailty, and the vulnerability and the mortality of the individuals. In this way even death cannot be feared because it is a part of the inevitable process of life, and it does not mean an ending but a new kind of beginning. Each one who dies becomes a part of history—a part of the immortality of the ancestors.

It is a joyous occasion and one of reaffirmation, renewed commitments, reconnections, and renewal. It reconnects everyone to the past, to each other, and to a shared future. In this way, I cannot participate with them. But it does not matter because I help to make the connections possible. It really doesn't matter who sits in the paloquine. The important thing is the ceremony, the ritual. The important thing is that someone sits in the paloquine who is called Nana, who wears kente, and who carries a sword.

It is an important event and a great honor. I am touched, as I continue to be, by the willingness of Abaasians to take me into their village and their family. I leave feeling tired but with a renewed faith in humanity. Here in Abaasa there remains the ability for human beings to relate to each other, to accept each other, and to connect. There are still people who will insist that we are all one, we are all the same, and that, despite some superficial characteristics of difference, I still belong to these people and my ancestors still came from this place. Chagnon wrote a book called *The Fierce People,* and although I understand the hazards, I am tempted to call these people The Gentle

People. The day after I arrive back at my bungalow, Nkrumah is at my door. Nana is leaving for Kumasi, he tells me. He must say farewell to me before he leaves. They return the next day. Nana is dressed in a black cloth, and Nkrumah is agitated. There is a great tragedy. Our great Muslim friend, Mr. Mohammed, has died. He went to his field with his wife to prepare it for planting. It is nearing the big rainy season, and people are burning their fields in preparation. While he was burning, his clothing caught on fire, and he burned to death. I couldn't believe it. I asked, "Do you mean Mr. Mohammed who was just in the hospital with a hernia?" We worked so hard to get him well. He held my hand in the hospital and wept because he thought he would die. He lived, only to be burned in his field. His wife is prostrate, they tell me. It happened only yesterday when Nkrumah was heading home from my house. The funeral is Sunday. I must attend. Nana will return to Kumasi, so he cannot be there. I tell him I will attend although I am still in disbelief.

Life is very perilous here. People die all the time. They get sick, they do not have money to take care of their sickness, and they die. They die young and old. We are always amazed, those of us from the West, at how many young people die. Here is a man, clearing off his fields, and he dies. His wife went to and from the hospital during his illness, carrying food and trying to find money. Now she is left with a small son and no money because everything they had was spent on his illness. What will she do? "Well," says Nkrumah, "It is up to us, her family, to care for her." But in the meantime, there is the funeral. It will cost money, and who has it? I can't bear to hear it. How do they stand it? How do you go from trouble to trouble? Mr. Nkrumah tells me that he just turns it all over to God. He says that we, in Africa, have to turn it over to God. God does what is best and helps us through.

Where is God? I want to know.

THE FUNERAL

Black and red figures descend from taxis and tro tros. Women, at least a dozen, are pounding fu fu with their long pestles and large wooden mortars. They are laughing, punching, and joking. They are outside in a group like a factory of pounders. Men wear black, red, yellow, and gold cloths; flowing white, yellow, and blue Muslim dress with caps; or jeans or slacks and shirts. They are counting the money, or they are sitting in family groups, drinking apeteche, laughing, and talking.

It is a clear, bright Sunday. The sky is vivid blue. It has not rained, so roads are dusty as we make our way to the village of Mohammed's family. Mr. Nkrumah is dressed in a knit shirt of contemporary design with khaki trousers and new black boots. I ask him why he is not in black or red and why he does not wear his cloth. I think that for such an occasion he would be thus clad. He says that he would wear the cloth, but because he will be called on to run about here and there, to serve people, and to make sure things are going well, he cannot wear the cloth. The cloth is too cumbersome and does not allow for enough movement.

As we enter the village, we see many men in the cloth. They tug on it and adjust it as they sit, stand, and talk. The funeral is going on, but it seems confusing. There are groups of people scattered around the village. In the center is a palm frond and bamboo canopy under which sit Mohammed's family. They seem to be having a service. The bereaved wife is huddled in a corner of a room where she receives guests. We join the family gathering and shake hands while someone speaks in the center. He has spoken already about the deceased and is now speaking about Islam, I am told. We sit for some time. It is hot. The sun forces its way through the palm and provides us no rest. After some time, we ask to be excused, and I am led to a room where I am served drinks and food. The room is dark and stifling. There is a fan, but it only stirs around the hot air. The room is typical with chairs, a table, and a bed. It is dirty. There are clothes and piles of things around. I am greeted by different groups of people who come to welcome me. Just before I eat the rice, fish, and meat, the family of the man come to greet me. The leader carries the staff of the clan with a parrot on the top. They are all in styles of cloth with black in it. They stop at the door, extend formal greetings, and say that they have come to greet Nana. I am not expected to say anything. I am here representing the village of Abaasa. They bring two bottles of soft drink as a welcoming gesture. Because they are Muslim, they bring no alcohol. My linguist thanks them on my behalf and accepts the drinks with my gratitude. They sit for only a few minutes and say that they must meet others.

When they leave, all others leave the room, and I am left to eat. When this is accomplished, I am led back to the center where the man's family sits. My linguist now presents my money offering. He holds up the money to let everyone know how much I have contributed to the family. Their spokesman accepts the money on behalf of the family and expresses gratitude. Shortly thereafter, my linguist stands before the assembled crowd (mostly men) and begs them to allow us to leave. We are to visit the family of the wife. We are granted permission and travel to another section of the village where the family of the wife sits. These are all men. My linguist again greets them formally and again presents our offering. I give the same amount to each side of the family. They thank me through my linguist. I never say a word. There are more drinks and some apeteche. One of the family members then wishes to formally dismiss the group. He comes before us, takes off one shoe in respect, and presents apeteche and four bottles of Sprite. All agree that this group can now disassemble.

Nkrumah, however, goes to a meeting where they decide who will take the place of the deceased. He says that the husband's family agrees to take care of her and her children for 3 months. After that, her care will revert back to her family. They have not decided yet whether or not she is allowed to stay in the house. Her husband has fields, orange groves, and a house, but because the Fante are matrilineal, this all belongs to the family of the man. I am told that if it rains in the next week or two, the citrus can be saved. However, if the rains do not come on time, all will be ruined, and there will be no income until the next growing season. The widow and her children do not belong to the deceased's clan, so she does not inherit from her husband. The senior member of her family, a teacher, looks to me and says that after the 3 months, if the family makes her leave the house, then it is up to him and me to take care of her. He looks meaningfully at me when he says this. In other words, we have both inherited a wife and children. Her family is now responsible for this woman who has not only lost a husband, but who has lost a livelihood, a place to stay, property, and social security. When I express sorrow at this great tragedy, I am always given the same response: God knows everything. God does what is best.

We have come full circle. We end where we began, with a funeral. Birth, mar-riage, queen mother ceremonies, death, and back again. The cycle repeats itself. Life is a preparation for death, but death is not an end—it is a new kind of beginning. Death is a part of life. The Sankofa bird is an important Akan symbol. It reminds the Fante that they must keep an eye on what went before, remember from where they come, and recognize that the past is part of the present. In life it is important is to be able to look back with grace. Gold or diamonds are not what count. What counts is to be able to look back at a life lived well. When one dies, one must be prepared. One must have one's life in order and must have lived one's life with care. You never know when God will take you, so you must always be prepared. You must always live your life well. You must watch and pray.

Bibliography

Aidoo, Ama Ata. 1993. *Changes: A Love Story*. New York: Feminist Press at the City of New York.

Ake, Claude. 1981. *A Political Economy of Africa*. Harlow, Essex: Longman Group, Ltd.

Appiah, Kwame Anthony. 1992. *In My Father's House: Africa in the Philosophy of Culture*. New York: Oxford University Press.

Asamoa, Ansa. 1989. *The Ewe of Ghana and Togo on the Eve of Colonialism*. Accra, Ghana: Ghana Publishing Corporation.

———. 1996. *Socio-Economic Development Strategies of Independent African Countries: The Ghana Experience*. Accra: Ghana Universities Press.

Ayittey, George. 1998. *Africa in Crisis*. New York: St. Martin's Press.

Benedict, Ruth. 1934. *Patterns of Culture*. New York: Houghton Mifflin

Berreman, Gerald, ed. 1981. *Social Inequality: Comparative and Developmental Approaches*. New York: Academic Press.

Boas, Franz. 1938. *The Mind of the Primitive*. New York: Macmillan Co.

Bohannan, Paul. 1964. *Africa and Africans*. New York: Natural History Press.

Bowles, Samuel and Herbert Gintis. 1976. *Schooling in Capitalist America: Educational Reform and the Contradictions of Economic Life*. New York: Basic Books, Inc.

Brazelton, T. Berry and Bertrand G. Cramer. 1990. *The Earliest Relationship: Parents, Infants and the Drama of Early Attachment*. Reading, MA: Addison-Wesley.

Brogger, Jan. 1992. Nazare: *Women and Men in a Prebureacratic Portuguese Fishing Village*. New York: Harcourt Brace.

Bronfenbrenner, Uri. 1970. *Two Worlds of Childhood: U.S. and U.S.S.R.* New York: Russell Sage Foundation.

Bruner, J.S. 1961. The Cognitive Consequences of Early Sensory Deprivation. In *Sensory Deprivation*. Solomon, P., et al, eds. Cambridge, MA: Harvard University Press.

Cabral, Amilcar. 1979. *Unity and Struggle*. New York: Monthly Review Press.

Clark, Gracia. 1994. *Onions Are My Husband: Survival and Accumulation in West African Market Women*. Chicago: University of Chicago Press.

———. 1999. Mothering, Work and Gender in Urban Asante Ideology and Practice. *American Anthropologist*, 101(4):717-729.

Daily Graphic. 1999. September 26, Accra, Ghana.

Davidson, Basil. 1970. *The African Genius: An Introduction to African Cultural and Social History*. Boston: Atlantic Monthly Press.

———. 1992. *The Black Man's Burden: Africa and the Curse of the Nation-State*. New York: Random House, Inc.

Dubois, W.E.B. 1969. *The Soul of Black Folk*. New York: Penguin Books.

Eboyi-Anza. 1997. *Religious Practices in Ghana*. Accra: Ghana Universities Press.

Ellison, Ralph. 1993. *Invisible Man*. New York: Book of the Month Club.

Evans-Pritchard, E.E. 1951. *Social Anthropology*. New York: Free Press.

Fanon, Franz. 1967. *Black Skin, White Masks*. New York: Norton.

Fernandez-Kelly, Maria Patricia. 1983. *For We Are Sold, I and My People*. Albany, NY: State University of New York Press.

Forde, Daryll and A.R. Radcliffe-Brown. 1950. *African Systems of Kinship and Marriage*. London: Oxford University Press.

Forde, Daryll and G.I. Jones. 1950. *The Igbo and Ibibio-Speaking Peoples of South-Eastern Nigeria.* London: International African Institute.

Fortes, Myer. 1949. *The Web of Kinship among the Tallensi.* London: Oxford University Press.

Fortes, M. and E.E. Evans-Pritchard, eds. 1940. *African Political Systems.* London: Oxford University Press.

Frank, Andre Gunder. 1967. *Capitalism and Underdevelopment in Latin America. Historical Studies of Chile and Brazil.* New York: Monthly Review Press.

Freire, Paulo. 1981. *Pedagogy of the Oppressed.* New York: Continuum.

———. 1983. *Education for Critical Consciousness.* New York: Continuum.

Gates, Henry Louis, Jr. 1989. *The Signifying Monkey: A Theory of African-American Literary Criticism.* New York: Oxford University Press.

Geertz, Clifford. 1973. *The Interpretation of Cultures: Selected Essays.* New York: Basic Books.

Goffman, Erving. 1974. *Frame Analysis: An Essay on the Organization of Experience.* New York: Harper and Row.

Gould, Stephen Jay. 1981. *The Mismeasure of Man.* New York and London: W.W. Norton and Co.

Gyeke, Kwame. 1996. *African Cultural Values: An Introduction.* Philadelphia, Pa./Accra, Ghana: Sankofa Publishing Company.

Harris, Marvin. 1980. *Cultural Materialism: The Struggle for a Science of Culture.* New York: Vintage Books.

Herskovits, Melville and Harwitz, M., eds. 1964. *Economic Transition in Africa.* Evanston, Il: Northwestern University Press.

Hurston, Zora Neale. 1990. *Tell My Horse.* New York: Perennial Library

———. 1991. *Their Eyes Were Watching God.* Urbana, IL: University of Illinois Press.

Jenkins, Richard. 1997. *Rethinking Ethnicity: Arguments and Explorations.* London: Sage Publications.

Kroeber, A. 1939. *Cultural and Natural Areas of Native North America.* Berkeley: University of California Publications in American Archaeology and Ethnology.

Little, Kenneth. 1965. *Race and Society.* Paris: Unesco.

———. 1973. *African Women in Towns: An Aspect of Africa's Social Revolution.* London, New York: Cambridge University Press.

Lundgren, Nancy. 1999. Learning to Become. In Competent: Children in Belize Speak Out. In Jenkins, Richard, ed. *Questions of Competence: Culture, Classification and Intellectual Ability.* Cambridge, MA: Cambridge University Press.

———. 1992. Children, Race, and Inequality: The Colonial Legacy in Belize. *Journal of Black Studies,* 23(1), 86-106.

Magubane, Bernard. 1981. *The Political Economy of Race and Class in South Africa.* New York: Monthly Review Press.

Malinowski, Bronislaw. 1964. *Argonauts of the Western Pacific.* London: G. Routledge and Sons, Ltd; New York: E.P. Dutton and Co.

Marable, Manning. 1983. *How Capitalism Underdeveloped Black America.* Boston: South End Press.

Mazrui, Ali A. 1986. *The Africans: A Triple Heritage.* Boston: Little Brown.

Mead, Margaret. 1928. *Coming of Age in Samoa.* New York: Morrow.

———. 1935. *Sex and Temperament in Three Primitive Societies.* New York: Morrow.

Memmi, A. 1965. *The Colonizer and the Colonized.* Boston: Beacon.

Mies, Maria. 1986. *Patriarchy and Accumulation on a World Scale: Women in the International Division of labor.* London: Zed Books.

Montagu, Ashley. 1974. *Man's Most Dangerous Myth: The Fallacy of Race.* New York: Oxford University Press.

Morrison, Toni. 1994. *The Bluest Eye.* New York: Knopf: Distributed by Random House.

Naipaul, V.S. 1984, c1959. *Miguel Street.* New York: Vintage Books.

Prah, Kwesi. 1998. *Beyond the Color Line.* New York: Africa World Press.

Prah, Mansah. 1999. Women and Girl's Responses to Violence. In Appiah, Dorcas Coker and Kathy Cusack, ed. *Breaking the Silence and Challenging Myths of Violence Against Women in Ghana.* Accra: Gender Studies and Human Rights Documentation Centre.

Quarm, S.E. 1999. The Daily Graphic, Thursday, July 22, Accra, Ghana.

Quarshie, Stephen Aidoo. 1999. The Mirror, Saturday, July 10, Accra, Ghana.

Radcliffe-Brown, A.R. and C.D. Forde, eds. 1950. *African Systems of Kinship and Marriage.* London: Oxford University Press.

Robertson, Claire and Iris Berger, eds. 1986. *Women and Class in Africa.* New York: Africana Publishing Co.

Rodney, Walter. 1981. *How Europe Underdeveloped Africa.* Washington, D.C: Howard University Press.

Rostow, W.W. 1962. *The Stages of Economic Growth: A Non-Communist Manifesto.* Cambridge, MA: Cambridge University Press.

Said, Edward. 1994. *Orientalism.* New York: Vintage Books.

Sapir, E. 1921. *Language.* New York: Harcourt Brace.

Saul, John S. and Colin Leys. 1999. Sub-Saharan Africa in Global Capitalism. *Monthly Review Press,* (51)3:13-30.

Tronick, E.G., et al. 1987. Multiple Caretaking of Efe (Pygmy) Infants. *American Anthropologist,* 89(1):96-104.

Uchendu, Victor C. 1965. *The Igbo of Southeast Nigeria.* New York: Holt, Rinehart and Winston.

Wallerstein, Immanuel. 1980. *The Modern World-System II.* New York: Academic Press.

Watkins, Kevin. 1995. World Bank and IMF Responsible for African Misery. Notebooks for Study and Research. *International Institute for Research and Education,* 24/25: 93-99.

Weber, Max. 1975. *The Protestant Ethic and the Spirit of Capitalism.* Translated by T. Parsons. New York: Scribners.

Whiting, Beatrice B. and Carolyn P. Edwards. 1988. *Children of Different Worlds: The Formation of Social Behavior.* Cambridge, MA: Harvard University Press.

Waldman, Linda. 1993. *My Neighborhood: The Words and Pictures of Inner-City Children.* Chicago: Hyde Park Bank Foundation.

Wolf, Eric. 1982. *Europe and the People Without History.* Berkeley: University of California Press.

Glossary

Abusua: Matrilineal clan

Akwaaba: Directly translated, this means "You are welcome." It is used to welcome someone into your home or on their return from an absence.

Apeteche: A home brewed alcoholic beverage usually made from corn but sometimes from
bananas.

Asafo: CompanyAll male military group.

Bore Hole: The underground source of water created by digging a deep hole and tapping
the underlying water with a pump.

Bronyi: A term used to refer to foreigners of European or American extraction. It can mean
"white" person or it can mean foreigner. Ghanaians typically say that the term is de-
scriptive and complimentary, possessing neither negative nor positive connotations.
Usually it is used to mean "white" person and Americans are frequently surprised when
the term is used to refer to an American of African descent. Pronounced: Brooni.

Cedi: Ghanaian currency. It is weak against the dollar and declines in value almost daily.
Pronounced: C.D.

Chop: A term used for food. It may be used as a noun or a verb: "To go chop," "A chop
bar." It can also be used in other contexts such as "He chopped the money."

Cloth: In its broad sense, it is a length of fabric, usually African. Often it is used in refer-
ence to the long piece of traditional cloth used by men as a garment.

Coal Pot: A small outdoor brazier type cooking apparatus. It is made of clay or iron with a
section for coal, on top of which is set a pot, with or without a grille.

Day Names: The name every child acquires at birth by virtue of his or her gender and day
upon which she or he is born. Usually this name is used at home and a "Christian"
name is used at school and in other public contexts.

Foo Foo: A common and favored food made by pounding yam or cassava and plantain with
a very large mortar and pestle. It is served fresh and hot with a soup or stew.

Foos: Colloquial word meaning used, imported clothing. Someone told me that it literally
means, "dead white men's clothes." I have never seen it written and am spelling it the
way it is pronounced in English.

Gari: Ground cassava. A staple food used also with soup or stew or as a kind of cereal.

Gong Gong Man: The man who beats the gong gong to announce coming events or give instructions to the village. The gong is a piece of metal hollowed out and beaten with a
metal stick. This person is akin to the town crier. He is important as a messenger and a
kind of spokesperson for the village. Simple messages can be understood simply from the
rhythm of the gong gong, in a manner akin to that of talking drums or telegraph machines.

Ground Nuts: Americans call these "peanuts."

JSS: The initials used for Junior Secondary School. It is comparable with "middle School"
in the United States.

Kaaba: A woman's garment worn as a top to a long skirt. The Kaaba and slit are considered
the "traditional" dress of Ghanaian women. The Kaaba can be simple or very elaborate,
usually with full sleeves, worn by almost all women at some time. In villages and in
the market, women wear them for work. Other women may wear them only for their almost compulsory use at weddings, funerals, church and other formal occasions.

Kenky: A very popular and cheap food made from fermented corn and wrapped in plantain
leaves.

Kente: The special woven cloth used traditionally by chiefs but also by all men for weddings
and other special events and given as gifts and traded. It is usually worn by men, but is
also used by women. Men wear it draped as a cloth. Women may wrap it around their
slits, but more usually wear it as an accessory over their shoulders. These days it may also
be made into a coat or dress or trim on a dress, but this is not its traditional use.

Malta: A malt-based, non-alcoholic drink that is very popular. It is more expensive than a soft drink, or mineral as it is called, and, therefore, more prestigious to offer guests.

Nana: The name reserved for a chief. Because the Queen Mother is also a chief, the title is likewise given to her. It is, however, sometimes used as a name for both boys and girls.

Omanhen: One of several titles given to chiefs, usually reserved for paramount chief. The local chief is usually referred to as Ohen, the queen mother as Obaahemba.

Paanu: Bread

Palanquine: A sled-like conveyance decorated with various types of cloth, often kente. It is used to carry chiefs, including queen mothers, during important celebrations. While seated in the paloquine, chiefs, and usually two small girls, dance in a particular manner, telling the people that "to my right and to my left, all belongs to me" and God watches over us all. Eight men are enlisted to carry it on their shoulders. Pronounced: Paroquin

Politin rubber: The common name for the black plastic bag that is used by market women and shop owners. The bag usually must be bought and is useful as a suitcase and for other carrying needs. Sometimes it is shortened to simply "rubber," which is a term also used for plastic receptacles of many kinds. It probably is a local derivation of polyurethane. I am spelling it as it sounds to American ears.

Pouring libation: Literally pouring an alcoholic beverage, usually gin or schnapps, while praying to God. It is done on special occasions, usually by the chief's linguist and is a way of paying homage to God and evoking the good will, guidance and support of whoever watches over the lives of living people.

Slit: A long skirt, usually to the ankle, worn by women. It is traditionally made by seam-stresses who use two uncut yards of a piece of wax print fabric. The traditional wax print fabrics are usually sold by the "half piece" (six yards) or by the "whole piece" (twelve yards). Out of this is made a two yard slit and a two yard kaaba. The other two yards is used to wrap around the skirt, as a shawl if it is cool or as a carrying vessel for a baby. A drawstring is used at the waist of the slit. Sometimes if the cloth is very fancy and the occasion is dressy, the two extra yards may be folded and worn over the shoulder. The traditional wax print cloth is different from other fabrics such as Batik in that its design conveys particular messages and certain colors and styles are worn for particular occasions. For example, a white and blue print is used to mark the birth of a child. A particular favorite of mine conveys the message "good beads don't rattle," re-ferring to the beads that a girl child wears around her hips. If the beads are authentic, good ones, they will not make a noise when she walks. It carries the same meaning as the proverb "an empty drum makes the most noise."

SSS: Abbreviation for Senior Secondary School. It is comparable with High School in the United States.

Stool: When a chief (or queen mother) becomes enstooled, he or she receives a "stool." It is carved of one piece of wood, is sometimes passed down from their predecessors, and is decorated with various appropriate symbols. Chiefs (or queen mothers) must always have their stools with them, should sit on them when entertaining guests, and should use a stool when visiting. There is a long history of stools and stool making and meaning.

Tro Tro: A contemporary means of transportation. It is a small bus that, for a small sum, conveys its occupants around town and from village to village and town to town. These buses are always very crowded and are usually in poor repair, sometimes traveling in the crablike sideways style referred to in this text and by others.

AKAN DAY NAMES

DAY	BOY	GIRL
Monday	Kojo/Kodwo/Kwadwo/Kwadjo	Adwoa
Tuesday	Kwabena/Kobena	Abena/Araba
Wednesday	Kwaku	Akua/Ekuwa
Thursday	Yaw/Dow	Yaa/Aba
Friday	Kofi	Afua/Efuwa
Saturday	Kwame	Ama
Sunday	Kwesi/Akwesi	Akosua/Esi

Index

A

Abaasa, 54-56
  people of, 13, 20
Abokyi, Efuwa, 73
Aboradze clan, 73
Abura Dunkwa, 96
Accidents, 26
Accra, 1, 28
Action, call to, 54
Adams, Mr., 19
African anthem, 10
African tradition, 34
Afua, 6
AIDS, 98
Akan group, 72
Akotokyir, 54-56, 69
  founding, 73
  new chief, 140-141
  people, 13
Akotokyir Catholic Church, 7
Akrah, Mr., 20
Altar boys, 8
Animosity, between brothers, 84
Anthony, 108
Anthropologists, structural-functionalists, 37
Appearance, 18
Assembly Man, 24
Ato, 3-5, 7
Automobile repairs, 28

B

Babies
  African compared with Western, 79
  carrying, 77
  nursing, 77-78
Baidoo family, 3, 5, 7
  background, 72
  Mary, 35
  Mr., 37
  thinking, 33
Banking, 1, 9
Bargaining, 24-25
Batik, 15
Big Men
  appeal, 94-95
  corruption, 98
  status, 94-95
Bird cage, 41-45
  bargaining for, 45
  factory, 43-44
  makers, 43
  purchasing, 44
Birkenstock sandals, 16
Boas, Franz, 38

Boys, 66
Brass band, 12
Broom, sending, 54
Brothers, animosity between, 84
Bronyi, 34, 40, 43
Bucket bath, 61
Buildings
  construction, 70
  lean-to style, 83
  modern, 83

C

Cape Coast
  atmosphere, 1
  schools, 102
Capitalism principles, 25
Caring, 49
Carrying, 139, 144-148
  dressing for, 146
  purpose, 147
  success, 146-147
Cassava, 9, 21
Catholic ceremony, 8-9
Cedis, 9, 20
Celebration
  carrying, 144-148
  preparation for, 137
Chairman, 20
Change, 34-35, 137
  effects, 37
  responses, 37
Charles, 109
Chief
  obligations, 53
  qualities, 52
  palace, 46-58, 83
  role in disputes, 58
  visits to, 53-54
Children
  adult protection, 115
  behavior, 114
  education, 116-120
  Fante view, 123
  play and, 114
  problems with, 82
  socialization, 114-122
  stories of, 106-109
  voices of, 107-109
Choirs, 3, 10
Choristers, 5-6
Christian hymn, 10
Christmas, 140
Churches. *See also* Worship, houses of
  in Abassa, 127
  drumming and dancing in, 128

Churches, cont'd
  services, 62-63
  speeches in, 128
Church of Pentecost, 63
Church of Twelve Apostles, 42
Clans, Aboradze, 73
Clarke, Ben, 22, 96-97
Classrooms
  described, 117-118
  fan installation, 1
Clothing, 34-35, 59. *See also* Dress
  change in, 16-17
  Ghanaian concept, 16-17
  imports, 15
  industry, 15-16
  rules regarding, 16
  T-shirts, 56
Coal, for cooking, 103
Colonialism, 8
  experience of, 49-50
  modernity of, 7
  race and, 120-121
Confidence, 114-116
Consensus, 51
Cooking, coal and, 103
Corruption, 98
Courage, 66, 67
Courtship, 75-79
Culture
  awareness, 92-93
  behavior and, 93-94
  infant care and, 79
  identity, 17
  shock, 94
  tradition and, 94
  understanding, 38

D
Daily Graphic, 86
Death, causes, 3
Decision making, 51
  skills, 64
Development, 32
Dignity, 47
Discussions, animated, 49
Disputes
  resolving, 57-58
  supporters in, 57-58
Dormitory, 103
Dress. *See also* Clothing
  codes, 17
  social behavior and, 16
  vestments, 8

E
Easter Monday, 140
Economy, 31
  mixed strategy, 33
Education
  calendar, 116

culture and, 119-120
curriculum, 116
fees, 117
monetary support, 117
quality of, 117
system, 116-118
tertiary, 117
view of, 116
Efutu Afehe, 107
Elders, 5
Electricity, 106
  acquiring, 30
  company, 26
  need for, 21
Electricity poles, 18
  price negotiations, 24
  purchase, 21-25
English, using, 12
Enstooling ceremony, 40
Esoteric, Philip, 15, 17
Essies, 12
Evil, 129

F
Family
  -oriented society, 78
  planning, 6
  relations, 85
  ties, 93
  workings of, 74
Fante, 22
Farm produce, 20-21
Fathers,
 death of, 104
 and sons, 4, 81
Fear, 55
Female. *See also* Women
  Ghanaian definition,
    123
  qualities, 98
  work, 9
Fighting, verbal, 66
Food, 113
  industry, 16
Foos, 16
Foreign aid, 32
Foreign missionaries, 8
Forgiveness, 29, 49, 85
Fra Fra, 69
Francis, 1
Funerals, 104-106, 148-150
  cloth, 3
Future, 143

G
Gender, 86-94, 122-123
Ghana
  anniversary celebration, 141-142
  colonial, 32
  imports and exports, 32

language, 12
matrilineal groups, 72
people, 6
regions, 72
Ghanaian reality, 39
Ghanaian Wax Print fabric, 2
Gifts, 45
Global economy, 17, 88
competing in, 18
Gloria, 107
God, concept of, 131
Good Friday, 140
Government, 30
politics and, 57-58
popular, 49
services, 30
system, 32
Greetings, 83-84
Gregorian chant, 10
Grinding machine, 21

H
Health care, 98
Holy Child, 95
Homecoming, typical, 2
Homo sapiens, 49
Horticulture
groups, 74
societies, 78
Hospitality, 25
Hospitalization
costs, 28
recuperating from, 139
Humility, 67
Hygiene, 26

I
Identity, 65
IFPRI. *See* International Food Policy Research
Institute
IMF. *See* International Monetary Fund
Industrial Revolution, 142
Infants
care and cultural change, 79
mortality rate, 98
Insults, 83
International Food Policy Research Institute
(IFPRI), 86
International Monetary Fund (IMF), 31
Intervillage affairs, 64
Issues, resolving, 57

J
Jersey cattle, 7
Jewkwa, 21, 22
Jokes, 44
Joyce, 108-109
Junior Secondary School, 23, 72, 82,
102

K
Kaaba, 15
Kente cloth, 9
Kente Kaaba, 58
Kinship, 79
Kissing, in public, 91-92
Kobina, 85-86
Eight, 19
Kofis, 7-8, 12
Kojo, 1, 45
Kotokuraba market, 1
Kumasi, 4, 18
Kwaku, 19
Kwesis, 1, 3, 7, 12
Kyirba, Nna Ama, 73

L
Labeling, 17
Labor
cost, 32
force, 15-16
presence, 25
Land ownership, 74
Learning, described, 117-118
Life cycle, 150
Life expectancy rate, 98
Linguist, 19
Lodgings, 58

M
Macho, 95
Maize, 21
Malaria, 26
Male. *See also* Men
culture, 97
Ghanian definition, 123
qualities, 98
work, 8-9
Margaret, 108
Mark, 107-108
Market
activity, 89-90
economy impact, 78-79
as woman's place, 89-94
Marriage
Christian impact, 80
contractual system, 76
expectation, 87
as family affair, 76
family benefits, 76
fees, 75
mates, choosing, 76
post-marital residence, 77
readiness for, 75
religious ceremony, 77
rites, 77
Masculine style, 19
Medicinal herbs, 27
Meetings, 51-54
permission to leave, 52

Melanin, 34
Men. *See also* Male
    roles, 88
    spheres, 87
Mensah, Nana, 47
Methodology, 38
Migration, 88
Mime, 44
Mirror, The, 31
Modernization, 17, 141-143
    vs. tradition, 18
Mohammed, Mr., 20, 22
Money, 34-35, 142
    absconding of, 97
    as offering, 149
    role of, 119
Monogamy, 76
    belief in, 81
    virtues, 77
Morbidity rate, 98
Multiculturalism, 39
Music, 128
Muslims, 20

N
Nana, 40
Newspapers, 64
NGOs. *See* Nongovernmental organizations
Nicole, 2
Nim, 82-86
    people of, 13
Nkame family, 2
Nkrumah, Kwame, 18, 22, 37, 47
Nobility, levels of, 40
Nongovernmental organizations (NGOs),
    20-21
Nuclear family, neolocal, 76

O
Obaapanyier Dokee, 73
Obedience, 115
Oguaa Traditional Council, 73
Omanhene greeting, 47
Opanyin Yaboah, 73

P
Pakap Hotel, 109, 141
Pa, Kun, 73
Parables, 29
Paradoxes, 8
Palanquine, 60
Participant observation, 38
Pastoral societies, 78
Pentecostal churches, 128
People, characterized, 34
Personality, concept of, 131
Peter, 109
Politics, 57-58

Polygamy, 74, 81
Population, 34
Prayer, 128
Pregnancy, teenage, 75
Priests, 133
Progress, 31
Property, 74
Proverbs, 29
Public spaces, 78

Q
Quashie, Mr., 50
Queen mother, 18, 22
    assistants, 41
    becoming, 40-45
    building house for, 138
    celebration, 56, 58-62
    ceremony, 61
    installation ceremonies, 54-55
    job description, 54
    literature on, 40
    qualifications, 49

R
Race, 49-50, 120-122
    concept, 50
    hatred, 122
    literature on, 121
Rains, 149
Reflexive anthropology, 38
Refreshment, 83-84
Relationships
    brothers, 84
    father-son, 4, 81
    transition of, 88-89
Religion
    Catholic, 127
    cultural messages and, 133-134
    dress for, 130
    Ghanaian view of, 129-130
    holidays, 140
    messages, 131
    music and, 130
    Muslim, 127
    Protestant, 127
    ritual, 131
    work and, 140
Residence, post-marital, 77
Resolutions, of issues, 57
Respect, 47, 115
Road conditions, 42
Rostow, W.W., 38

S
Sacrifice, 55
Salvage anthropology, 37-38
Scholars, 39
Schools
    location of, 71

Scripture, 6
Self Help Electricity Program (SHEP), 139
Senior Secondary School, 72, 82, 102
Sensibility, 49
Sensitivity, 47
Sexual activities, extramarital, 80
SHEP. *See* Self Help Electricity Program
Shirts, 47
Shower, 61
Skin color, 18
Snow-White Pigeon, The, 112
Soccer, 62
Social behavior, dress and, 16
Sons, fathers and, 4, 81
Soul, concept of, 131-134
Sound system locking fee, 137
Spirit, concept of, 131
St. Augustine Secondary School, 95
Stillness, 23
Stool
   description of, 60
   duties, 55-56
Supplication position, 86

T
Tailoring, 15
Tallensi, 69
Third World people, 12-13
Thomas, 5
Thompson, Elizabeth, 73
Thompson, J.H., 73
Time, 142
   sense of, 23
Tortoise, 113
Tradition, 141-143
   vs. modern, 18
Transportation costs, 28
Travel, 26
Trust, 67
Tuwohofo Holly International School, 71-72
Twelve Apostles Church, 18

U
Unification, 35
University Guest House, 112
University of Cape Coast, 69
University Primary School, 4, 111

V
Vestments, 8
Villages, 64
   appearance of, 71
   family and, 6
   organization of, 70
Visiting day, 64

W
Wages, 32
Wake, 5
Wallerstein, 12
Weddings, 132
West African markets, 1
White Chicken, The, 112
White superiority, 49
Wisdom, 51
Wolf, Eric, 12
Women. *See also* Female
   as economic unit, 86
   as market merchants, 89-94
   spheres of, 87
Work
   female, 9
   male, 8-9
World Bank, 31
World market, 65
Worship, houses of, 130-134. *See also*
   Churches
Worshippers, seating of, 128

Y
Yeboah, Nana, 73